THE FABER BOOK
OF MODERN VERSE

Also edited by Michael Roberts

THE FABER BOOK OF COMIC VERSE

THE FABER BOOK
OF MODERN VERSE

edited by

MICHAEL
ROBERTS

This new edition has a
supplement of poems
chosen by
ANNE RIDLER

London
FABER AND FABER
24 Russell Square

First published in mcmxxxvi
By Faber and Faber Limited
24 Russell Square London W.C.1
Fifteenth impression mcmxlviii
This new edition mcmli
Second impression mcmliv
Third impression mcmlix
Printed in Great Britain by
R. MacLehose and Company Limited
The University Press Glasgow
All Rights Reserved

EDITOR'S NOTE

I wish to thank those poets who have helped me in the selection and arrangement of their work. The opinions which some of them have expressed on the subject of anthologies are well known, and their collaboration in the present book does not indicate any change in that general attitude. Where the text of the poems in this book differs from that of earlier printed versions, the change has been made at the author's request.

CONTENTS

xii

xv

xvi

xviii

xvii

xx

INTRODUCTION TO THE
FIRST EDITION

More often than prose or mathematics, poetry is received in a hostile spirit, as if its publication were an affront to the reader; yet most of the poetry which is published probably appears because, at the time of writing, it delighted the writer and convinced him that it held some profound significance or some exact description which he hoped that others, too, might see. One might expect that any poetry depending upon a very personal experience or a relatively private use of words would be ignored; and certainly a great deal of new poetry does meet with indifference because it seems private and incomprehensible. There remains, however, a considerable body of poetry which excites an active animosity, not because it states opinions and expresses feelings which are repugnant to the ordinary man, but because the reader feels compelled to argue that it is not poetry at all: many of the poems in this book aroused that animosity on their first appearance. Much of that hostility has now vanished: it is seen that these poets were saying things which were true, and important, and which could not be said as well in any other way. In that sense, it might be claimed that this collection represents the most significant poetry of this age; but the omission of Charles Sorley, Walter de la Mare, Edmund Blunden, Edwin Muir,[1] William Plomer, Roy Campbell, all of whom seem to me to have written good poems without having been compelled to make any notable development of poetic technique, is suffi-

[1] See Introduction to Second Edition.—A.R.

cient evidence that this is not intended to be a comprehensive anthology of the best poems of our age.

The poems in the book were, with few exceptions, first printed after 1910. This date is arbitrary, and so are some of the inclusions and omissions. I have included only poems which seem to me to add to the resources of poetry, to be likely to influence the future development of poetry and language, and to please me for reasons neither personal nor idiosyncratic. But the capacity to provoke controversy has been neither a necessary nor a sufficient condition for inclusion. Mr. Yeats is included, although the breadth of his appeal has always placed him beyond controversy, but it is worth noting that in his images, approximations to ordinary speech rhythms, political implications and private references, and in his strictly poetic[1] use of myth and legend, he has anticipated many of the devices of the younger men. The earlier poems of some of the older poets are omitted, and the later included, when it is in the later work that a significant development appears. A number of young poets who have written good poems are included, although the full significance of their innovations is not yet wholly clear. Perhaps the most general characteristic of the poems in this book is that they seldom record a recognized 'poetical' experience.

To most readers it will not be surprising that an anthology of modern poetry should begin with Hopkins: but I do not mean to suggest that his poetry made a complete break with the poetry of the past and marked the inauguration of a new age. In rhythm and

[1] The word 'poetic' is here used to describe a special concentration of sensuous impression, idea and evocation in a word or phrase. The word 'poetical' is used to describe an attempted evocation by conventional symbols, of a state of mind sometimes called mystical.

2

in imagery, as well as in the thoughts and feelings which he intended to express, he differed from most of the English poets of his time, but there was no sharp discontinuity. Doughty, born only a year before Hopkins, resembled him in his inversions, his alliteration, the violence of his syntax, and above all in the emphasis which he succeeded in placing on accumulated masses of nouns, verbs, adjectives and adverbs, often unleavened by prepositions or conjunctions. Doughty's poetry is massive and uneven: a strong case could have been made out for including it; but it lacks that intensity which, in the poetry of Hopkins, was the expression of an important moral conflict, related to an outer social and intellectual conflict.

It is not possible to compile an anthology of serious poetry without reflecting the social and moral problems of our time; but writing may be poetic without being either moral or didactic. Poetry may be intended to amuse, or to ridicule, or to persuade, or to produce an effect which we feel to be more valuable than amusement and different from instruction; but primarily poetry is an exploration of the possibilities of language. It does not aim directly at consolation or moral exhortation, nor at the expression of exquisite moments, but at an extension of significance; and it might be argued that a too self-conscious concern with 'contemporary' problems deflects the poet's effort from his true objective. The technical merit of a poem is measured by its accuracy, not by the importance of a rough approximation to what is being said, nor by the number of people to whom it is immediately intelligible. If a poet is incomprehensible to many people, but clearly intelligible to a few, as Hopkins appeared to be when his collected poems were first published, it may be be-

3

cause he is speaking of things not commonly experienced and is using subtleties of rhythm and imagery not used in ordinary speech, and therefore not widely understood. If it can be shown that a poet's use of language is valid for some people, we cannot dismiss his way of speaking as mere 'obscurity' and idiosyncrasy, though we may regret the necessity for such a rhetoric as we regret the necessity for scientific jargon and mathematical notation.

The significant point about Hopkins was, however, not that he invented a style different from the current poetic style, but that, working in subterranean fashion, he moulded a style which expressed the tension and disorder that he found inside himself. Good poetry is more likely to be written about subjects which are, to the writer, important, than about unimportant subjects, because only on subjects of personal importance to himself does he feel the need for that accuracy of speech which itself lessens the tension which it describes. Deliberately to imitate a style arising from one poet's crisis would be absurd, but something similar is likely to appear when a crisis of a general kind arouses a personal conflict in many poets. The conflict may be the product of a fractured personality or a decaying society, or, like some of the 'problems' of academic philosophy, a result of the deficiencies of language. The terms of the conflict may be intellectual, when people are torn between conflicting systems of ideas. They may be theological, when people argue that they themselves should be perfect, being the children of God, but are perplexed by the recognition that they are evil. The terms may be political and aesthetic, when people cling to some features of the existing state, but see that there can be no good future until that state is

4

overthrown. Sometimes, as in Donne, several of these terminologies are superimposed, serving as metaphors for each other, and concentrating, intensifying, and ultimately simplifying the problems by this poetic identification. For 'problems' of this kind are seldom independent; there is a relation between the personal and moral problem and the political and intellectual.

To those who have not felt some adumbration of such a crisis, the expression and resolution of conflict and disorder must appear like the strained muscles and distorted features of a strong man pretending to lift stupendous but non-existent weights. But for those who have come near to feeling the crisis themselves, the poetry is important. Words do something more than call up ideas and emotions out of a lumber-room: they call them up, but they never replace them exactly where they were. A good descriptive poem may enable us to be more articulate, to perceive more clearly, and to distinguish more readily between sensitive and sentimental observation, than before. But a poem may do more than that: even though we may not accept the poet's explicit doctrine, it may change the configuration of the mind and alter our responses to certain situations: it may harmonize conflicting emotions just as a good piece of reasoning may show the fallacy of an apparent contradiction in logic.

But the poetic use of language can cause discord as easily as it can cure it. A bad poem, a psychologically disordered poem, if it is technically effective may arouse uneasiness or nausea or anger in the reader. A sentimental poem, which deals with a situation by ignoring some of the factors, is offensive in this way; and a poem is equally confusing if it takes into account greater complexities of thought and intricacies of feeling

5

than the reader has ever noticed. It unsettles the mind —and by the mind I mean more than the conscious mind; and the reader expends the energy he originally brought to the poem in trivial irritation with the poet.

It is very natural that this should be the first response of many readers to 'new' poetry, but in so far as the poet is a good poet, the situation will remedy itself. The problem which worried the poet will worry other people, or the new grounds which he saw for delight and hope will become apparent to them too: perhaps their recognition of the new element will be accelerated by his writing. But in either case they will welcome the way of speech which makes them articulate. Sometimes, as in the case of Hopkins, the problem which is his today is the world's tomorrow. Sometimes his writing is significant primarily for only a few of each generation, as when it is evoked by some remote place or rare experience or an intricate thought which few can follow. Sometimes it expresses only the problem of few or many people at one particular moment. But in each case, if the writer is a good poet, good in the sense of being rhetorically effective, his writing has a value over and above that of its immediate appeal: he has added to the possibilities of speech, he has discovered evocative rhythms and image-sequences unknown before. It may happen that in some future state of society there will be no people in the position of Mr. Eliot's Prufrock, and therefore no people for whom the poem is actual. But the rhetorical merit of the poem remains: it has said something which could not be said in ordinary speech, and said it exactly, and people who are interested in effective expression will read it. Pope and Erasmus Darwin both wrote poems which were chiefly of didactic interest

6

in their own time, but the elegance of Pope's writing keeps it alive today, whereas the poetry of Erasmus Darwin is almost forgotten. Chaucer has influenced English poetry and English language more than Langland, though Langland was, and is, the nearer to the thought and feeling of the common people.

In contrast to the previous twenty years, when the 'decadence' of the content of certain poems was continually discussed, critical discussion for the past thirty years has been concerned most often with the form, or alleged formlessness, of modern poetry. In the narrow sense, the word 'form' is used to describe special metrical and stanzaic patterns: in a wider sense it is used for the whole set of relationships involving the sensuous imagery and the auditory rhetoric of a poem. A definite 'form' in the narrower (and older) sense is not an asset unless it is an organized part of the 'form' in the wider sense, for the final value of a poem always springs from the inter-relation of form and content. In a good poet a change or development of technique always springs from a change or development of subject-matter.

If, then, we are to discuss technical innovations effectively, we must also discuss content; and here, at once, an important point appears. Roughly speaking, the poets in this book may be divided into two classes: those whose poetry is primarily a defence and vindication of existing cultural values, and those who, using the poetic qualities of the English language, try to build up poetry out of the realities implicit in the language, and which they find in their own minds rather than base it upon humanistic learning and memories of other poetry. The poets of the first kind possess what

7

might be called a 'European' sensibility: they are aware of Baudelaire, Corbière, Rimbaud, Laforgue and the later Symbolists (it is notable that German poetry has had little influence upon them), they turn to Dante or Cavalcanti more readily than to Milton, they are more likely to be interested in a Parisian movement in poetry, such as Surrealism, than in the corresponding tendency in *Alice Through the Looking Glass* or Young's *Night Thoughts*. Most of them are Americans by birth, but their appeal is as much to the English as to the American reader. Among their English predecessors they might number Donne, Crashaw and Pope.

Poets in whose work the 'English' element predominates take the language as they find it, developing the implications of its idioms, metaphors and symbols. They are 'first order' poets: that is to say, it is not necessary to have a wide acquaintance with European literature, or even with English literature, to appreciate their work. They may be given an ancestry in Langland, Skelton, Doughty, on the one hand, and Blake, Shelley and perhaps Edward Lear, on the other, but their work does not depend upon a knowledge of literary history: it is an intensification of qualities inherent in the English language itself, and for this reason it is less easy to translate than that of the 'European' poets, in whose poems the specific properties of the language they are using is a more casual element.

These classes are not exclusive: they represent two moods of poetry rather than two kinds of poet. The poetry of W. B. Yeats, for example, must be considered under both headings: but the work of Ezra Pound and T. S. Eliot is clearly 'European' in cast. Robert Graves for a time hesitated between the two, then identified himself with that view of poetry which

8

Laura Riding has increasingly emphasized—poetry as the final residue of significance in language, freed from extrinsic decoration, superficial contemporaneity, and didactic bias.

The 'European' poet is acutely aware of the social world in which he lives, he criticizes it, but in a satirical rather than in an indignant manner, he adjusts himself to it, he is interested in its accumulated store of music, painting, sculpture, and even in its bric-à-brac. There is something of the dandy, something of the dilettante, in his make-up, but he is aware of the futility and evanescence of all this, and of the irresponsibility of big business, conventional politics and mass education. He is witty, and acutely self-conscious. His attitude is the outcome of a genuine care for much that is valuable in the past, and it gains its strength from a desire to preserve these things: to preserve them, not by violence, but by exercise, for they are not 'things' at all, but certain attitudes and activities.

Every vital age, perhaps, sees its own time as crucial and full of perils, but the problems and difficulties of our own age necessarily appear more urgent to us than those of any other, and the need for an evaluating, clarifying poetry has never been greater than it appears to be today. Industrial changes have broken up the old culture, based on an agricultural community in which poor and wealthy were alike concerned, and on a Church which bore a vital relation to the State. Parallel with this, and related to it, there has been a decay of the old moral and religious order, and a change in the basis of education, which has become more and more strictly scientific. Religion and classical learning, which once provided myths and legends symbolizing the purposes of society and the role of the individual, have declined, and the disorder weighs heavily upon the serious poet, whether in England or America.

It is the theme of many of the poems of Mr. Pound, and of Mr. Eliot's *Waste Land*. We find the American poets, Hart Crane and Allen Tate, seeing the situation in these terms:

'The Parthenon in stucco, art for the sake of death'.

And the poets—Mr. Yeats among them—have attempted to clarify their own vision by expressing the disorder which they see about them, and by finding and defining those things in the older tradition which they hold to be valuable and necessary:

Things fall apart; the centre cannot hold;
Mere anarchy is loosed upon the world,
The blood-dimmed tide is loosed, and everywhere
The ceremony of innocence is drowned;
The best lack all conviction, while the worst
Are full of passionate intensity.

If the poet is in the 'European' tradition, he describes the elements of civilization wherever he finds them: in Rome, in Greece, in Confucius, or in the Church of the Middle Ages; and against these he contrasts the violence and disorder of contemporary life. It is inevitable that poetry concerned with such issues should have political implications; but the poet is not arguing for one party against another: he is remodelling the basis upon which political creeds are founded, though sometimes immediate implications may appear in his poems.

Younger poets than Mr. Eliot and Mr. Pound may feel more acutely the inter-relation of culture and politics, but nevertheless they would agree with Mr. Auden that 'poetry is not concerned with telling people what to do, but with extending our knowledge of good and evil, perhaps making the necessity for action more urgent and its nature more clear, but only leading us to the point where it is possible for us to make a rational and moral choice'.

The problem, as we see on turning to Clough's *Amours de Voyage* (1849), is not wholly new. Clough had, as Bagehot says, 'an unusual difficulty in forming a creed as to the unseen world; he could not get the visible world out of his head; his strong grasp of plain facts and obvious matters was a difficulty to him. . . . He has himself given us in a poem, now first published, a very remarkable description of this curious state of mind. He has prefixed to it the characteristic motto, '*Il doutait de tout, même de l'amour*'. It is the delineation of a certain love-passage in the life of a hesitating young gentleman, who was in Rome at the time of the revolution of 1848; who could not make up his mind about the revolution, who could not make up his mind whether he liked Rome, who could not make up his mind whether he liked the young lady, who let her go away without him, who went in pursuit of her and could not make out which way to look for her, who, in fine, has some sort of religion but cannot tell himself what it is. . . .'

Amours de Voyage was written in conversational hexameters, in a tone of semi-satire and half-belief,

Rome disappoints me much; I hardly as yet understand, but
Rubbishy seems the word that most exactly would suit it.

Luther, they say, was unwise; like a half-taught Ger-
        man, he could not
See that old follies were passing most tranquilly out
        of remembrance;
Leo the Tenth was employing all efforts to clear out
        abuses;
Jupiter, Juno, and Venus, Fine Arts, and Fine Letters,
        the Poets,
Scholars, and Sculptors, and Painters, were quietly
        clearing away the
Martyrs, and Virgins, and Saints, or at any rate
        Thomas Aquinas:
He must forsooth make a fuss and distend his huge
        Wittenberg lungs, and
Bring back Theology once yet again in a flood upon
        Europe.

The resemblance to Mr. Pound's *Cantos*, in tone and
intention, is obvious, and there is the same detachment,
the same denial of commonly-accepted responsibility
that is found in *Mauberley* and *Prufrock*:

Dulce it is, and *decorum*, no doubt, for the country to
        fall,—to
Offer one's blood an oblation to Freedom, and die
        for the Cause; yet
Still, individual culture is also something. . . .

and the detachment passes easily into a kind of semi-
serious raillery, which springs from a feeling that the
generally-accepted code is all wrong, and yet that there
is no other to take its place:

Am I prepared to lay down my life for the British
        female?
Really, who knows? One has bowed and talked, till,
        little by little,

All the natural heat has escaped of the chivalrous
      spirit.
Oh, one conformed, of course; but one doesn't die
      for good manners,
Stab or shoot, or be shot, by way of graceful attention.
No, if it should be at all, it should be on the
      barricades there . . . .
Sooner far by the side of the damned and dirty
      plebeians.
Ah, for a child in the street I could strike; for the
      full-blown lady—
Somehow, Eustace, alas! I have not felt the vocation.

There is the same introspection, the same self-mockery
that is found in the poetry of Jules Laforgue, the same
dissatisfaction with ready-made analysis, and the same
intense conviction that there is an underlying problem
which is not to be laughed away:

I am in love, meantime, you think; no doubt you
      would think so.
I am in love, you say; with those letters, of course,
      you would say so.
I am in love, you declare. . . .
I am in love, you say: I do not think so, exactly.

There are lines which recall the more 'metaphysical'
passages of T. S. Eliot with their echoes of Chapman
and Webster:

I do not like being moved: for the will is excited; and
      action
Is a most dangerous thing; I tremble for something
      factitious,
Some malpractice of heart and illegitimate process;
We are so prone to these things, with our terrible
      notions of duty.

and there are passages of lyrical fine writing, such as we find in *The Waste Land* and the *Cantos*:

> Tibur is beautiful, too, and the orchard slopes, and
>   the Anio
> Falling, falling yet, to the ancient lyrical cadence;
> Tibur and Anio's tide; . . .

There are obvious technical resemblances (I am not denying the obvious differences) in tempo, pitch and rhythm, but Eliot and Pound differ from Clough in their greater compression and intensity. Although Clough's poem sustains its narrative interest, his hexameters, however freely handled, become irritating, and his imagery is often diffuse and unexciting. Browning and Walt Whitman, both of whom anticipated many of the habits of the modern poets, suffer from the same long-windedness. They do not compress a situation into a single memorable image, and Clough did not feel the problem of his young man as intensely as Ezra Pound and T. S. Eliot felt it in 1912. Clough suspected that the *malaise* was due to a fault in himself, and Bagehot, a sensitive critic, agreed with him; but for Pound and Eliot the problem was external: it was society and its standards that were crumbling. A culture adapted to the older aristocratic system of landed proprietors was falling to pieces in a world governed by big business. Civilization was becoming 'a few score of broken statues, an old bitch gone in the teeth' or 'a heap of broken images'. It was necessary to sift out from the mass of habits, institutions and conventions the traditions which were worth preserving.

For the moment all that the poet could do was to concentrate upon surfaces: in a world in which moral,

intellectual and aesthetic values were all uncertain, only sense impressions were certain and could be described exactly. From such minute particulars perhaps something could be built up. In 1913 a few poets, shocked at the vagueness and facility of the poetry of the day, determined:

1. To use the language of common speech, but to employ always the *exact* word, not the merely decorative word.

2. To create new rhythms—as the expression of new moods. We do not insist upon 'Free-verse' as the only method of writing poetry. . . . We do believe that the individuality of a poet may often be better expressed in free verse than in conventional forms.

3. To allow absolute freedom in the choice of subject.

4. To present an image. We are not a school of painters, but we believe that poetry should render particulars exactly and not deal with vague generalities.

5. To produce poetry that is hard and clear, never blurred or indefinite.

6. Finally, most of us believe that concentration is the very essence of poetry.

Edited by Ezra Pound, a number of 'Imagist' anthologies appeared; T. E. Hulme wrote some of the earliest Imagist poems. Amy Lowell, F. S. Flint, H.D., J. G. Fletcher, Richard Aldington, T. S. Eliot and Ezra Pound himself at one time or other were members of the group, and the later development of the movement appears in the work of Marianne Moore. T. S. Eliot had been influenced by Baudelaire, Laforgue and Rimbaud. Ezra Pound was impressed by the work of

Villon and the Provençal and early Italian poets. F. S. Flint was interested in the later Symbolists—Samain, Kahn, Jammes, Rodenbach and the earlier Verhaeren —as well as more recent writers, Vildrac, Romains, Duhamel. The name 'Imagist' itself recalls 'Symbolist', and the Imagists themselves sometimes confused the image, the clear evocation of a material thing, with the symbol, the word which stirs subconscious memories. Such, indeed, was their intention: their poetry was meant to widen outwards like the ripples from a stone dropped in clear water. But the scope of 'pure' Imagist poetry was limited to clear renderings of visual experience: the poetry of H.D. shows both the possibilities and the limitations of the method.

It was natural that there should be a movement away from poeticality of subject and from the direct expression of emotion when the poets were in doubt about standards of art and morals: for the moment *any* emotion seemed sentimental to their realism. But the realism itself was often deceptive. Wallace Stevens in *The Emperor of Ice-Cream* writes a poem to insist that only the commonplace is real: let 'be' be the end of 'seem'; but the reality he describes is itself highly-coloured, and the poem contains more than a clear visual image. When he writes:

> Take from the dresser of deal,
> Lacking the three glass knobs, that sheet
> On which she embroidered fantails once
> And spread it so as to cover her face.
> If her horny feet protrude, they come
> To show how cold she is, and dumb—

I am fairly sure that he is writing with some vague memory of Mantegna's picture of the dead Christ

16

and certainly that recollection makes the image more impressive.

The poetry of Wallace Stevens and Miss Sitwell still shows the Imagist concentration upon the sensuous surface of things, but even with the latitude which they allow themselves, Imagism is limited in scope; and as Mr. Pound has recorded: 'at a particular date in a particular room, two authors, neither engaged in picking the other's pocket, decided that the dilution of *vers libre*, Amygism, Lee Masterism, general floppiness had gone too far and that some counter-current must be set going. Parallel situation centuries ago in China. Remedy prescribed *Emaux et Camées* (or the Bay State Hymn Book). Rhyme and regular strophes.

'Results: Poems in Mr. Eliot's *second* volume, not contained in his first *Prufrock* (Egoist, 1917), also *H. S. Mauberley*.'

Between 1920 and 1926, many poets were trying to write long poems which would present a unified view of the social crisis as they saw it, and imply their criticism of it. Conrad Aiken, who had been for a brief time influenced by the ideals of the Imagists, began to work for something which would lead to more profound and more highly organized poems, and turned to music. The predominant pattern of his poems is musical, whereas the more important pattern of some poems, as St. J. Perse's *Anabase* (translated by T. S. Eliot), is one of vivid visual and tactile images.

Conrad Aiken's *Senlin* (1918), T. S. Eliot's *The Waste Land* (1922), Richard Aldington's *Fool i' the Forest* (1925), and Archibald MacLeish's *Hamlet of A. Mac-Leish* (1928), were all poems of this kind. *The Waste Land* is the most concise, the most evocative, the widest in scope, and the most highly organized of these poems. It possesses 'imaginative order', by which I mean, that to some minds it is cogent even before its narrative and argumentative continuity is grasped. This 'imaginative order' is not something arbitrary, specific and inexplicable. If the images which are used to denote complex situations were replaced by abstractions much of the apparent incoherence of the poem would vanish. It would become a prose description of the condition of the world, a restatement of a myth and a defence of the tragic view of life. But being a poem it does more than this; a poem expresses not merely the idea of a social or scientific fact, but also the sensation of thinking or knowing, and it does not merely defend the tragic view, it may communicate it.

The images and rhythms of *The Waste Land* are not conventionally poetical: their aura of suggestion radiates from a definite meaning relating to the ordinary world, and their full significance is not seen until the essentially tragic attitude of the poem is grasped. The omission of explanatory connecting matter when contrasting a 'modern' situation with an old or the life of one class with that of another may be puzzling at first, but given a general understanding of the poem it becomes clear. Thus one situation may be described in the terms and rhythms appropriate to another, so that both the similarities and the differences are illuminated.

It is not only the 'European' poets who are concerned with these problems, nor are they the only poets who aim at poetic concentration and whose work therefore presents initial difficulties. These spring from several sources. There is the intellectual

18

difficulty which arises from the poet's use of some little-known fact, or some idea hard to grasp; there is the difficulty which comes from the unusual use of metaphor; and there is the difficulty which arises when the poet is making a deliberately fantastic use of words.

The obscurity which arises from the use of little-known or intricate ideas is easily removed. Some of the obscurity of Mr. Eliot's poetry and Mr. Empson's is of this kind: it needs only elucidatory notes to make it vanish, and it should be remembered that, because the ideas of science are widely known and generally believed, the poet who uses them is on safer ground than the man who makes classical allusions which, although they are accepted as poetical, are neither exactly appreciated nor fully understood.

The difficulty which arises from an unusual use of metaphor is less easy to remove: it depends far more upon the goodwill of the reader. Metaphor and simile are fundamental to civilized speech: but they have one serious disadvantage, the moment you say one thing is 'like' another, you remind the reader that the two things are, after all, different; and there may be an effect of dilution and long-windedness which is inimical to poetry. The poet, therefore, condenses his metaphor. Hart Crane in *Voyages III*, referring to the rhythm of the motion of a boat through a thickly clustered archipelago, speaks of 'adagios of islands'. Similarly, in *Faustus and Helen III*, the speed and altitude of an aeroplane are suggested by the idea of 'nimble blue plateaus'. This kind of compressed metaphor is also found in the poetry of Stephen Spender:

> Eye, gazelle, delicate wanderer,
> Drinker of horizon's fluid line.

This condensation may demand an initial effort of understanding in the reader, but once the meaning is understood, the aptness and convenience of the phrase is obvious; it becomes part of one's habit of thought, and the understanding of these compressed analogies becomes, after a time, no more difficult than the understanding of a simile or a more prosaic and long-winded metaphor.

The condensation of metaphor involves no denial of logic: it is simply an extension of the implications of grammar, the development of a notation which, being less cumbersome, enables us to think more easily. It may be compared to the invention of a new notation, say that of Leibnitz or Hamilton, in mathematics: the new is defined in terms of the old, it is a shorthand which must be learned by patient effort, but, once learnt, it makes possible the solution of problems which were too complicated to attack before. The human head can only carry a certain amount of notation at any one moment, and poetry takes up less space than prose.

The third difficulty, that which springs from a deliberately fantastic use of words, is less than one might imagine. We accept, willingly, the fantastic sequences of nursery-rhyme and fairy-tale; and only a confusion of thought makes us demand, as we grow older, that poetry should always give us enlightenment or high moral doctrine. The poet has a right to play, and the reader to enjoy that play. The solemn attacks on the more riotously comic of Mr. Cummings' poems are themselves ridiculous. There is in all poetry an element of verbal play; and in nonsense verses, in the poetry of Mr. Cummings, in Mr. Madge's *Lusty Juventus*, and in the early poetry of Miss Sitwell, this element often predominates. It is found in Miss Riding's *Tillaquils* which, because it actualizes a strange experience of a kind which the reader has been accustomed to regard as 'abstract', tends to be read, like her better-known poem, *The Quids*, as a satire upon academic metaphysics.

Verbal play is a form of fantasy, and when we relax and abandon ourselves to such poetry we find that some of it makes too deep an impression on our minds to be called 'play' at all. In the joke-poem we may give ourselves up to the casual association of words, but many readers find this abandonment difficult when something more serious appears to be involved. They are prepared to enjoy poetry which tells a story or states a moral, but they distrust the abandonment of common sense and accepted habits of language, believing, rightly, that if common sense is abandoned, then the way is open to all nonsense, incoherence and private fantasy.

'There is a mental existence within us . . . which is not less energetic than the conscious flow, an absent mind which haunts us like a ghost or a dream and is an essential part of our lives. Incidentally . . . the unconscious life of the mind bears a wonderful resemblance to the supposed feature of imagination. . . . To lay bare the automatic or unconscious action of the mind is indeed to unfold a tale which outvies the romances of giants and ginns, wizards in their palaces, and captives in the Domdaniel roots of the sea.'[1]

There are no rules to guide us, no histories to enable us to check our facts: but it is a simple experimental fact that certain people do agree that 'imaginative order' is found in certain specified poems, and not in

[1] E. S. Dallas, *The Gav Science* (1866).

others. In so far as those people are normal, it therefore seems that the poem, though 'subjective' in the old sense, is 'objective' in so far as it describes something which is part of the experience of a number of people. Poetry changes in its emphasis from one time to another, and just as, in recent years, there has been a decline in the writing of descriptive poetry (a decline which the Imagists attempted to check), so in the near future we may see greater emphasis placed on poetry as a means of appealing directly to the subconscious mind, and less on poetry as a conscious criticism of life.

As we see from the quotation from Dallas, the critical theory appropriate to such poetry is not new. Hints of its method are found in the older critics, and in Shelley. 'Poetry', said Shelley, 'differs in this respect from logic, that it is not subject to the control of the active powers of the mind, and that its birth and recurrence have no necessary connexion with the consciousness or will.' Sometimes the reason for the order of the images of such poems and the cause of their effectiveness are fairly obvious. Their power and order may come from casual memory, or from the make-up of the mind, from the deep impressions of early childhood, or from the influence of the birth trauma, or from the structure of the language itself. The meaning of a word is never a simple thing, a 'standing-for' an object or relation: it is the whole complex set of grammatical habits and associations of ideas which have grown up from our first hearing of it, and the poet exploits this symbolism of words as he exploits the more directly 'psychological' symbolism or substitution value of images. It is possible, therefore, for a poem to be professedly realistic and yet to

22

have the vigour and insistence of a dream or night-mare. Good poetry always has something of this quality, but the nightmare may be directly verbal, rather than visual. Robert Graves is, I think, a poet whose poetry is mainly verbal. That is to say, although there is often a visual picture corresponding to his poems, the effect of the poem depends upon the direct evocative effect of the words, not on the visual stimulus.

Among the poems which deliberately free them-selves from logic there are not only the joke-poems, which are simply an exercise of poetic energy showing the word-sense of the poet; but also the relaxation-poems, which range from those in which words as-sociate themselves mainly according to relations and similarities of sound (as in Miss Sitwell's *Hornpipe*[1]), to those which are day-dream narratives. Of these, one of the more obvious types is the wandering-ego poem in which the 'I'—'On a bat's back I do fly'—paces beside the ocean, passes through caves and dis-mal gorges, is prisoned in miserable dungeons, rises to craggy heights and is carried upon the wind. A poem of this kind has often a tremendous self-importance which becomes inflated until the ego dominates the entire world and we arrive at the great passages in Whitman, where, Charles Madge has pointed out, the ego passes over all the earth and eventually 'dissolves in lacy jags'.

Then again, there are the poems which, like *Kubla Khan* or, to take a modern example, Dylan Thomas's '*Light breaks where no sun shines*', correspond to dream-fantasies of a sexual type. The woods, the hills, the

[1] Omitted from the second edition. But see *When Sir Beelzebub*, which remains. A.R.

rushing stream—all become substitutes for other things, and the reader (and perhaps the poet), unaware of what is happening in his own mind, is puzzled at the strange excitement which he finds in the succession of images.

In some poems, the dream-quality is exaggerated and the structure which is believed to characterize the fantasies of the deeper levels in sleep is deliberately made the model for the structure of the poem. The *Parade Virtues for a Dying Gladiator* of Sacheverell Sitwell is of that kind, and so, too, are the poems which the Surrealists, and their English admirer, David Gascoyne, aim at producing. Such poems, if they are the product of a normal mind, may become fascinating when we get over their initial strangeness; but the 'order' of such poems is not necessarily identical with the 'imaginative order' of myth and legend. The poem may be a good one without being socially important, or it may be fascinating without being specifically poetic. It might, for example, be more effective as a film than it is in printed words.

But although good poems may sometimes be shown to correspond to standard types of dream, good poetry is not likely to be written by working to fit a standard pattern. Even allegory, which would seem to require constant reference to a preconceived design, cannot be written in cold blood: the writer must be interested in the story itself, not merely in the underlying 'meaning', and the story must develop with the overpowering inevitability of a dream. There are some writers who might say that if a poem has this kind of inevitability, it need not have commonsense logic or narrative sense as well. Certainly good poems of this kind have been written, though personally I prefer poems in which the compulsion of the image sequence is

24

matched by a natural development of argument or narrative. *Kubla Khan* owes its force to its image-order, but it owes its popularity to the fact that it possesses a loose narrative order which saves the reader from the awkward fear of being taken in by nonsense. Furthermore, the two currents, the narrative and the fantastic, reinforce each other, just as the coalescence of narrative and imaginative pattern give life and force to myth and legend.

To myths, rather than to dreams, many poets still turn for the content of their poems, and the researches of Sir James Frazer and other anthropologists have provided the *motif* of a few good poems and many bad ones. Myths are more than fumbling attempts to explain historical and scientific facts: they control and organize the feeling, thought and action of a people: their function is symbolic as well as significant. But often the stories have become the conventional material of second-rate poetry, and have become perverted so that the symbolism has been lost, and we are left with the mere husk of a story, a story easily discredited by scientific and historical research. When Mr. Yeats turned to the myth as a means of giving shape and significance to his vision of the world, he was returning to the essential purpose of the myth and setting an example which Mr. Eliot, among others, has followed. But the modern reader cannot be expected to be influenced by a myth whose plain narrative sense is counter to his everyday beliefs. Either the poet must break away from any such direct narrative, or he must attempt, as I think Mr. Day Lewis has attempted in his *Flight* poem, to present a story credible in the ordinary everyday sense. If the poet turns to an existing myth or legend, however shop-soiled, and sees in it a

25

profound significance, he will see the legend itself exemplified and symbolized in the world about him.

'So', says Hart Crane, in an unpublished manuscript, 'I found "Helen" sitting in a street car; the Dionysian revels of her court and her seduction were transferred to a Metropolitan roof garden with a jazz orchestra: and the *katharsis* of the fall of Troy I saw approximated in the recent world war. . . .

'It is a terrific problem that faces the poet today—a world that is so in transition from a decayed culture toward a reorganization of human evaluations that there are few common terms, general denominators of speech, that are solid enough or that ring with any vibration or spiritual conviction. The great mythologies of the past (including the Church) are deprived of enough façade even to launch good raillery against. Yet much of their traditions are operative still—in millions of chance combinations of related and unrelated detail, psychological reference, figures of speech, precepts, etc. These are all part of our common experience and the terms, at least partially, of that very experience when it defines or extends itself.

'The deliberate program, then, of a "break" with the past or tradition seems to me to be a sentimental fallacy. . . . The poet has a right to draw on whatever practical resources he finds in books or otherwise about him. He must tax his sensibility and his touchstone of experience for the proper selections of these themes and details, however,—and that is where he either stands, or falls into useless archaeology.

'I put no particular value on the simple objective of "modernity". . . . It seems to me that a poet will accidentally define his time well enough simply by reacting honestly and to the full extent of his sensibilities

26

to the states of passion, experience and rumination that fate forces on him, first hand. He must, of course, have a sufficiently universal basis of experience to make his imagination selective and valuable. . . .

'I am concerned with the future of America . . . because I feel persuaded that here are destined to be discovered certain as yet undefined spiritual quantities, perhaps a new hierarchy of faith not to be developed so completely elsewhere. And in this process I like to feel myself as a potential factor; certainly I must speak in its terms. . . .

'But to fool one's self that definitions are being reached by merely referring frequently to skyscrapers, radio antennae, steam whistles, or other surface phenomena of our time is merely to paint a photograph. I think that what is interesting and significant will emerge only under the conditions of our submission to, and examination and assimilation of the organic effects on us of these and other fundamental factors of our experience. It can certainly not be an organic expression otherwise. And the expression of such values may often be as well accomplished with the vocabulary and blank verse of the Elizabethans as with the calligraphic tricks and slang used so brilliantly at times by an impressionist like Cummings.'

If a poet is to give new life to a legend, if indeed he is to write good poetry at all, he must charge each word to its maximum poetic value. It must appeal concurrently to all the various levels of evocation and interpretation: experiments in new rhythms and new images, if they are not used in this specifically poetic way, are of no more than technical interest. In discussing new technical devices a distinction must be drawn between those which produce an effect upon the reader even before he has noticed them, and those which, like some of the devices of Mr. Cummings, attract the reader's attention and lead him to infer, by ordinary reasoning, what effect the poet intended to produce. There are, I think, many examples of the first kind in this book, and of the many auditory devices of this kind, none, perhaps, are more effective, or have had greater effect upon later poets, than those of Wilfred Owen.

In Owen's poetry, the use of half-rhymes is not merely the result of an attempt to escape from the over-obviousness of rhyme-led poetry, though Owen probably discovered its possibilities in that way. His innovations are important because his sound-effects directly reinforce the general effect which he is trying to produce. In Owen's war poetry, the half-rhymes almost invariably fall from a vowel of high pitch to one of low pitch, producing an effect of frustration, disappointment, hopelessness. In other poets, rising half-rhymes are used, which produce the opposite effect, without reaching out to the full heartiness of rhyme. Full end-rhyme itself is felt by many modern poets to be too arbitrary and too noisy for serious poetry, unless modified, as Hopkins modifies it, by taking some of the stress off the last syllable of the line either by stressing earlier syllables, or by placing the emphasis of meaning, as distinct from metre, elsewhere. If they use end-rhymes at all, it is often for satiric purposes, or in a modified form, rhyming stressed with unstressed syllables, as Sacheverell Sitwell has done, and thus producing an uncertain, tentative, hesitating effect in keeping with the poet's purpose.

Nevertheless rhyme, like meaning and metre, is one of the possible elements in a verbal pattern, and few poets abandon it entirely. The sense of order in complication is part of the fascination of poetry, and often, as in the poetry of C. Day Lewis, internal rhymes, carefully but not obviously placed, are used to produce a pattern running counter to sense and rhythm and to add that intricacy and richness which marks the difference between part-song and unison.

Even when the poet writes, apparently, in a regular metre, he may use effects ignored in the formal rules of prosody and grammar. Thus Owen, in the second stanza of *Futility*, retards the movement of the first four lines by punctuation and intricacy of syntax, so that the fifth line, unimpeded, comes out with a terrific force, continued, though less vigorously and a little more slowly, as though one added a conclusive after-thought, in the final couplet. Similarly, in William Empson's *Note on Local Flora* the first seven lines form a single intricate sentence, retarding the pace, so that the eighth line, again an unimpeded sentence, is stamped with the emphasis of conviction, and the con-cluding couplet comes strongly, but comparatively quietly, as a conclusive deduction might do.

Often an effect of logic in a poem which, when ex-amined, proves illogical, is due to auditory rhetoric[1] rather than to fantasy. The poetry of Edith and Sache-verell Sitwell shows, for example, not only an unusually vivid use of sensuous impressions, and of image-patterns based, like nursery rhymes, on the compelling

[1] I use the word 'rhetoric' here, as elsewhere, in the technical, not the popular sense. There is good rhetoric and bad rhetoric, and there is rhetoric used in a good cause and in a bad, but rhetoric itself is not necessarily bad.

force of dreams, but also an effective use of sound-patterns having this convincing facility of speech. The poetry of Edith Sitwell, like the poetry of Vachel Lindsay and E. E. Cummings, needs to be read aloud, with careful changes of rhythm, volume, pitch and tempo. A practised reader will be able to determine these variations for himself: in a good poem they are usually implied, but the pointing of the Psalms is an example of the use of typography to help the reader. Similarly, Hopkins, in his effort to extract the utmost poetic value from the varied stress of words, resorts to a system of accents and markings; and Mr. Cummings takes a great deal of trouble to show, by typographical devices, how his poems should be read. More conventional poets are less violent in their fluctuations, and less helpful in their methods. To read poetry as it should be read requires considerable practice. Most people tend to over-emphasize any regular metrical pattern which may be the background to the rhythm of the poem, and at the same time they raise the voice to a deliberately 'poetical' key and make use of fluctuations of pitch which bring their reading nearer to singing than to talking. It is characteristic of modern poets in general that they fight as hard as they can against this tendency, which seems to them not to increase the significance of the poetry, but to diminish it by asserting an arbitrary music at the expense of meaning, and to read their poems as songs, and necessarily bad songs, is to misread them completely.

When in pre-war days a few poets began to write, not in regular metres, but in cadences, as Whitman and the translators of the Bible had done, it was objected that this practice would destroy the art of verse entirely. It is true that a more delicate sensibility and a more careful training are necessary if we are to appreciate cadenced verse, and it is true that the existence of cadenced verse blurs the distinction between prose and poetry; but the critical vocabulary must be revised to fit the facts: to deny the facts and close your ears to the rhythms is to behave like the Inquisitor who refused to look through Galileo's telescope. Every discovery creates disorder: it is not the duty of the critic to prevent discovery or to deny it, but to create new order to replace the older. Today, the quarrel over cadenced verse has died down, and it is very hard to draw a sharp line, or to see any purpose in trying to draw a sharp line, between 'free' verse and *varied* regular verse. One or two points may be noted, however. There is verse which is intended to be 'free': that is to say, whose rhythm is composed to please the ear alone; there is verse which is quantitative, depending on a recurrent pattern of long and short syllables; there is verse which is accentual, depending on a recurrent pattern of accented and unaccented syllables; and there is syllabic verse. In the latter (some of the poems of Marianne Moore and Herbert Read are examples) the lines are evaluated by the number of syllables they contain, and the pattern will be something like this—11:11:11:6. It is not very difficult to train the ear to recognize and enjoy syllabic patterns, and if it is objected that this training is 'unnatural' it must be pointed out that all training is 'unnatural' and yet inevitable. Even the writer of 'free' verse has been trained to enjoy and detect certain patterns, and his 'free' verse often shows the skeleton of a 'regular' pattern underneath.

These effects are not felt by every reader: to some,

the devices are merely evidence of technical incompetence. It is, however, demonstrable that some people respond to them without having them pointed out; the only possible conclusion is that these people are more sensitive to language than the others. The only objection to such devices is that it would never be possible to teach everyone to respond to them, therefore they tend to cut off one section of the community from another. But the same objection could be brought against the theory of tensors, and it is as necessary that some members of the community should explore the possibilities of language and use it to control and clarify emotional, spiritual and sensuous experience, as it is that others should use their mathematical notation to codify and organize our scientific knowledge.

Modern poets have been decreasingly concerned with sound-effects as independent entities, and today the auditory rhetoric of poetry is dictated, not by its own rules, but by the central impulse of the poem. Perhaps for this reason, no adequate study of auditory rhetoric exists. Prosody is little more than an enumeration and naming of all the possible combinations of stressed and unstressed syllables. It takes no account of the variety of stresses, or of the quantitative patterns interwoven with accentual patterns, and it ignores the 'laws' of consonant and vowel sequences. It becomes useless if it loses sight of its original purpose and erects itself into a system of unchanging orthodoxy. In criticism all general rules and classifications are elucidatory: and new discoveries or the introduction of matters previously thought to be irrelevant may compel us to amend them or admit their limitations.

The critic tries to make distinctions and to discover rules valid for the widest possible variety of purpose; but for different purposes different classifications may be necessary, and this is true not only of the classifications which we use in discussing the technique of poetry, but also of those which we use when speaking of the poets. Where, as in the criticism of poetry, we are dealing with something as complex as personalities, any division must be arbitrary. An historical or categorical label never prescribes the ultimate achievements of the poet, it merely tells us where to look for them; and from time to time, if we are to recognize the poet as a mobile force, new categories are needed.

Often the new dividing line between the categories may not be far removed from the old; and it may be objected that the classification which results from a distinction between the 'English' sensibility and 'European' sensibility does not differ very much from the distinction between 'romantic' and 'classic' writers, or between 'pure' poetry and 'didactic and descriptive' poetry. There is, however, a difference in the points on which it focusses our attention. Any distinction in terms of schools and tendencies is misleading if we use it for any purpose beyond concentrating our attention for a moment on one aspect of the work of one or two selected writers; and if for the moment I have classified poets, it is merely as a shop-window arrangement, a tactful use of contrasts to focus attention on certain qualities, and to lessen some of the difficulty which readers find when they approach modern poetry for the first time.

New poetry is never popular unless it accepts the prejudices of the immediate past, and, giving an aura of heroism to actions which are already inevitable, stifles those misgivings out of which the real decisions of the present are to grow. Often in reading poems for this anthology, I have come upon one which, though its beginning seemed to show an apprehension beyond the commonplace, lapsed at the end into a false simplicity: a statement in familiar terms which had been given no new significance and depth. I have found Mr. Aldington's poems, in spite of their innovations, disappointing in that way; the earlier poems of Mr. Monro, and many of the poems of Mr. Cummings affect me similarly. The poet has seen something, and almost seen it clearly; and then at the end, unable to say it, he has been content to say some lesser thing, and the true poem remains unwritten.

For a time, the false poem may be more popular than the true one could have been. 'The poet', Johnson said, 'must divest himself of the prejudice of his age and country; he must consider right and wrong in their abstracted and invariable state; he must disregard present laws and opinions, and rise to general and transcendental truths, which will always be the same. He must, therefore, content himself with the slow progress of his name, contemn the praise of his own time, and commit his claims to the justice of posterity.'

Sometimes it is argued that readers, too, must leave the judgment of contemporary literature to posterity; but the judgment of posterity is only another name for the accumulated judgments of those who read most carefully and with least prejudice and preconception. To read merely to concur in the judgments of our ancestors is to inhibit all spontaneous response and to miss the pleasure of that reading which moulds the opinions, tastes and actions of our time. The first important thing about contemporary literature is that it *is* contemporary: it is speaking to us and for us, here, now. Judgment can only follow an act of sympathy and understanding, and to let our appreciation grow outwards from that which immediately appeals to us is both wiser and more enjoyable than to echo the judgments of others or to restrict and sour our appreciation by hastily attacking anything which at first seems difficult or irritating.   MICHAEL ROBERTS, 1936

INTRODUCTION TO THE SECOND EDITION

THE *Faber Book of Modern Verse* was made some sixteen years ago, and has been the most influential of all collections of contemporary poetry: in fact, as J. Isaacs has pointed out, it formed the taste of a generation. Its compiler said in his Introduction that he had chosen the poems because they pleased him for reasons 'neither personal nor idiosyncratic'. But I question whether any anthology which gave an entirely impersonal choice would have sufficient character to survive, any more than a periodical could do so, and it was natural that Michael Roberts's criteria of originality in poetic thought or technique should reflect his personal preferences. By his two earlier collections, *New Signatures* and *New Country*, he had introduced his contemporaries to the public: as a poet himself, he had an instinctive understanding of their aims; as a trained thinker, he was able to rationalize them. He has set a shape upon his book which no subsequent editions will be able to distort.

However, a new generation of poets has grown up since the book appeared, and it has accordingly lost its contemporary character. Michael Roberts had planned to bring it up to date, but had not advanced farther in the project than to make the few notes, which I shall describe later. If he had lived to carry out the work, he might have made a drastic reshaping such as no other hand has the liberty to attempt. As it is, I have deleted no poet without his authority, but have tried to record important developments in the work of some older writers, and to give a representative selection of new ones.

It is always misleading to make clear-cut divisions of date or movement, but it happens that the war years come more or less in the centre of the period covered by my supplement, and most of the poems which I have chosen were written during those years (a time when many people bought books of poetry, though it is a question how many can have read them), or later. The original edition, then, could be taken as representative up to the end of the 'thirties. Then *New Verse* came to an end; *Poetry, London* began: it is tempting to make the division thus, though it is a false simplification. But even the editor of the first-named, who detested everything about the other periodical, found it representative of its period. It is easier to affix a label to the poetry of *New Verse*, concerned with exact reporting and 'the universe of objects and events'[1] than to that of *Poetry, London*, which was a hotch-potch. Yet this very eclecticism was a virtue, at a time when other poetry periodicals were brought to an end by the war: it became a growing-point, and most of the younger poets in this book have at some time been published in

[1] Geoffrey Grigson: Preface to *New Verse* Anthology.

36

its pages. In a reaction towards a stricter editorial direction and a more disciplined metric, the periodical *Nine* was started, but it is too early yet to say what value the movement will have, or whether it will seem to a later generation to be representative of its period. More than one of this group is included here, but I found that none among the poets I had chosen was under thirty, and I could see no sufficient reason to alter my choice. This, it seems, is not the moment in which to judge the post-war generation, or even to distinguish it clearly. But as we consider the time which has passed since Michael Roberts chose his anthology, we can see that he was right in prophesying an increase of poetry appealing directly to the sub-conscious mind: of the kinds of poetry represented among the youngest in his book, this was the one that developed most rapidly, for good or ill. I do not think that anyone comparing the new edition with the old would feel that the poets of Roberts's own generation had quite fulfilled their promise, except Auden, and even there I found myself very reluctant to sacrifice any of his early poetry to make room for his later. William Empson published a second admirable book, in 1940, but no collection of his has appeared since then. But of the youngest generation who appeared in the *Faber Book*, there is much to record.

When we re-read the section of Roberts's Introduction which deals with technical devices, I think we feel a change in attitude at the present time. I doubt whether anyone writing now would speak so emphatically against treating poetry as if it were song. He rightly decries the sing-song method of reading aloud, but Coleridge pointed out the dangers of the opposite extreme in his *Biographia*, and better the chanting than the chatty style. The lyrical tone is stronger in this second edition than it was in the first: when that was published, Auden had not reached the zenith of his musical powers, and Eliot had not written the wonderful lyrics in traditional metrics for the fourth movements of his *Quartets*. Taught by these two masters, by Yeats, and by Empson's use of the Villanelle, poets have learnt to use traditional forms again. The effect is not like that of a medium suddenly speaking with a borrowed voice (that effect was largely exhausted by *The Waste Land*), for although the metric is borrowed, the diction is not, and even the metric is altered to fit its new purpose: a resonance is added to the new thing said, by overtones from earlier poems in the form, as harmonics give resonance to a note, and there is an added poignancy, where the poetry is expressing strong emotion, from the strict technical restraint.

'Full end-rhyme', Roberts said, 'is felt by many modern poets to be too arbitrary and too noisy for serious poetry.' But if poets shunned full rhymes, it was surely not so much because of their noisiness as because of their scarcity in English, which made so many of them too stale for further use. So poets resorted to assonance, dissonance and off-rhyme, and as a result of this enlargement of scope, full rhyme has lost some of its staleness. Poets so diverse as David Gascoyne and Vernon Watkins can use it continuously: in Gascoyne's poetry, where the virtue is emotional intensity rather than music, its directness helps the directness of his speech; in that of Watkins, his wide verbal resource enables him to use it without constraint—see the sonnet *A Christening Remembered*, which is perfectly conventional in form except for a slight alteration in the order and one dissonant rhyme.

As to the various tricks of rhyme (none was

unprecedented in English verse, though the consistent use of them was unprecedented), they have become so far domesticated that they cease to attract the reader's attention: they enabled an academic poet, Laurence Binyon, to translate Dante into English terza-rima without a bad artificiality. Dissonance is used in all its varieties, and the Welsh poets are, as we should expect, among the most skilful in it. Rhymes on the off-beat enable George Barker to make a remarkable resuscitation of the sonnet-form, and even to get away with such a rhyme as peninsula-star, which would be excruciating if it were fully emphasized. Assonance, which normally has an effect like that of discord in music (and is brilliantly used thus in MacNeice's *Bagpipe Music* and Auden's *Song for St. Cecilia's Day*), is also surprisingly used for the clinching effect natural to full rhyme—for example, in Keyes's *Glaucus* (wreck-set) ; in Barker's *Love Poem* (feet-weep); and in Comfort's *Fifth Elegy* (leaves-seeds), where it actually ends the poem. There are conventional rhymes interrupted by the slight surprise which redeems the poem from academicism, as with G. S. Fraser; there are rhymes touched so lightly as hardly to be noticeable, as in Kathleen Raine's *The Silver Stag*; there are full rhymes used with a clinching and epigrammatic effect, as in Lawrence Durrell's *Coptic Poem* and *Green Coconuts* (he achieves, surprisingly, nearly the same effect without the aid of rhyme in two other of the poems printed here). Often, full rhyme and dissonance alternate, as in Vernon Watkins's marvellous *White Blossom*. Another technique, which Eliot perfected—the sequence of images without a logical connexion, has become as natural to poetry as it is to the cinema under the name of montage: again, the consistent use of it was the innovation.

Michael Roberts noticed a decline in descriptive poetry. The description of a scene for its own sake, with no *pathetic fallacy* to turn our eyes to man, was rare enough at any time, and it is not often to be found in this book; yet it does exist, though evocation would seem a more accurate word than description, when E. J. Scovell writes of swans or W. S. Graham of the sea. Landscape here often teaches a lesson, reflects or contrasts with a mood: so in the war poems it provides a comment, wistful or satirical, on the insanities of war.

It is still possible to use the classification made by Roberts of predominantly 'European' and predominantly 'English' sensibilities. John Heath-Stubbs might be taken as an example of the first, and Kathleen Raine of the second: we should probably classify Lawrence Durrell's early poetry as belonging to the second type, whereas his later poetry belongs rather to the first. But Roberts was careful to point out that such classifications are only useful in order to emphasize some aspects of a poet's work. Certainly they do not help us to enjoy unfamiliar poetry, and in order to judge contemporary poetry, you must first be able to enjoy it. Useless to approach it as a dramatic critic approaches a new play, with a motto of No Surrender on your shield. And herein lies the difficulty of contemporary judgement: that the first surrender has to be complete. It is true that with earlier poetry, our critical classifications into major, minor, and so on, are forgotten as we read, so that—for instance—we do not care, while we enjoy the amateur poet Robert Hayman's *Sir Francis Drake*, whether he ever wrote another successful poem or not; but because the form and matter are familiar, it is easy for us to preserve a certain detachment, which does the poem no injury.

But the same sort of detachment in reading, for instance, Vernon Watkin's *White Blossom*, would be fatal to the poem's effect: not only because it appeals to the sub-conscious mind, but also because the effort of comparison and analysis, when form and matter are new to us, preoccupies just those faculties which should be responding to the poetry.

Michael Roberts's division might also seem to separate those who tend to look inward (the 'pure' or 'English' sensibility) from those who tend to look outward. But those who look inward may, like Charles Williams in *The Crowning of Arthur*, produce a visual scene no less vivid for being unlike anything in the exterior world; and a poem like E. J. Scovell's *The Swan's Feet*, which is minutely observed from the exterior world, derives its power from our sense of a meaning, implied though not explicit, in the whole picture which she sets before us. Swans are a recurrent symbol in contemporary poetry, and the reader if he chooses may compare their appearances in this book. Edith Sitwell's poem is a feast for the senses, yet her swans have appeared before the inward eye, and their perfection is of the imagination. E. J. Scovell's are, as I say, observed from those birds which are the property of the Crown or the Worshipful Company of Vintners, are liable to contamination by tar, and have dark webbed feet. Lawrence Durrell's are intellectual, almost geometrical, symbols (fraudulent because their source of movement is hidden, followed about by empty space): almost, but not quite, because they remind us of human myths.

I must now describe briefly the difference between the new edition and the old. Mrs. Roberts gave me the fragmentary notes that her husband had made of his intentions, which were as follows: that Edwin Muir, who had originally been omitted for reasons given in the Introduction, should now be included; that Kathleen Raine should have a place among the younger generation; that two of the younger poets in the original book should now be omitted; and that one of T. S. Eliot's *Quartets* should be included instead of *Ash Wednesday*. He also mentioned Empson's *Missing Dates* as one of the poems that he wished to include. These intentions I have, of course, carried out. Where the selections had become out of date because of a development in the poets' work, I have cut out some poems in order to make room for new, although as the length had to be the same as before, I could not work with much freedom. When the space given to a poet was obviously now inadequate, as in the case of Edith Sitwell, I have taken from others in order to correct it. But of course the amount of space given is not always a measurement of importance, in spite of our ridiculous though inevitable custom of paying for poetry by the page. I have chosen a long poem or a short one because of the merits of the work. Where the selections were still representative, I have left them as they stood, without taking account of an altered taste which might now on occasion choose rather differently. I have been allowed 64 pages for additional poets, among whom I have included Roberts himself. From an older generation I have also added Charles Williams, whose *Taliessin through Logres* was published two years after this book first appeared. Williams's poetry is not flattered by the anthologist, for it needs to be read as a whole, but it ought in its own right to be included in any contemporary survey, and not merely—as some have maintained—

because of its influence on young poets. My choice of these last will inevitably seem arbitrary. Perhaps there are three or four who have as good a right to inclusion as some who are printed here; but one of the virtues of the anthology was the generous length of its selections, and although I could not be so lavish as Roberts was, I limited my list of poets, rather than allot a couple of pages each to a greater number. For the same reason, I have not attempted to represent the latest American poets: I could not have done justice to them in the space, and should have had to be even more arbitrary in my choice. I have tried to apply Roberts's test, that the poems included should be those which 'add to the resources of poetry', or are 'likely to influence the future development of poetry and language'. It is not always an easy test to make, and it has helped me more in deciding on my exclusions than on my inclusions; but I make the point again here, to remind the reader that while this is a collection of *modern* verse, it does not necessarily include all the best poems written in this period, 1910-1951.

Certain poems cry out to be included because they speak for their time, and even if they have often been reprinted, it is impossible to omit them without leaving a hole in the anthology. Such poems of the war —on their very different levels—are Edith Sitwell's *Still Falls the Rain*, David Gascoyne's *Miserere*, and Henry Reed's *Lessons of the War*. Or one may wish to avoid a well-known poem, and find that a selection would not sufficiently describe a poet's work without it—such is Dylan Thomas's *After the Funeral*. Sometimes it is only a poet's early work which seems fully typical of him, for the anthology may come at a time when he is feeling after a new style: if I have not always

43

included later work, it does not mean that I have not read it. But one is most unsafe when trying to be most impersonal: to choose the best work in a kind of writing which one does not personally like.

I have sometimes felt impelled, probably unnecessarily, to avoid the poems which I chose for my *Little Book of Modern Verse* ten years ago. This was not because I had come to think less of them, but rather because of the impulse which makes one avoid using the same words twice, in describing anything. Because an anthology *is* a description—its editor's description of a given period; and perhaps his desire to show the merits of his chosen poets (however often thwarted by copyright or printing costs) is akin to that which Mozart expressed, when he said that he liked to fit a singer with an aria as neatly as a tailor fits his customer with a suit of clothes. To make another musical analogy, an editor must consider the metrical juxtaposition of his chosen poems, in order to try to avoid monotony, just as a programme-planner will avoid giving two consecutive works in the same key. It requires some self-control to read an anthology as it was meant to be read—leisurely, and with a pause after each poet: yet if one does not, it is as if one added to apple-pie not only cheese but also mustard and chestnuts and avocado pear.

Michael Roberts began and ended his Introduction with a plea for sympathy towards contemporary poetry. It is no less necessary to-day, although the danger is indifference rather than hostility, if the sales of new books of verse are any proof. But his book helped to break down the barrier between poets and audience, and I hope that this new edition may bring the younger generation some fresh readers. ANNE RIDLER, 1951

44

POETRY

GERARD MANLEY HOPKINS

THE WRECK OF THE DEUTSCHLAND

To the
happy memory of five Franciscan Nuns
exiles by the Falk Laws
drowned between midnight and morning of
Dec. 7th, 1875

PART THE FIRST

1

Thou mastering me
God! giver of breath and bread;
World's strand, sway of the sea;
Lord of living and dead;
Thou hast bound bones and veins in me, fastened me
flesh,
And after it almost unmade, what with dread,
Thy doing: and dost thou touch me afresh?
Over again I feel thy finger and find thee.

2

I did say yes
O at lightning and lashed rod;
Thou heardst me truer than tongue confess
Thy terror, O Christ, O God;
Thou knowest the walls, altar and hour and night:
The swoon of a heart that the sweep and the hurl of
thee trod
Hard down with a horror of height:
And the midriff astrain with leaning of, laced with fire
of stress.

47

The frown of his face
Before me, the hurtle of hell
Behind, where, where was a, where was a place?
I whirled out wings that spell
And fled with a fling of the heart to the heart of the
Host.
My heart, but you were dovewinged, I can tell,
Carrier-witted, I am bold to boast,
To flash from the flame to the flame then, tower from
the grace to the grace.

4

I am soft sift
In an hourglass—at the wall
Fast, but mined with a motion, a drift,
And it crowds and it combs to the fall;
I steady as a water in a well, to a poise, to a pane,
But roped with, always, all the way down from the
tall
Fells or flanks of the voel, a vein
Of the gospel proffer, a pressure, a principle, Christ's
gift.

5

I kiss my hand
To the stars, lovely-asunder
Starlight, wafting him out of it; and
Glow, glory in thunder;
Kiss my hand to the dappled-with-damson west:
Since, tho' he is under the world's splendour and
wonder,
His mystery must be instressed, stressed;

For I greet him the days I meet him, and bless when I
understand.

6

Not out of his bliss
Springs the stress felt
Nor first from heaven (and few know this)
Swings the stroke dealt—
Stroke and a stress that stars and storms deliver,
That guilt is hushed by, hearts are flushed by and
melt—
But it rides time like riding a river
(And here the faithful waver, the faithless fable and
miss).

7

It dates from day
Of his going in Galilee ;
Warm-laid grave of a womb-life grey ;
Manger, maiden's knee ;
The dense and the driven Passion, and frightful
sweat ;
Thence the discharge of it, there its swelling to be,
Though felt before, though in high flood yet—
What none would have known of it, only the heart,
being hard at bay.

8

Is out with it! Oh,
We lash with the best or worst
Word last! How a lush-kept plush-capped sloe
Will, mouthed to flesh-burst,
Gush!—flush the man, the being with it, sour or
sweet,

Brim, in a flash, full!—Hither then, last or first,
To hero of Calvary, Christ's feet—
Never ask if meaning it, wanting it, warned of it—men
go.

9

Be adored among men,
God, three-numberèd form;
Wring thy rebel, dogged in den,
Man's malice, with wrecking and storm.
Beyond saying sweet, past telling of tongue,
Thou art lightning and love, I found it, a winter and
warm;
Father and fondler of heart thou hast wrung:
Hast thy dark descending and most art merciful then.

10

With an anvil-ding
And with fire in him forge thy will
Or rather, rather then, stealing as Spring
Through him, melt him but master him still:
Whether at once, as once at a crash Paul,
Or as Austin, a lingering-out sweet skill,
Make mercy in all of us, out of us all
Mastery, but be adored, but be adored King.

PART THE SECOND

11

'Some find me a sword; some
The flange and the rail; flame,
Fang, or flood' goes Death on drum,
And storms bugle his fame.

But wé dream we are rooted in earth—Dust!
Flesh falls within sight of us, we, though our flower
    the same,
    Wave with the meadow, forget that there must
The sour scythe cringe, and the blear share come.

12

On Saturday sailed from Bremen,
    American-outward-bound,
Take settler and seamen, tell men with women,
    Two hundred souls in the round—
O Father, not under thy feathers nor ever as guess-
        ing
The goal was a shoal, of a fourth the doom to be
        drowned;
    Yet did the dark side of the bay of thy blessing
Not vault them, the millions of rounds of thy mercy
        not reeve even them in?

13

Into the snows she sweeps,
    Hurling the haven behind,
The Deutschland, on Sunday; and so the sky
        keeps,
    For the infinite air is unkind,
And the sea flint-flake, black-backed in the regular
        blow,
Sitting Eastnortheast, in cursed quarter, the wind;
    Wiry and white-fiery and whirlwind-swivellèd
        snow
Spins to the widow-making unchilding unfathering
        deeps.

51

She drove in the dark to leeward,
She struck—not a reef or a rock
But the combs of a smother of sand: night drew
her
Dead to the Kentish Knock;
And she beat the bank down with her bows and the
ride of her keel:
The breakers rolled on her beam with ruinous
shock;
And canvas and compass, the whorl and the wheel
Idle for ever to waft her or wind her with, these she
endured.

15

Hope had grown grey hairs,
Hope had mourning on,
Trenched with tears, carved with cares,
Hope was twelve hours gone;
And frightful a nightfall folded rueful a day
Nor rescue, only rocket and lightship, shone,
And lives at last were washing away:
To the shrouds they took,—they shook in the hurling
and horrible airs.

16

One stirred from the rigging to save
The wild woman-kind below,
With a rope's end round the man, handy and
brave—
He was pitched to his death at a blow,
For all his dreadnought breast and braids of thew:
They could tell him for hours, dandled the to and fro

Through the cobbled foam-fleece, what could he do GERARD
With the burl of the fountains of air, buck and the   MANLEY
flood of the wave?   HOPKINS

17

They fought with God's cold—
And they could not and fell to the deck
(Crushed them) or water (and drowned them) or
rolled
With the sea-romp over the wreck.
Night roared, with the heart-break hearing a heart-
broke rabble,
The woman's wailing, the crying of child without
check—
Till a lioness arose breasting the babble,
A prophetess towered in the tumult, a virginal tongue
told.

18

Ah, touched in your bower of bone
Are you! turned for an exquisite smart,
Have you! make words break from me here all
alone,
Do you!—mother of being in me, heart.
O unteachably after evil, but uttering truth,
Why, tears! is it? tears; such a melting, a madriga.
start!
Never-eldering revel and river of youth,
What can it be, this glee? the good you have there of
your own?

19

Sister, a sister calling
A master, her master and mine !—

And the inboard seas run swirling and hawling;
The rash smart sloggering brine
Blinds her; but she that weather sees one thing, one;
Has one fetch in her: she rears herself to divine
Ears, and the call of the tall nun
To the men in the tops and the tackle rode over the
storm's brawling.

20

She was first of a five and came
Of a coifèd sisterhood.
(O Deutschland, double a desperate name!
O world wide of its good!
But Gertrude, lily, and Luther, are two of a town,
Christ's lily and beast of the waste wood:
From life's dawn it is drawn down,
Abel is Cain's brother and breasts they have sucked the
same.)

21

Loathed for a love men knew in them,
Banned by the land of their birth,
Rhine refused them. Thames would ruin them;
Surf, snow, river and earth
Gnashed: but thou art above, thou Orion of light;
Thy unchancelling poising palms were weighing the
worth,
Thou martyr-master: in thy sight
Storm flakes were scroll-leaved flowers, lily showers—
sweet heaven was astrew in them.

22

Five! the finding and sake
And cipher of suffering Christ.

Mark, the mark is of man's make
    And the word of it Sacrificed.
But he scores it in scarlet himself on his own be-
        spoken,
Before-time-taken, dearest prizèd and priced—
    Stigma, signal, cinquefoil token
For lettering of the lamb's fleece, ruddying of the-rose
        flake.

23

Joy fall to thee, father Francis,
    Drawn to the Life that died;
With the gnarls of the nails in thee, niche of the
        lance, his
    Lovescape crucified
And seal of his seraph-arrival! and these thy
        daughters
And five-livèd and leavèd favour and pride,
    Are sisterly sealed in wild waters,
To bathe in his fall-gold mercies, to breathe in his all-
        fire glances.

24

Away in the loveable west,
    On a pastoral forehead of Wales,
I was under a roof here, I was at rest,
    And they the prey of the gales;
She to the black-about air, to the breaker, the
        thickly
Falling flakes, to the throng that catches and quails
    Was calling 'O Christ, Christ, come quickly':
The cross to her she calls Christ to her, christens her
        wild-worst Best.

55

25

The majesty! what did she mean?
Breathe, arch and original Breath.
Is it love in her of the being as her lover had been?
Breathe, body of lovely Death.
They were else-minded then, altogether, the men
Woke thee with a *we are perishing* in the weather of
Gennesareth.
Or is it that she cried for the crown then,
The keener to come at the comfort for feeling the
combating keen?

26

For how to the heart's cheering
The down-dugged ground-hugged grey
Hovers off, the jay-blue heavens appearing
Of pied and peeled May!
Blue-beating and hoary-glow height; or night, still
higher,
With belled fire and the moth-soft Milky Way,
What by your measure is the heaven of desire,
The treasure never eyesight got, nor was ever guessed
what for the hearing?

27

No, but it was not these.
The jading and jar of the cart,
Time's tasking, it is fathers that asking for ease
Of the sodden-with-its-sorrowing heart,
Not danger, electrical horror; then further it finds
The appealing of the Passion is tenderer in prayer
apart:

Other, I gather, in measure her mind's
Burden, in wind's burly and beat of endragonèd seas.

28

But how shall I . . . make me room there:
Reach me a . . . Fancy, come faster—
Strike you the sight of it? look at it loom there,
Thing that she . . . there then! the Master,
Ipse, the only one, Christ, King, Head:
He was to cure the extremity where he had cast her;
Do, deal, lord it with living and dead;
Let him ride, her pride, in his triumph, despatch and
have done with his doom there.

29

Ah! there was a heart right!
There was single eye!
Read the unshapeable shock night
And knew the who and the why;
Wording it how but by him that present and past,
Heaven and earth are word of, worded by?—
The Simon Peter of a soul! to the blast
Tarpeian-fast, but a blown beacon of light.

30

Jesu, heart's light,
Jesu, maid's son,
What was the feast followed the night
Thou hadst glory of this nun?—
Feast of the one woman without stain.
For so conceivèd, so to conceive thee is done;
But here was heart-throe, birth of a brain,
Word, that heard and kept thee and uttered thee out-
right.

31

Well, she has thee for the pain, for the
Patience; but pity of the rest of them!
Heart, go and bleed at a bitterer vein for the
Comfortless unconfessed of them—
No not uncomforted: lovely-felicitous Providence
Finger of a tender of, O of a feathery delicacy, the
breast of the
Maiden could obey so, be a bell to, ring of it, and
Startle the poor sheep back! is the shipwrack then a
harvest, does tempest carry the grain
for thee?

32

I admire thee, master of the tides,
Of the Yore-flood, of the year's fall;
The recurb and the recovery of the gulf's sides,
The girth of it and the wharf of it and the wall;
Stanching, quenching ocean of a motionable mind;
Ground of being, and granite of it: past all
Grasp God, throned behind
Death with a sovereignty that heeds but hides, bodes
but abides;

33

With a mercy that outrides
The all of water, an ark
For the listener; for the lingerer with a love
glides
Lower than death and the dark;
A vein for the visiting of the past-prayer, pent in
prison,
The-last-breath penitent spirits—the uttermost
mark

Our passion-plungèd giant risen,
The Christ of the Father compassionate, fetched in the
storm of his strides.

GERARD
MANLEY
HOPKINS

34

Now burn, new born to the world,
Double-naturèd name,
The heaven-flung, heart-fleshed, maiden-furled
Miracle-in-Mary-of-flame,
Mid-numbered He in three of the thunder-throne!
Not a dooms-day dazzle in his coming nor dark as he
came;
Kind, but royally reclaiming his own;
A released shower, let flash to the shire, not a lightning
of fire hard-hurled.

35

Dame, at our door
Drowned, and among our shoals,
Remember us in the roads, the heaven-haven of
the Reward:
Our King back, oh, upon English souls!
Let him easter in us, be a dayspring to the dimness
of us, be a crimson-cresseted east,
More brightening her, rare-dear Britain, as his reign
rolls,
Pride, rose, prince, hero of us, high-priest,
Our hearts' charity's hearth's fire, our thoughts'
chivalry's throng's Lord.

GERARD
MANLEY
HOPKINS

FELIX RANDAL

Felix Randal the farrier, O he is dead then? my duty
    all ended,
Who have watched his mould of man, big-boned and
    hardy-handsome
Pining, pining, till time when reason rambled in it and
    some
Fatal four disorders, fleshed there, all contended?

Sickness broke him. Impatient he cursed at first, but
    mended
Being anointed and all; though a heavenlier heart began
    some
Months earlier, since I had our sweet reprieve and
    ransom
Tendered to him. Ah well, God rest him all road ever
    he offended!

This seeing the sick endears them to us, us too it en-
    dears.
My tongue had taught thee comfort, touch had
    quenched thy tears,
Thy tears that touched my heart, child, Felix, poor
    Felix Randal;

How far from then forethought of, all thy more
    boisterous years,
When thou at the random grim forge, powerful amidst
    peers,
Didst fettle for the great grey drayhorse his bright and
    battering sandal!

PIED BEAUTY

GERARD
MANLEY
HOPKINS

Glory be to God for dappled things—
    For skies of couple-colour as a brinded cow;
        For rose-moles all in stipple upon trout that swim;
Fresh-firecoal chestnut-falls; finches' wings;
    Landscape plotted and pieced—fold, fallow, and
           plough;
        And áll trádes, their gear and tackle and trim.

All things counter, original, spare, strange;
    Whatever is fickle, freckled (who knows how?)
        With swift, slow; sweet, sour; adazzle, dim;
He fathers-forth whose beauty is past change:
           Praise him.

ANDROMEDA

Now Time's Andromeda on this rock rude,
With not her either beauty's equal or
Her injury's, looks off by both horns of shore,
Her flower, her piece of being, doomed dragon's food.
    Time past she has been attempted and pursued
By many blows and banes; but now hears roar
A wilder beast from West than all were, more
Rife in her wrongs, more lawless, and more lewd.

    Her Perseus linger and leave her tó her extremes?—
Pillowy air he treads a time and hangs
His thoughts on her, forsaken that she seems,
    All while her patience, morselled into pangs,
Mounts; then to alight disarming, no one dreams,
With Gorgon's gear and barebill, thongs and fangs.

61

THE CANDLE INDOORS

Some candle clear burns somewhere I come by.
I muse at how its being puts blissful back
With yellowy moisture mild night's blear-all black,
Or to-fro tender trambeams truckle at the eye.
By that window what task what fingers ply,
I plod wondering, a-wanting, just for lack
Of answer the eagerer a-wanting Jessy or Jack
There—God to aggrándise, God to glorify.—

Come you indoors, come home; your fading fire
Mend first and vital candle in close heart's vault:
You there are master, do your own desire;
What hinders? Are you beam-blind, yet to a fault
In a neighbour deft-handed? are you that liar
And, cast by conscience out, spendsavour salt?

INVERSNAID

This darksome burn, horseback brown,
His rollrock highroad roaring down,
In coop and in comb the fleece of his foam
Flutes and low to the lake falls home.

A windpuff-bonnet of fáwn-fróth
Turns and twindles over the broth
Of a pool so pitchblack, féll-frówning,
It rounds and rounds Despair to drowning.

Degged with dew, dappled with dew
Are the groins of the braes that the brook treads
    through,

62

Wiry heathpacks, flitches of fern,
And the beadbonny ash that sits over the burn.

What would the world be, once bereft
Of wet and of wildness? Let them be left,
O let them be left, wildness and wet;
Long live the weeds and the wilderness yet.

GERARD
MANLEY
HOPKINS

THE WINDHOVER:

To Christ our Lord

I caught this morning morning's minion, king-
    dom of daylight's dauphin, dapple-dawn-drawn
        Falcon, in his riding
    Of the rolling level underneath him steady air, and
        striding
High there, how he rung upon the rein of a wimpling
        wing
In his ecstasy! then off, off forth on swing,
    As a skate's heel sweeps smooth on a bow-bend: the
        hurl and gliding
    Rebuffed the big wind. My heart in hiding
Stirred for a bird,—the achieve of, the mastery of the
        thing!

Brute beauty and valour and act, oh, air, pride, plume,
    here
    Buckle! AND the fire that breaks from thee then, a
        billion
Times told lovelier, more dangerous, O my chevalier!

    No wonder of it: shéer plód makes plough down
        sillion
Shine, and blue-bleak embers, ah my dear,
    Fall, gall themselves, and gash gold-vermilion.

'AS KINGFISHERS CATCH FIRE, DRAGON-FLIES DRAW FLAME'

As kingfishers catch fire, dragonflies dráw fláme;
As tumbled over rim in roundy wells
Stones ring; like each tucked string tells, each hung
      bell's
Bow swung finds tongue to fling out broad its name;
Each mortal thing does one thing and the same:
Deals out that being indoors each one dwells;
Selves—goes itself; *myself* it speaks and spells,
Crying *Whát I do is me: for that I came.*

Í say móre: the just man justices;
Kéeps gráce: thát keeps all his goings graces;
Acts in God's eye what in God's eye he is—
Chríst—for Christ plays in ten thousand places,
Lovely in limbs, and lovely in eyes not his
To the Father through the features of men's faces.

HARRY PLOUGHMAN

Hard as hurdle arms, with a broth of goldish flue
Breathed round; the rack of ribs; the scooped flank;
      lank
Rope-over thigh; knee-nave; and barrelled shank—
            Head and foot, shoulder and shank—
By a grey eye's heed steered well, one crew, fall to;
Stand at stress. Each limb's barrowy brawn, his thew
That onewhere curded, onewhere sucked or sank—
            Soared or sank—,
Though as a beechbole firm, finds his, as at a roll-call,
      rank
And features, in flesh, what deed he each must do—
            His sinew-service where do.

He leans to it, Harry bends, look. Back, elbow, and
    liquid waist
In him, all quail to the wallowing o' the plough:
    's cheek crimsons; curls
Wag or crossbridle, in a wind lifted, windlaced—
            See his wind- lilylocks-laced;
Churlsgrace, too, child of Amansstrength, how it hangs
    or hurls
Them—broad in bluff hide his frowning feet lashed!
    raced
With, along them, cragiron under and cold furls—
            With-a-fountain's shining-shot furls.

'NO WORST, THERE IS NONE. PITCHED PAST PITCH OF GRIEF'

No worst, there is none. Pitched past pitch of grief,
More pangs will, schooled at forepangs, wilder wring.
Comforter, where, where is your comforting?
Mary, mother of us, where is your relief?
My cries heave, herds-long; huddle in a main, a chief
Woe, world-sorrow; on an age-old anvil wince and
    sing—
Then lull, then leave off. Fury had shrieked 'No ling-
ering! Let me be fell: force I must be brief'.

    O the mind, mind has mountains; cliffs of fall
Frightful, sheer, no-man-fathomed. Hold them cheap
May who ne'er hung there. Nor does long our small
Durance deal with that steep or deep. Here! creep,
Wretch, under a comfort serves in a whirlwind: all
Life death does end and each day dies with sleep.

SPELT FROM SIBYL'S LEAVES

Earnest, earthless, equal, attuneable, | vaulty, vol-
    uminous, . . . stupendous

Evening strains to be tíme's vást, | womb-of-all, home-
    of-all, hearse-of-all night.

Her fond yellow hornlight wound to the west, | her
    wild hollow hoarlight hung to the height

Waste; her earliest stars, earl-stars, | stárs principal,
    overbend us,

Fíre-féaturing heaven. For earth | her being has un-
    bound, her dapple is at an end, as-

tray or aswarm, all throughther, in throngs; | self ín
    self steepèd and páshed—qúite

Disremembering, dísmémbering | áll now. Heart,
    you round me right

With: Óur évening is over us; óur night | whélms,
    whélms, ánd will end us.

Only the beak-leaved boughs dragonish | damask the
    tool-smooth bleak light; black,

Ever so black on it. Óur tale, O óur oracle! |.Lét life,
    wáned, ah lét life wind

Off hér once skéined stained véined varíety | upon, áll
    on twó spools; párt, pen, páck

Now her áll in twó flocks, twó folds—black, white; |
    right, wrong; reckon but, reck but, mind

But thése two; wáre of a wórld where bút these | twó
    tell, each off the óther; of a rack

Where, selfwrung, selfstrung, sheathe- and shelterless, |
    thóughts agaínst thoughts ín groans grínd.

'MY OWN HEART LET ME MORE HAVE PITY ON; LET'

Gerard Manley Hopkins

My own heart let me more have pity on; let
Me live to my sad self hereafter kind,
Charitable; not live this tormented mind
With this tormented mind tormenting yet.
　　I cast for comfort I can no more get
By groping round my comfortless, than blind
Eyes in their dark can day or thirst can find
Thirst's all-in-all in all a world of wet.

Soul, self; come, poor Jackself, I do advise
You, jaded, let be; call off thoughts awhile
Elsewhere; leave comfort root-room; let joy size
At God knows when to God knows what; whose smile
's not wrung, see you; unforeseen times rather—as
　　　skies
Betweenpie mountains—lights a lovely mile.

THAT NATURE IS A HERACLITEAN FIRE AND OF THE COMFORT OF THE RESURRECTION

Cloud-puffball, torn tufts, tossed pillows |
　　flaunt forth, then chevy on an air-
built thoroughfare: heaven-roysterers, in gay-gangs |
　　they throng: they glitter in marches.
Down roughcast, down dazzling whitewash, | wher-
　　ever an elm arches,
Shivelights and shadowtackle in long | lashes lace, lance,
　　and pair.
Delightfully the bright wind boisterous | ropes,
　　wrestles, beats earth bare

67

GERARD MANLEY HOPKINS Of yestertempest's creases; in pool and rut peel
　　　parches
Squandering ooze to squeezed | dough, crust, dust;
　　　stanches, starches
Squadroned masks and manmarks | treadmire toil there
Footfretted in it. Million-fuelèd, | nature's bonfire
　　　burns on.
But quench her bonniest, dearest | to her, her clearest-
　　　selvèd spark
Man, how fast his firedint, | his mark on mind, is gone!
Both are in an unfathomable, all is in an enormous dark
Drowned. O pity and indig | nation! Manshape, that
　　　shone
Sheer off, disseveral, a star, | death blots black out;
　　　nor mark
　　　　　Is any of him at all so stark
But vastness blurs and time | beats level. Enough! the
　　　Resurrection,
A heart's-clarion! Away grief's gasping, | joyless days,
　　　dejection.
　　　　　Across my foundering deck shone
A beacon, an eternal beam. | Flesh fade, and mortal
　　　trash
Fall to the residuary worm; | world's wildfire, leave
　　　but ash:
　　　　　In a flash, at a trumpet crash,
I am all at once what Christ is, | since he was what I am,
　　　and
This Jack, joke, poor potsherd, | patch, matchwood,
　　　immortal diamond,
　　　　　Is immortal diamond.

W. B. YEATS

RED HANRAHAN'S SONG ABOUT IRELAND

The old brown thorn-trees break in two high over
    Cummen Strand,
Under a bitter black wind that blows from the left
    hand;
Our courage breaks like an old tree in a black wind
    and dies,
But we have hidden in our hearts the flame out of the
    eyes
Of Cathleen, the daughter of Houlihan.

The wind has bundled up the clouds high over Knock-
    narea,
And thrown the thunder on the stones for all that
    Maeve can say.
Angers that are like noisy clouds have set our hearts
    abeat;
But we have all bent low and low and kissed the quiet
    feet
Of Cathleen, the daughter of Houlihan.

The yellow pool has overflowed high up on Clooth-na-
    Bare,
For the wet winds are blowing out of the clinging air;
Like heavy flooded waters our bodies and our blood;
But purer than a tall candle before the Holy Rood
Is Cathleen, the daughter of Houlihan.

AN IRISH AIRMAN FORESEES HIS DEATH

I know that I shall meet my fate
Somewhere among the clouds above;
Those that I fight I do not hate,
Those that I guard I do not love;
My country is Kiltartan Cross,
My countrymen Kiltartan's poor,
No likely end could bring them loss
Or leave them happier than before.
Nor law, nor duty bade me fight,
Nor public men, nor cheering crowds,
A lonely impulse of delight
Drove to this tumult in the clouds;
I balanced all, brought all to mind,
The years to come seemed waste of breath,
A waste of breath the years behind
In balance with this life, this death.

EASTER, 1916

I have met them at close of day
Coming with vivid faces
From counter or desk among grey
Eighteenth-century houses.
I have passed with a nod of the head
Or polite meaningless words,
Or have lingered awhile and said
Polite meaningless words,
And thought before I had done
Of a mocking tale or a gibe
To please a companion
Around the fire at the club,

Being certain that they and I
But lived where motley is worn:
All changed, changed utterly:
A terrible beauty is born.

That woman's days were spent
In ignorant good-will,
Her nights in argument
Until her voice grew shrill.
What voice more sweet than hers
When, young and beautiful,
She rode to harriers?
This man had kept a school
And rode our wingèd horse;
This other his helper and friend
Was coming into his force;
He might have won fame in the end,
So sensitive his nature seemed,
So daring and sweet his thought.
This other man I had dreamed
A drunken, vainglorious lout.
He had done most bitter wrong
To some who are near my heart,
Yet I number him in the song;
He, too, has resigned his part
In the casual comedy;
He, too, has been changed in his turn,
Transformed utterly:
A terrible beauty is born.

Hearts with one purpose alone
Through summer and winter seem
Enchanted to a stone
To trouble the living stream.

The horse that comes from the road,
The rider, the birds that range
From cloud to tumbling cloud,
Minute by minute they change;
A shadow of cloud on the stream
Changes minute by minute;
A horse-hoof slides on the brim,
And a horse plashes within it;
The long-legged moor-hens dive,
And hens to moor-cocks call;
Minute by minute they live:
The stone's in the midst of all.

Too long a sacrifice
Can make a stone of the heart.
O when may it suffice?
That is Heaven's part, our part
To murmur name upon name,
As a mother names her child
When sleep at last has come
On limbs that had run wild.
What is it but nightfall?
No, no, not night but death;
Was it needless death after all?
For England may keep faith
For all that is done and said.
We know their dream; enough
To know they dreamed and are dead;
And what if excess of love
Bewildered them till they died?
I write it out in a verse—
MacDonagh and MacBride
And Connolly and Pearse
Now and in time to be,

Wherever green is worn,
Are changed, changed utterly:
A terrible beauty is born.

W. B.
YEATS

September 25, 1916

THE SECOND COMING

Turning and turning in the widening gyre
The falcon cannot hear the falconer;
Things fall apart; the centre cannot hold;
Mere anarchy is loosed upon the world,
The blood-dimmed tide is loosed, and everywhere
The ceremony of innocence is drowned;
The best lack all conviction, while the worst
Are full of passionate intensity.

Surely some revelation is at hand;
Surely the Second Coming is at hand.
The Second Coming! Hardly are those words out
When a vast image out of *Spiritus Mundi*
Troubles my sight: somewhere in sands of the
    desert
A shape with lion body and the head of a man,
A gaze blank and pitiless as the sun,
Is moving its slow thighs, while all about it
Reel shadows of the indignant desert birds.
The darkness drops again; but now I know
That twenty centuries of stony sleep
Were vexed to nightmare by a rocking cradle,
And what rough beast, its hour come round at last,
Slouches towards Bethlehem to be born?

THE TOWER

I

What shall I do with this absurdity—
O heart, O troubled heart—this caricature,
Decrepit age that has been tied to me
As to a dog's tail?
                    Never had I more
Excited, passionate, fantastical
Imagination, nor an ear and eye
That more expected the impossible—
No, not in boyhood when with rod and fly,
Or the humbler worm, I climbed Ben Bulben's back
And had the livelong summer day to spend.
It seems that I must bid the Muse go pack,
Choose Plato and Plotinus for a friend
Until imagination, ear and eye,
Can be content with argument and deal
In abstract things; or be derided by
A sort of battered kettle at the heel.

II

I pace upon the battlements and stare
On the foundations of a house, or where
Tree, like a sooty finger, starts from the earth;
And send imagination forth
Under the day's declining beam, and call
Images and memories
From ruin or from ancient trees,
For I would ask a question of them all.

Beyond that ridge lived Mrs. French, and once
When every silver candlestick or sconce
Lit up the dark mahogany and the wine,
A serving-man, that could divine

That most respected lady's every wish,
Ran and with the garden shears
Clipped an insolent farmer's ears
And brought them in a little covered dish.

W. B.
YEATS

Some few remembered still when I was young
A peasant girl commended by a song,
Who'd lived somewhere upon that rocky place,
And praised the colour of her face,
And had the greater joy in praising her,
Remembering that, if walked she there,
Farmers jostled at the fair
So great a glory did the song confer.

And certain men, being maddened by those rhymes,
Or else by toasting her a score of times,
Rose from the table and declared it right
To test their fancy by their sight;
But they mistook the brightness of the moon
For the prosaic light of day—
Music had driven their wits astray—
And one was drowned in the great bog of Cloone.

Strange, but the man who made the song was blind;
Yet, now I have considered it, I find
That nothing strange; the tragedy began
With Homer that was a blind man,
And Helen has all living hearts betrayed.
O may the moon and sunlight seem
One inextricable beam,
For if I triumph I must make men mad.

And I myself created Hanrahan
And drove him drunk or sober through the dawn
From somewhere in the neighbouring cottages.
Caught by an old man's juggleries

W. B. He stumbled, tumbled, fumbled to and fro
YEATS And had but broken knees for hire
And horrible splendour of desire;
I thought it all out twenty years ago:

Good fellows shuffled cards in an old bawn;
And when that ancient ruffian's turn was on
He so bewitched the cards under his thumb
That all but the one card became
A pack of hounds and not a pack of cards,
And that he changed into a hare.
Hanrahan rose in frenzy there
And followed up those baying creatures towards—

O towards I have forgotten what—enough!
I must recall a man that neither love
Nor music nor an enemy's clipped ear
Could, he was so harried, cheer;
A figure that has grown so fabulous
There's not a neighbour left to say
When he finished his dog's day:
An ancient bankrupt master of this house.

Before that ruin came, for centuries,
Rough men-at-arms, cross-gartered to the knees
Or shod in iron, climbed the narrow stairs,
And certain men-at-arms there were
Whose images, in the Great Memory stored,
Come with loud cry and panting breast
To break upon a sleeper's rest
While their great wooden dice beat on the board.

As I would question all, come all who can;
Come old, necessitous, half-mounted man;
And bring beauty's blind rambling celebrant;
The red man the juggler sent

Through God-forsaken meadows; Mrs. French,
Gifted with so fine an ear;
The man drowned in a bog's mire,
When mocking muses chose the country wench.

Did all old men and women, rich and poor,
Who trod upon these rocks or passed this door,
Whether in public or in secret rage
As I do now against old age?
But I have found an answer in those eyes
That are impatient to be gone;
Go therefore; but leave Hanrahan,
For I need all his mighty memories.

Old lecher with a love on every wind,
Bring up out of that deep considering mind
All that you have discovered in the grave,
For it is certain that you have
Reckoned up every unforeknown, unseeing
Plunge, lured by a softening eye,
Or by a touch or a sigh,
Into the labyrinth of another's being;

Does the imagination dwell the most
Upon a woman won or woman lost?
If on the lost, admit you turned aside
From a great labyrinth out of pride,
Cowardice, some silly over-subtle thought
Or anything called conscience once;
And that if memory recur, the sun's
Under eclipse and the day blotted out.

III

It is time that I wrote my will;
I choose upstanding men

77

That climb the streams until
The fountain leap, and at dawn
Drop their cast at the side
Of dripping stone; I declare
They shall inherit my pride,
The pride of people that were
Bound neither to Cause nor to State,
Neither to slaves that were spat on,
Nor to the tyrants that spat,
The people of Burke and of Grattan
That gave, though free to refuse—
Pride, like that of the morn,
When the headlong light is loose,
Or that of the fabulous horn,
Or that of the sudden shower
When all streams are dry,
Or that of the hour
When the swan must fix his eye
Upon a fading gleam,
Float out upon a long
Last reach of glittering stream
And there sing his last song.
And I declare my faith:
I mock Plotinus' thought
And cry in Plato's teeth,
Death and life were not
Till man made up the whole,
Made lock, stock and barrel
Out of his bitter soul,
Aye, sun and moon and star, all,
And further add to that
That, being dead, we rise,
Dream and so create
Translunar Paradise.

I have prepared my peace   W. B.
With learned Italian things   Yeats
And the proud stones of Greece,
Poet's imaginings
And memories of love,
Memories of the words of women,
All those things whereof
Man makes a superhuman
Mirror-resembling dream.

As at the loophole there
The daws chatter and scream,
And drop twigs layer upon layer.
When they have mounted up,
The mother bird will rest
On their hollow top,
And so warm her wild nest.

I leave both faith and pride
To young upstanding men
Climbing the mountain side,
That under bursting dawn
They may drop a fly;
Being of that metal made
Till it was broken by
This sedentary trade.

Now shall I make my soul,
Compelling it to study
In a learned school
Till the wreck of body,
Slow decay of blood,
Testy delirium
Or dull decrepitude,
Or what worse evil come—

The death of friends, or death
Of every brilliant eye
That made a catch in the breath—
Seem but the clouds of the sky
When the horizon fades;
Or a bird's sleepy cry
Among the deepening shades.

1926

A DIALOGUE OF SELF AND SOUL

I

MY SOUL. I summon to the winding ancient stair;
Set all your mind upon the steep ascent,
Upon the broken, crumbling battlement,
Upon the breathless starlit air,
Upon the star that marks the hidden pole;
Fix every wandering thought upon
That quarter where all thought is done:
Who can distinguish darkness from the soul?

MY SELF. The consecrated blade upon my knees
Is Sato's ancient blade, still as it was,
Still razor-keen, still like a looking-glass
Unspotted by the centuries;
That flowering, silken, old embroidery, torn
From some court-lady's dress and round
The wooden scabbard bound and wound,
Can, tattered, still protect, faded adorn.

MY SOUL. Why should the imagination of a man
Long past his prime remember things that are
Emblematical of love and war?
Think of ancestral night that can,

If but imagination scorn the earth
And intellect its wandering
To this and that and t'other thing,
Deliver from the crime of death and birth.

MY SELF. Montashigi, third of his family, fashioned it
Five hundred years ago, about it lie
Flowers from I know not what embroidery—
Heart's purple—and all these I set
For emblems of the day against the tower
Emblematical of the night,
And claim as by a soldier's right
A charter to commit the crime once more.

MY SOUL. Such fullness in that quarter overflows
And falls into the basin of the mind
That man is stricken deaf and dumb and blind,
For intellect no longer knows
Is from the *Ought*, or *Knower* from the *Known*—
That is to say, ascends to Heaven;
Only the dead can be forgiven;
But when I think of that my tongue's a stone.

II

MY SELF. A living man is blind and drinks his drop.
What matter if the ditches are impure?
What matter if I live it all once more?
Endure that toil of growing up;
The ignominy of boyhood; the distress
Of boyhood changing into man;
The unfinished man and his pain
Brought face to face with his own clumsiness;

The finished man among his enemies?—
How in the name of Heaven can he escape

That defiling and disfigured shape
The mirror of malicious eyes
Casts upon his eyes until at last
He thinks that shape must be his shape?
And what's the good of an escape
If honour find him in the wintry blast?

I am content to live it all again
And yet again, if it be life to pitch
Into the frog-spawn of a blind man's ditch,
A blind man battering blind men;
Or into that most fecund ditch of all,
The folly that man does
Or must suffer, if he woos
A proud woman not kindred of his soul.

I am content to follow to its source,
Every event in action or in thought;
Measure the lot; forgive myself the lot!
When such as I cast out remorse
So great a sweetness flows into the breast
We must laugh and we must sing,
We are blest by everything,
Everything we look upon is blest.

FOR ANNE GREGORY

'Never shall a young man,
Thrown into despair
By those great honey-coloured
Ramparts at your ear,
Love you for yourself alone
And not your yellow hair.'

82

'But I can get a hair-dye
And set such colour there,
Brown, or black, or carrot,
That young men in despair
May love me for myself alone
And not my yellow hair.'

'I heard an old religious man
But yesternight declare
That he had found a text to prove
That only God, my dear,
Could love you for yourself alone
And not your yellow hair.'

BYZANTIUM

The unpurged images of day recede;
The Emperor's drunken soldiery are abed;
Night resonance recedes, night-walkers' song
After great cathedral gong;
A starlit or a moonlit dome disdains
All that man is,
All mere complexities,
The fury and the mire of human veins.

Before me floats an image, man or shade,
Shade more than man, more image than a shade;
For Hades' bobbin bound in mummy-cloth
May unwind the winding path;
A mouth that has no moisture and no breath
Breathless mouths may summon;
I hail the superhuman;
I call it death-in-life and life-in-death.

W. B.
YEATS

Miracle, bird or golden handiwork,
More miracle than bird or handiwork,
Planted on the star-lit golden bough,
Can like the cocks of Hades crow,
Or, by the moon embittered, scorn aloud
In glory of changeless metal
Common bird or petal
And all complexities of mire or blood.

At midnight on the Emperor's pavement flit
Flames that no faggot feeds, nor steel has lit,
Nor storm disturbs, flames begotten of flame,
Where blood-begotten spirits come
And all complexities of fury leave,
Dying into a dance,
An agony of trance,
An agony of flame that cannot singe a sleeve.

Astraddle on the dolphin's mire and blood,
Spirit after spirit! The smithies break the flood,
The golden smithies of the Emperor!
Marbles of the dancing floor
Break bitter furies of complexity,
Those images that yet
Fresh images beget,
That dolphin-torn, that gong-tormented sea.

1930

T. E. HULME

AUTUMN

A touch of cold in the Autumn night—
I walked abroad,
And saw the ruddy moon lean over a hedge
Like a red-faced farmer.
I did not stop to speak, but nodded,
And round about were the wistful stars
With white faces like town children.

MANA ABODA

*Beauty is the marking-time, the stationary
vibration, the feigned ecstasy of an arrested
impulse unable to reach its natural end.*

Mana Aboda, whose bent form
The sky in archèd circle is,
Seems ever for an unknown grief to mourn.
Yet on a day I heard her cry:
'I weary of the roses and the singing poets—
Josephs all, not tall enough to try'.

ABOVE THE DOCK

Above the quiet dock in midnight,
Tangled in the tall mast's corded height,
Hangs the moon. What seemed so far away
Is but a child's balloon, forgotten after play.

T. E.
HULME

THE EMBANKMENT

*(The fantasia of a fallen gentleman on a
cold, bitter night.)*

Once, in finesse of fiddles found I ecstasy,
In a flash of gold heels on the hard pavement.
Now see I
That warmth's the very stuff of poesy.
Oh, God, make small
The old star-eaten blanket of the sky,
That I may fold it round me and in comfort lie.

CONVERSION

Light-hearted I walked into the valley wood
In the time of hyacinths,
Till beauty like a scented cloth
Cast over, stifled me. I was bound
Motionless and faint of breath
By loveliness that is her own eunuch.

Now pass I to the final river
Ignominiously, in a sack, without sound,
As any peeping Turk to the Bosphorus.

EZRA POUND

NEAR PERIGORD

A Perigord, pres del muralh
Tan que i puosch' om gitar ab malh.

You'd have men's hearts up from the dust
And tell their secrets, Messire Cino,
Right enough? Then read between the lines of Uc St.
    Circ,
Solve me the riddle, for you know the tale.

Bertrans, En Bertrans, left a fine canzone:
'Maent, I love you, you have turned me out.
The voice at Montfort, Lady Agnes' hair,
Bel Miral's stature, the viscountess' throat,
Set all together, are not worthy of you . . .'
And all the while you sing out that canzone,
Think you that Maent lived at Montaignac,
One at Chalais, another at Malemort
Hard over Brive—for every lady a castle,
Each place strong.

       Oh, *is* it easy enough?
Tairiran held hall in Montaignac,
His brother-in-law was all there was of power
In Perigord, and this good union
Gobbled all the land, and held it later for some hun-
    dred years.
And our En Bertrans was in Altafort,
Hub of the wheel, the stirrer-up of strife,
As caught by Dante in the last wallow of hell—
The headless trunk 'that made its head a lamp',

EZRA For separation wrought out separation,
POUND And he who set the strife between brother and brother
And had his way with the old English king,
Viced in such torture for the 'counterpass'.
How would you live, with neighbours set about you—
Poictiers and Brive, untaken Rochecouart,
Spread like the finger-tips of one frail hand;
And you on that great mountain of a palm—
Not a neat ledge, not Foix between its streams,
But one huge back half-covered up with pine,
Worked for and snatched from the string-purse of
            Born—
The four round towers, four brothers—mostly fools:
What could he do but play the desperate chess,
And stir old grudges?
                'Pawn your castles, lords!
Let the Jews pay.'
                And the great scene—
(That, maybe, never happened!)
                Beaten at last,
Before the hard old king:
                'Your son, ah, since he died
My wit and worth are cobwebs brushed aside
In the full flare of grief. Do what you will.'

    Take the whole man, and ravel out the story.
He loved this lady in castle Montaignac?
The castle flanked him—he had need of it.
You read to-day, how long the overlords of Perigord,
The Talleyrands, have held the place; it was no transient
            fiction.
And Maent failed him? Or saw through the scheme?

    And all his net-like thought of new alliance?
Chalais is high, a-level with the poplars.

88

Its lowest stones just meet the valley tips
Where the low Dronne is filled with water-lilies.
And Rochecouart can match it, stronger yet,
The very spur's end, built on sheerest cliff,
And Malemort keeps its close hold on Brive,
While Born, his own close purse, his rabbit warren,
His subterranean chamber with a dozen doors,
A-bristle with antennae to feel roads,
To sniff the traffic into Perigord.
And that hard phalanx, that unbroken line,
The ten good miles from there to Maent's castle,
All of his flank—how could he do without her?
And all the road to Cahors, to Toulouse?
What would he do without her?

'Papiol,
Go forthright singing—Anhes, Cembelins.
There is a throat; ah, there are two white hands;
There is a trellis full of early roses,
And all my heart is bound about with love.
Where am I come with compound flatteries—
What doors are open to fine compliment?'
And every one half jealous of Maent?
He wrote the catch to pit their jealousies
Against her; give her pride in them?

Take his own speech, make what you will of it—
And still the knot, the first knot, of Maent?

Is it a love poem? Did he sing of war?
Is it an intrigue to run subtly out,
Born of a jongleur's tongue, freely to pass
Up and about and in and out the land,
Mark him a craftsman and a strategist?
(St. Leider had done as much at Polhonac,

EZRA
POUND

89

EZRA Singing a different stave, as closely hidden.)
POUND Oh, there is precedent, legal tradition,
To sing one thing when your song means another,
'*Et albirar ab lor bordon*—'
Foix' count knew that. What is Sir Bertrans' singing?
Maent, Maent, and yet again Maent,
Or war and broken heaumes and politics?

II

End fact. Try fiction. Let us say we see
En Bertrans, a tower-room at Hautefort,
Sunset, the ribbon-like road lies, in red cross-light,
Southward toward Montaignac, and he bends at a table
Scribbling, swearing between his teeth; by his left
    hand
Lie little strips of parchment covered over,
Scratched and erased with *al* and *ochaisos*.
Testing his list of rhymes, a lean man? Bilious?
With a red straggling beard?
And the green cat's-eye lifts toward Montaignac.

    Or take his 'magnet' singer setting out,
Dodging his way past Aubeterre, singing at Chalais
    In the vaulted hall,
Or, by a lichened tree at Rochecouart
Aimlessly watching a hawk above the valleys,
Waiting his turn in the midsummer evening,
Thinking of Aelis, whom he loved heart and soul . . .
To find her half alone, Montfort away,
And a brown, placid, hated woman visiting her,
Spoiling his visit, with a year before the next one.
Little enough?
Or carry him forward. 'Go through all the courts,
My Magnet,' Bertrans had said.

We came to Ventadour   EZRA
POUND
In the mid love court, he sings out the canzon,
No one hears save Arrimon Luc D'Esparo—
No one hears aught save the gracious sound of compli-
      ments.
Sir Arrimon counts on his fingers, Montfort,
Rochecouart, Chalais, the rest, the tactic,
Malemort, guesses beneath, sends word to Cœur-de-
      Lion:
The compact, de Born smoked out, trees felled
About his castle, cattle driven out!
Or no one sees it, and En Bertrans prospered?

And ten years after, or twenty, as you will,
Arnaut and Richard lodge beneath Chalus:
The dull round towers encroaching on the field,
The tents tight drawn, horses at tether
Farther and out of reach, the purple night,
The crackling of small fires, the bannerets,
The lazy leopards on the largest banner,
Stray gleams on hanging mail, an armourer's torch-flare
Melting on steel.

And in the quietest space
They probe old scandals, say de Born is dead;
And we've the gossip (skipped six hundred years).
Richard shall die to-morrow—leave him there
Talking of *trobar clus* with Daniel.
And the 'best craftsman' sings out his friend's song,
Envies its vigour . . . and deplores the technique,
Dispraises his own skill?—That's as you will.
And they discuss the dead man,
Plantagenet puts the riddle: 'Did he love her?'
And Arnaut parries: 'Did he love your sister?

91

EZRA True, he has praised her, but in some opinion
POUND He wrote that praise only to show he had
         The favour of your party; had been well received.'
         'You knew the man.'
                    '*You* knew the man.'
         'I am an artist, you have tried both métiers.'
         'You were born near him.'
                    'Do we know our friends?'
         'Say that he saw the castles, say that he loved Maent!'
         'Say that he loved her, does it solve the riddle?'
      End the discussion, Richard goes out next day
   And gets a quarrel-bolt shot through his vizard,
   Pardons the bowman, dies,

                    Ends our discussion. Arnaut ends
   'In sacred odour'—(that's apocryphal!)
   And we can leave the talk till Dante writes:
   Surely I saw, and still before my eyes
   Goes on that headless trunk, that bears for light
   Its own head swinging, gripped by the dead hair,
   And like a swinging lamp that says, 'Ah me!
   I severed men, my head and heart
   Ye see here severed, my life's counterpart.'

   Or take En Bertrans?

                         III

                    Ed eran due in uno, ed uno in due;
                       Inferno, XXVIII, 125

   Bewildering spring, and by the Auvezere
   Poppies and day's eyes in the green émail
   Rose over us; and we knew all that stream,
   And our two horses had traced out the valleys;

                         92

Knew the low flooded lands squared out with poplars,
In the young days when the deep sky befriended.
    And great wings beat above us in the twilight,
And the great wheels in heaven
Bore us together . . . surging . . . and apart . . .
Believing we should meet with lips and hands,
    High, high and sure . . . and then the counter-thrust:
'Why do you love me? Will you always love me?
But I am like the grass, I cannot love you.'
Or, 'Love, and I love and love you,
And hate your mind, not *you,* your soul, your hands.'

        So to this last estrangement, Tairiran!

        There shut up in his castle, Tairiran's,
She who had nor ears nor tongue save in her hands,
Gone—ah, gone—untouched, unreachable!
She who could never live save through one person,
She who could never speak save to one person,
And all the rest of her a shifting change,
A broken bundle of mirrors . . . !

EXILE'S LETTER

To So-Kin of Rakuyo, ancient friend, Chancellor of
        Gen.
Now I remember that you built me a special tavern
By the south side of the bridge at Ten-Shin.
With yellow gold and white jewels, we paid for songs
        and laughter
And we were drunk for month on month, forgetting
        the kings and princes.

Intelligent men came drifting in from the sea and from
      the west border,
And with them, and with you especially
There was nothing at cross purpose,
And they made nothing of sea-crossing or of mountain-
      crossing,
If only they could be of that fellowship,
And we all spoke out our hearts and minds, and with-
      out regret.
And then I was sent off to South Wei,
            smothered in laurel groves,
And you to the north of Raku-hoku
Till we had nothing but thoughts and memories in
      common.

And then, when separation had come to its worst,
We met, and travelled into Sen-Go,
Through all the thirty-six folds of the turning and
      twisting waters,
Into a valley of the thousand bright flowers,
That was the first valley;
And into ten thousand valleys full of voices and pine-
      winds.
And with silver harness and reins of gold,
Out came the East of Kan foreman and his company.
And there came also the 'True man' of Shi-yo to meet
      me,
Playing on a jewelled mouth-organ.
In the storied houses of San-Ko they gave us more
      Sennin music,
Many instruments, like the sound of young phoenix
      broods.
The foreman of Kan Chu, drunk, danced
            because his long sleeves wouldn't keep still

With that music playing,
And I, wrapped in brocade, went to sleep with my head
 on his lap,
And my spirit so high it was all over the heavens,
And before the end of the day we were scattered like
 stars, or rain.
I had to be off to So, far away over the waters,
You back to your river-bridge.

And your father, who was brave as a leopard,
Was governor in Hei Shu, and put down the barbarian
 rabble.
And one May he had you send for me,
   despite the long distance.
And what with broken wheels and so on, I won't say it
 wasn't hard going,
Over roads twisted like sheep's guts.
And I was still going, late in the year,
   in the cutting wind from the North,
And thinking how little you cared for the cost,
   and you caring enough to pay it.
And what a reception:
Red jade cups, food well set on a blue jewelled table,
And I was drunk, and had no thought of returning.
And you would walk out with me to the western
 corner of the castle,
To the dynastic temple, with water about it clear as
 blue jade,
With boats floating, and the sound of mouth-organs
 and drums,
With ripples like dragon-scales, going grass-green on
 the water,
Pleasure lasting, with courtesans, going and coming
 without hindrance,

EZRA With the willow flakes falling like snow,
POUND And the vermilioned girls getting drunk about sunset,
And the water, a hundred feet deep, reflecting green
eyebrows
—Eyebrows painted green are a fine sight in young
moonlight,
Gracefully painted—
And the girls singing back at each other,
Dancing in transparent brocade,
And the wind lifting the song, and interrupting it,
Tossing it up under the clouds.
And all this comes to an end.
And is not again to be met with.
I went up to the court for examination,
Tried Layu's luck, offered the Choyo song,
And got no promotion,
and went back to the East Mountains
White-headed.

And once again, later, we met at the South bridge-head.
And then the crowd broke up, you went north to San
palace,
And if you ask how I regret that parting:
It is like the flowers falling at Spring's end
Confused, whirled in a tangle.
What is the use of talking, and there is no end of talk-
ing,
There is no end of things in the heart.
I call in the boy,
Have him sit on his knees here
To seal this,
And send it a thousand miles, thinking.

By Rihaku

POUR L'ELECTION DE SON SEPULCHRE

EzRA
PouND

I

For three years, out of key with his time,
He strove to resuscitate the dead art
Of poetry; to maintain 'the sublime'
In the old sense. Wrong from the start—

No, hardly, but seeing he had been born
In a half-savage country, out of date;
Bent resolutely on wringing lilies from the acorn;
Capaneus; trout for factitious bait;

Ἴδμεν γάρ τοι πάνθ᾽, ὅσ᾽ ἐνὶ Τροίῃ
Caught in the unstopped ear;
Giving the rocks small lee-way
The chopped seas held him, therefore, that year.

His true Penelope was Flaubert,
He fished by obstinate isles;
Observed the elegance of Circe's hair
Rather than the mottoes on sundials.

Unaffected by 'the march of events',
He passed from men's memory in *l'an trentiesme*,
De son eage; the case presents
No adjunct to the Muses' diadem.

II

The age demanded an image
Of its accelerated grimace,
Something for the modern stage,
Not, at any rate, an Attic grace;

Not, not certainly, the obscure reveries
Of the inward gaze;

EZRA
POUND

Better mendacities
Than the classics in paraphrase!

The 'age demanded' chiefly a mould in plaster,
Made with no loss of time,
A prose kinema, not, not assuredly, alabaster
Or the 'sculpture' of rhyme.

III

The tea-rose tea-gown, etc.
Supplants the mousseline of Cos,
The pianola 'replaces'
Sappho's barbitos.

Christ follows Dionysus,
Phallic and ambrosial
Made way for macerations;
Caliban casts out Ariel.

All things are a flowing,
Sage Heracleitus says;
But a tawdry cheapness
Shall outlast our days.

Even the Christian beauty
Defects—after Samothrace;
We see τὸ καλὸν
Decreed in the market-place.

Faun's flesh is not to us,
Nor the saint's vision.
We have the Press for wafer;
Franchise for circumcision.

All men, in law, are equals.
Free of Pisistratus,
We choose a knave or an eunuch
To rule over us.

O bright Apollo,
τίν' ἄνδρα, τίν' ἥρωα, τίνα θεὸν
What god, man, or hero
Shall I place a tin wreath upon!

IV

These fought in any case,
and some believing,
                    pro domo, in any case . . .

Some quick to arm,
some for adventure,
some from fear of weakness,
some from fear of censure,
some for love of slaughter, in imagination,
learning later . . .
some in fear, learning love of slaughter;

Died some, pro patria,
        non 'dulce' non 'et decor' . . .
walked eye-deep in hell
believing in old men's lies, then unbelieving
came home, home to a lie,
home to many deceits,
home to old lies and new infamy;
usury age-old and age-thick
and liars in public places.

Daring as never before, wastage as never before.
Young blood and high blood,
fair cheeks, and fine bodies;

fortitude as never before

frankness as never before,
disillusions as never told in the old days,
hysterias, trench confessions,
laughter out of dead bellies.

V

There died a myriad,
And of the best, among them,
For an old bitch gone in the teeth,
For a botched civilization,

Charm, smiling at the good mouth,
Quick eyes gone under earth's lid,

For two gross of broken statues,
For a few thousand battered books.

HOMAGE TO SEXTUS PROPERTIUS: XII

Who, who will be the next man to entrust his girl to
        a friend?
                Love interferes with fidelities;
The gods have brought shame on their relatives;
                Each man wants the pomegranate for himself;
Amiable and harmonious people are pushed incontinent
        into duels,
A Trojan and adulterous person came to Menelaus
        under the rites of hospitium,
And there was a case in Colchis, Jason and that woman
        in Colchis;
And besides, Lynceus,
                you were drunk.

Could you endure such promiscuity?
                She was not renowned for fidelity;
But to jab a knife in my vitals, to have passed on a swig
        of poison,
Preferable, my dear boy, my dear Lynceus,

Comrade, comrade of my life, of my purse, of my
      person;
But in one bed, in one bed alone, my dear Lynceus,
        I deprecate your attendance;
I would ask a like boon of Jove.

And you write of Acheloüs, who contended with
      Hercules,
You write of Adrastus' horses and the funeral rites of
      Achenor,
And you will not leave off imitating Aeschylus.
        Though you make a hash of Antimachus,
You think you are going to do Homer.
        And still a girl scorns the gods,
Of all these young women
        not one has enquired the cause of the world,
Nor the modus of lunar eclipses
        Nor whether there be any patch left of us
After we cross the infernal ripples,
        nor if the thunder fall from predestination;
Nor anything else of importance.

Upon the Actian marshes Virgil is Phoebus' chief of
      police,
        He can tabulate Caesar's great ships.
He thrills to Ilian arms,
        He shakes the Trojan weapons of Aeneas,
And casts stores on Lavinian beaches.
Make way, ye Roman authors,
           clear the street O ye Greeks,
For a much larger Iliad is in the course of construction
             (and to Imperial order)
Clear the streets O ye Greeks!

EZRA And you also follow him 'neath Phrygian pine shade':
POUND   Thyrsis and Daphnis upon whittled reeds,
And how ten sins can corrupt young maidens;
          Kids for a bribe and pressed udders,
Happy selling poor loves for cheap apples.

Tityrus might have sung the same vixen;
          Corydon tempted Alexis,
Head farmers do likewise, and lying weary amid their
    oats
They get praise from tolerant Hamadryads.

Go on, to Ascraeus' prescription, the ancient,
              respected, Wordsworthian:
'A flat field for rushes, grapes grow on the slope.'

And behold me, a small fortune left in my house.
          Me, who had no general for a grandfather!
I shall triumph among young ladies of indeterminate
    character,
My talent acclaimed in their banquets,
          I shall be honoured with yesterday's wreaths.

And the god strikes to the marrow.

          Like a trained and performing tortoise,
I would make verse in your fashion, if she should com-
    mand it,
With her husband asking a remission of sentence,
          And even this infamy would not attract
              numerous readers
Were there an erudite or violent passion,
For the nobleness of the populace brooks nothing
    below its own altitude.

One must have resonance, resonance and sonority . . . EZRA
like a goose. POUND

Varro sang Jason's expedition,
          Varro, of his great passion Leucadia,
There is song in the parchment; Catullus the highly
     indecorous,
Of Lesbia, known above Helen;
And in the dyed pages of Calvus,
          Calvus mourning Quintilia,
And but now Gallus had sung of Lycoris.
          Fair, fairest Lycoris—
The waters of Styx poured over the wound:
And now Propertius of Cynthia, taking his stand
     among these.

CANTO XIII

Kung walked
          by the dynastic temple
and into the cedar grove,
          and then out by the lower river,
And with him Khieu Tchi
          and Tian the low speaking
And 'we are unknown', said Kung,
You will take up charioteering?
          'Then you will become known,
'Or perhaps I should take up charioteering, or archery?
'Or the practice of public speaking?'
And Tseu-lou said, 'I would put the defences in order,'
And Khieu said, 'If I were lord of a province
I would put it in better order than this is.'
And Tchi said, 'I should prefer a small mountain
     temple,

103

'With order in the observances,
                with a suitable performance of the ritual,'
And Tian said, with his hand on the strings of his lute
The low sounds continuing
                after his hand left the strings,
And the sound went up like smoke, under the leaves,
And he looked after the sound:
                'The old swimming hole,
'And the boys flopping off the planks,
'Or sitting in the underbrush playing mandolins.'
                And Kung smiled upon all of them equally.
And Thseng-sie desired to know:
                'Which had answered correctly?'
And Kung said, 'They have all answered correctly,
'That is to say, each in his nature.'
And Kung raised his cane against Yuan Jang,
                Yuan Jang being his elder,
For Yuan Jang sat by the roadside pretending to
                be receiving wisdom.
And Kung said
                'You old fool, come out of it,
'Get up and do something useful.'
                And Kung said
'Respect a child's faculties
'From the moment it inhales the clear air,
'But a man of fifty who knows nothing
                'Is worthy of no respect.'
And 'When the prince has gathered about him
'All the savants and artists, his riches will be fully
                employed.'
And Kung said, and wrote on the bo leaves:
                'If a man have not order within him
'He can not spread order about him;
'And if a man have not order within him

EZRA
POUND

104

'His family will not act with due order;
        'And if the prince have not order within him
'He can not put order in his dominions.'
And Kung gave the words 'order'
and 'brotherly deference'
And said nothing of the 'life after death'.
And he said
        'Anyone can run to excesses,
'It is easy to shoot past the mark,
'It is hard to stand firm in the middle.'

And they said: 'If a man commit murder
        'Should his father protect him, and hide him?'
And Kung said:
        'He should hide him.'

And Kung gave his daughter to Kong-Tchang
        Although Kong-Tchang was in prison.
And he gave his niece to Nan-Young
        although Nan-Young was out of office.
And Kung said 'Wang ruled with moderation,
        'In his day the State was well kept,
'And even I can remember
'A day when the historians left blanks in their writings,
'I mean for things they didn't know,
'But that time seems to be passing.'
And Kung said, 'Without character you will
        be unable to play on that instrument
'Or to execute the music fit for the Odes.
'The blossoms of the apricot
        blow from the east to the west,
'And I have tried to keep them from falling.'

T. S. ELIOT

SWEENEY AMONG THE NIGHTINGALES

ὤμοι, πέπληγμαι καιρίαν πληγὴν ἔσω.

Apeneck Sweeney spreads his knees
Letting his arms hang down to laugh,
The zebra stripes along his jaw
Swelling to maculate giraffe.

The circles of the stormy moon
Slide westward toward the River Plate,
Death and the Raven drift above
And Sweeney guards the horned gate.

Gloomy Orion and the Dog
Are veiled; and hushed the shrunken seas;
The person in the Spanish cape
Tries to sit on Sweeney's knees

Slips and pulls the table cloth
Overturns a coffee-cup,
Reorganised upon the floor
She yawns and draws a stocking up;

The silent man in mocha brown
Sprawls at the window-sill and gapes;
The waiter brings in oranges
Bananas figs and hothouse grapes;

The silent vertebrate in brown
Contracts and concentrates, withdraws;
Rachel *née* Rabinovitch
Tears at the grapes with murderous paws;

She and the lady in the cape
Are suspect, thought to be in league;
Therefore the man with heavy eyes
Declines the gambit, shows fatigue,

Leaves the room and reappears
Outside the window, leaning in,
Branches of wistaria
Circumscribe a golden grin;

The host with someone indistinct
Converses at the door apart,
The nightingales are singing near
The Convent of the Sacred Heart,

And sang within the bloody wood
When Agamemnon cried aloud,
And let their liquid siftings fall
To stain the stiff dishonoured shroud.

THE WASTE LAND

'NAM Sibyllam quidem Cumis ego ipse oculis
meis vidi in ampulla pendere, et cum illi pueri
dicerent: Σιβυλλα τί θέλεις; respondebat illa:
ἀποθανεῖν θέλω.'

For Ezra Pound
il miglior fabbro

I. THE BURIAL OF THE DEAD

April is the cruellest month, breeding
Lilacs out of the dead land, mixing
Memory and desire, stirring
Dull roots with spring rain.
Winter kept us warm, covering
Earth in forgetful snow, feeding
A little life with dried tubers.
Summer surprised us, coming over the Starnbergersee
With a shower of rain; we stopped in the colonnade,
And went on in sunlight, into the Hofgarten,   10
And drank coffee, and talked for an hour.
Bin gar keine Russin, stamm' aus Litauen, echt deutsch.
And when we were children, staying at the archduke's,
My cousin's, he took me out on a sled,
And I was frightened. He said, Marie,
Marie, hold on tight. And down we went.
In the mountains, there you feel free.
I read, much of the night, and go south in the winter.

What are the roots that clutch, what branches grow
Out of this stony rubbish? Son of man,   20
You cannot say, or guess, for you know only
A heap of broken images, where the sun beats,
And the dead tree gives no shelter, the cricket no
      relief,

And the dry stone no sound of water. Only
There is shadow under this red rock,
(Come in under the shadow of this red rock),
And I will show you something different from either
Your shadow at morning striding behind you
Or your shadow at evening rising to meet you;
I will show you fear in a handful of dust.   30

> *Frisch weht der Wind*
> *Der Heimat zu,*
> *Mein Irisch Kind,*
> *Wo weilest du?*

'You gave me hyacinths first a year ago;
'They called me the hyacinth girl.'
—Yet when we came back, late, from the Hyacinth
    garden,
Your arms full, and your hair wet, I could not
Speak, and my eyes failed, I was neither
Living nor dead, and I knew nothing,   40
Looking into the heart of light, the silence.
Od' und leer das Meer.

Madame Sosostris, famous clairvoyante,
Had a bad cold, nevertheless
Is known to be the wisest woman in Europe,
With a wicked pack of cards. Here, said she,
Is your card, the drowned Phoenician Sailor,
(Those are pearls that were his eyes. Look!)
Here is Belladonna, the Lady of the Rocks,
The lady of situations.   50
Here is the man with three staves, and here the Wheel,
And here is the one-eyed merchant, and this card,
Which is blank, is something he carries on his back,

T. S. Which I am forbidden to see. I do not find
ELIOT The Hanged Man. Fear death by water.
I see crowds of people, walking round in a ring.
Thank you. If you see dear Mrs. Equitone,
Tell her I bring the horoscope myself:
One must be so careful these days.

Unreal City,   60
Under the brown fog of a winter dawn,
A crowd flowed over London Bridge, so many,
I had not thought death had undone so many.
Sighs, short and infrequent, were exhaled,
And each man fixed his eyes before his feet.
Flowed up the hill and down King William Street,
To where Saint Mary Woolnoth kept the hours
With a dead sound on the final stroke of nine.
There I saw one I knew, and stopped him, crying:
        'Stetson!
'You who were with me in the ships at Mylae!   70
'That corpse you planted last year in your garden,
'Has it begun to sprout? Will it bloom this year?
'Or has the sudden frost disturbed its bed?
'Oh keep the Dog far hence, that's friend to men,
'Or with his nails he'll dig it up again!
'You! hypocrite lecteur!—mon semblable,—mon
        frère!'

II. A GAME OF CHESS

The Chair she sat in, like a burnished throne,
Glowed on the marble, where the glass
Held up by standards wrought with fruited vines
From which a golden Cupidon peeped out   80
(Another hid his eyes behind his wing)
Doubled the flames of sevenbranched candelabra

Reflecting light upon the table as
The glitter of her jewels rose to meet it,
From satin cases poured in rich profusion;
In vials of ivory and coloured glass
Unstoppered, lurked her strange synthetic perfumes,
Unguent, powdered, or liquid—troubled, confused
And drowned the sense in odours; stirred by the air
That freshened from the window, these ascended   90
In fattening the prolonged candle-flames,
Flung their smoke into the laquearia,
Stirring the pattern on the coffered ceiling.
Huge sea-wood fed with copper
Burned green and orange, framed by the coloured
          stone,
In which sad light a carvèd dolphin swam.
Above the antique mantel was displayed
As though a window gave upon the sylvan scene
The change of Philomel, by the barbarous king
So rudely forced; yet there the nightingale   100
Filled all the desert with inviolable voice
And still she cried, and still the world pursues,
'Jug Jug' to dirty ears.
And other withered stumps of time
Were told upon the walls; staring forms
Leaned out, leaning, hushing the room enclosed.
Footsteps shuffled on the stair.
Under the firelight, under the brush, her hair
Spread out in fiery points
Glowed into words, then would be savagely still.   110

'My nerves are bad to-night. Yes, bad. Stay with me.
'Speak to me. Why do you never speak. Speak.
    'What are you thinking of? What thinking? What?
'I never know what you are thinking. Think.'

T. S. I think we are in rats' alley
ELIOT Where the dead men lost their bones.

'What is that noise?'
             The wind under the door.
'What is that noise now? What is the wind doing?'
             Nothing again nothing.   120
                 'Do
'You know nothing? Do you see nothing? Do you
    remember
'Nothing?'
        I remember
Those are pearls that were his eyes.
'Are you alive, or not? Is there nothing in your head?'
                     But

O O O O that Shakespeherian Rag—
It's so elegant
So intelligent   130
'What shall I do now? What shall I do?'
'I shall rush out as I am, and walk the street
'With my hair down, so. What shall we do tomorrow?
'What shall we ever do?'
             The hot water at ten.
And if it rains, a closed car at four.
And we shall play a game of chess,
Pressing lidless eyes and waiting for a knock upon the
    door.

When Lil's husband got demobbed, I said—
I didn't mince my words, I said to her myself,   140
HURRY UP PLEASE ITS TIME
Now Albert's coming back, make yourself a bit smart.
He'll want to know what you done with that money he
    gave you

To get yourself some teeth. He did, I was there.
You have them all out, Lil, and get a nice set,
He said, I swear, I can't bear to look at you.
And no more can't I, I said, and think of poor Albert,
He's been in the army four years, he wants a good time,
And if you don't give it him, there's others will, I said.
Oh is there, she said. Something o' that, I said.   150
Then I'll know who to thank, she said, and give me a
          straight look.
HURRY UP PLEASE ITS TIME
If you don't like it you can get on with it, I said,
Others can pick and choose if you can't.
But if Albert makes off, it won't be for lack of telling.
You ought to be ashamed, I said, to look so antique.
(And her only thirty-one.)
I can't help it, she said, pulling a long face,
It's them pills I took, to bring it off, she said.
(She's had five already, and nearly died of young
          George.)   160
The chemist said it would be all right, but I've never
          been the same.
You *are* a proper fool, I said.
Well, if Albert won't leave you alone, there it is, I
          said,
What you get married for if you don't want children?
HURRY UP PLEASE ITS TIME
Well, that Sunday Albert was home, they had a hot
          gammon,
And they asked me in to dinner, to get the beauty of it
          hot—
HURRY UP PLEASE ITS TIME
HURRY UP PLEASE ITS TIME
Goonight Bill. Goonight Lou. Goonight May. Goo-
          night.   170

T. S. Ta ta. Goonight. Goonight.
ELIOT Good night, ladies, good night, sweet ladies, good
        night, good night.

III. THE FIRE SERMON

The river's tent is broken: the last fingers of leaf
Clutch and sink into the wet bank. The wind
Crosses the brown land, unheard. The nymphs are
    departed.
Sweet Thames, run softly, till I end my song.
The river bears no empty bottles, sandwich papers,
Silk handkerchiefs, cardboard boxes, cigarette ends
Or other testimony of summer nights. The nymphs are
    departed.
And their friends, the loitering heirs of city direc-
    tors;   180
Departed, have left no addresses.
By the waters of Leman I sat down and wept . . .
Sweet Thames, run softly till I end my song,
Sweet Thames, run softly, for I speak not loud or long.
But at my back in a cold blast I hear
The rattle of the bones, and chuckle spread from ear to
    ear.
A rat crept softly through the vegetation
Dragging its slimy belly on the bank
While I was fishing in the dull canal
On a winter evening round behind the gashouse   190
Musing upon the king my brother's wreck
And on the king my father's death before him.
White bodies naked on the low damp ground
And bones cast in a little low dry garret,
Rattled by the rat's foot only, year to year.
But at my back from time to time I hear

The sound of horns and motors, which shall bring
Sweeney to Mrs. Porter in the spring.
O the moon shone bright on Mrs. Porter
And on her daughter   200
They wash their feet in soda water
Et O ces voix d'enfants, chantant dans la coupole!

Twit twit twit
Jug jug jug jug jug jug
So rudely forc'd.
Tereu
Unreal City
Under the brown fog of a winter noon
Mr. Eugenides, the Smyrna merchant
Unshaven, with a pocket full of currants   210
C.i.f. London: documents at sight,
Asked me in demotic French
To luncheon at the Cannon Street Hotel
Followed by a weekend at the Metropole.

At the violet hour, when the eyes and back
Turn upward from the desk, when the human engine
        waits
Like a taxi throbbing waiting,
I Tiresias, though blind, throbbing between two lives,
Old man with wrinkled female breasts, can see
At the violet hour, the evening hour that strives   220
Homeward, and brings the sailor home from sea,
The typist home at teatime, clears her breakfast, lights
Her stove, and lays out food in tins.
Out of the window perilously spread
Her drying combinations touched by the sun's last rays,
On the divan are piled (at night her bed)
Stockings, slippers, camisoles, and stays.

T. S.
ELIOT I Tiresias, old man with wrinkled dugs
Perceived the scene, and foretold the rest—
I too awaited the expected guest.   230
He, the young man carbuncular, arrives,
A small house agent's clerk, with one bold stare,
One of the low on whom assurance sits
As a silk hat on a Bradford millionaire.
The time is now propitious, as he guesses,
The meal is ended, she is bored and tired,
Endeavours to engage her in caresses
Which still are unreproved, if undesired.
Flushed and decided, he assaults at once;
Exploring hands encounter no defence;   240
His vanity requires no response,
And makes a welcome of indifference.
(And I Tiresias have foresuffered all
Enacted on this same divan or bed;
I who have sat by Thebes below the wall
And walked among the lowest of the dead.)
Bestows one final patronising kiss,
And gropes his way, finding the stairs unlit . . .

She turns and looks a moment in the glass,
Hardly aware of her departed lover;   250
Her brain allows one half-formed thought to pass:
'Well now that's done: and I'm glad it's over.'
When lovely woman stoops to folly and
Paces about her room again, alone,
She smoothes her hair with automatic hand,
And puts a record on the gramophone.

'This music crept by me upon the waters'
And along the Strand, up Queen Victoria Street.
O City city, I can sometimes hear

Beside a public bar in Lower Thames Street,
The pleasant whining of a mandoline
And a clatter and a chatter from within
Where fishmen lounge at noon: where the walls
Of Magnus Martyr hold
Inexplicable splendour of Ionian white and gold.

      The river sweats
      Oil and tar
      The barges drift
      With the turning tide
      Red sails   270
      Wide
      To leeward, swing on the heavy spar.
      The barges wash
      Drifting logs
      Down Greenwich reach
      Past the Isle of Dogs.
                  Weialala leia
                  Wallala leialala
      Elizabeth and Leicester
      Beating oars   280
      The stern was formed
      A gilded shell
      Red and gold
      The brisk swell
      Rippled both shores
      Southwest wind
      Carried down stream
      The peal of bells
      White towers
                  Weialala leia   290
                  Wallala leialala

'Trams and dusty trees.
Highbury bore me. Richmond and Kew
Undid me. By Richmond I raised my knees
Supine on the floor of a narrow canoe.'

'My feet are at Moorgate, and my heart
Under my feet. After the event
He wept. He promised "a new start."
I made no comment. What should I resent?'

'On Margate Sands.   300
I can connect
Nothing with nothing.
The broken fingernails of dirty hands.
My people humble people who expect
Nothing.'
            la la

To Carthage then I came

Burning burning burning burning
O Lord Thou pluckest me out
O Lord Thou pluckest   310

burning

IV. DEATH BY WATER

Phlebas the Phoenician, a fortnight dead,
Forgot the cry of gulls, and the deep sea swell
And the profit and loss.
                 A current under sea
Picked his bones in whispers. As he rose and fell
He passed the stages of his age and youth
Entering the whirlpool.
                Gentile or Jew

O you who turn the wheel and look to windward, 320 T. S.
Consider Phlebas, who was once handsome and tall as ELIOT
    you.

V. WHAT THE THUNDER SAID

After the torchlight red on sweaty faces
After the frosty silence in the gardens
After the agony in stony places
The shouting and the crying
Prison and palace and reverberation
Of thunder of spring over distant mountains
He who was living is now dead
We who were living are now dying
With a little patience 330

Here is no water but only rock
Rock and no water and the sandy road
The road winding above among the mountains
Which are mountains of rock without water
If there were water we should stop and drink
Amongst the rock one cannot stop or think
Sweat is dry and feet are in the sand
If there were only water amongst the rock
Dead mountain mouth of carious teeth that cannot spit
Here one can neither stand nor lie nor sit 340
There is not even silence in the mountains
But dry sterile thunder without rain
There is not even solitude in the mountains
But red sullen faces sneer and snarl
From doors of mudcracked houses
                         If there were water
  And no rock
  If there were rock

And also water
And water   350
A spring
A pool among the rock
If there were the sound of water only
Not the cicada
And dry grass singing
But sound of water over a rock
Where the hermit-thrush sings in the pine trees
Drip drop drip drop drop drop drop
But there is no water

Who is the third who walks always beside you?
When I count, there are only you and I together   360
But when I look ahead up the white road
There is always another one walking beside you
Gliding wrapt in a brown mantle, hooded
I do not know whether a man or a woman
—But who is that on the other side of you?

What is that sound high in the air
Murmur of maternal lamentation
Who are those hooded hordes swarming
Over endless plains, stumbling in cracked earth
Ringed by the flat horizon only   370
What is the city over the mountains
Cracks and reforms and bursts in the violet air
Falling towers
Jerusalem Athens Alexandria
Vienna London
Unreal

A woman drew her long black hair out tight
And fiddled whisper music on those strings
And bats with baby faces in the violet light

Whistled, and beat their wings
And crawled head downward down a blackened wall
And upside down in air were towers
Tolling reminiscent bells, that kept the hours
And voices singing out of empty cisterns and exhausted
    wells.

In this decayed hole among the mountains
In the faint moonlight, the grass is singing
Over the tumbled graves, about the chapel
There is the empty chapel, only the wind's home.
It has no windows, and the door swings,
Dry bones can harm no one.   390
Only a cock stood on the rooftree
Co co rico co co rico
In a flash of lightning. Then a damp gust
Bringing rain

Ganga was sunken, and the limp leaves
Waited for rain, while the black clouds
Gathered far distant, over Himavant.
The jungle crouched, humped in silence.
Then spoke the thunder
Da   400
Datta : what have we given?
My friend, blood shaking my heart
The awful daring of a moment's surrender
Which an age of prudence can never retract
By this, and this only, we have existed
Which is not to be found in our obituaries
Or in memories draped by the beneficent spider
Or under seals broken by the lean solicitor
In our empty rooms
Da   410

T. S. *Dayadhvam* : I have heard the key
ELIOT Turn in the door once and turn once only
We think of the key, each in his prison
Thinking of the key, each confirms a prison
Only at nightfall, aethereal rumours
Revive for a moment a broken Coriolanus
DA
Damyata : The boat responded
Gaily, to the hand expert with sail and oar
The sea was calm, your heart would have responded 420
Gaily, when invited, beating obedient
To controlling hands

                             I sat upon the shore
Fishing, with the arid plain behind me
Shall I at least set my lands in order?
London Bridge is falling down falling down falling
    down
Poi s'ascose nel foco che gli affina
Quando fiam ceu chelidon—O swallow swallow
Le Prince d'Aquitaine à la tour abolie
These fragments I have shored against my ruins   430
Why then Ile fit you. Hieronymo's mad againe.
Datta. Dayadhvam. Damyata.
                    Shantih   shantih   shantih

JOURNEY OF THE MAGI

T. S.
ELIOT

'A cold coming we had of it,
Just the worst time of the year
For a journey, and such a long journey:
The ways deep and the weather sharp,
The very dead of winter.'
And the camels galled, sore-footed, refractory,
Lying down in the melting snow.
There were times we regretted
The summer palaces on slopes, the terraces,
And the silken girls bringing sherbet.
Then the camel men cursing and grumbling
And running away, and wanting their liquor and
      women,
And the night-fires going out, and the lack of shelters,
And the cities hostile and the towns unfriendly
And the villages dirty and charging high prices:
A hard time we had of it.
At the end we preferred to travel all night,
Sleeping in snatches,
With the voices singing in our ears, saying
That this was all folly.

Then at dawn we came down to a temperate valley,
Wet, below the snow line, smelling of vegetation;
With a running stream and a water-mill beating the
      darkness,
And three trees on the low sky,
And an old white horse galloped away in the meadow.
Then we came to a tavern with vine-leaves over the
      lintel,
Six hands at an open door dicing for pieces of silver,
And feet kicking the empty wine-skins.
But there was no information, and so we continued

T. S. And arrived at evening, not a moment too soon
ELIOT Finding the place; it was (you may say) satisfactory.

All this was a long time ago, I remember,
And I would do it again, but set down
This set down
This: were we led all that way for
Birth or Death? There was a Birth, certainly,
We had evidence and no doubt. I had seen birth and
      death,
But had thought they were different; this Birth was
Hard and bitter agony for us, like Death, our death.
We returned to our places, these Kingdoms,
But no longer at ease here, in the old dispensation,
With an alien people clutching their gods.
I should be glad of another death.

MARINA

Quis hic locus, quae regio, quae mundi plaga?

What seas what shores what grey rocks and what
      islands
What water lapping the bow
And scent of pine and the woodthrush singing through
      the fog
What images return
O my daughter.

Those who sharpen the tooth of the dog, meaning
Death
Those who glitter with the glory of the humming bird,
      meaning
Death

Those who sit in the stye of contentment, meaning Death

T. S. ELIOT

Those who suffer the ecstasy of the animals, meaning Death

Are become unsubstantial, reduced by a wind,
A breath of pine, and the woodsong fog
By this grace dissolved in place

What is this face less clear and clearer
The pulse in the arm, less strong and stronger—
Given or lent? more distant than stars and nearer than
    the eye
Whispers and small laughter between leaves and
    hurrying feet
Under sleep, where all the waters meet.

Bowsprit cracked with ice and paint cracked with heat.
I made this, I have forgotten
And remember.
The rigging weak and the canvas rotten
Between one June and another September.
Made this unknowing, half conscious, unknown, my
    own.
The garboard strake leaks, the seams need caulking.
This form, this face, this life
Living to live in a world of time beyond me; let me
Resign my life for this life, my speech for that un-
    spoken,
The awakened, lips parted, the hope, the new ships.

What seas what shores what granite islands towards
    my timbers
And woodthrush calling through the fog
My daughter.

EAST COKER

I

In my beginning is my end. In succession
Houses rise and fall, crumble, are extended,
Are removed, destroyed, restored, or in their place
Is an open field, or a factory, or a by-pass.
Old stone to new building, old timber to new fires,
Old fires to ashes, and ashes to the earth
Which is already flesh, fur and faeces,
Bone of man and beast, cornstalk and leaf.
Houses live and die: there is a time for building
And a time for living and for generation
And a time for the wind to break the loosened pane
And to shake the wainscot where the field-mouse trots
And to shake the tattered arras woven with a silent
        motto.

In my beginning is my end. Now the light falls
Across the open field, leaving the deep lane
Shuttered with branches, dark in the afternoon,
Where you lean against a bank while a van passes,
And the deep lane insists on the direction
Into the village, in the electric heat
Hypnotised. In a warm haze the sultry light
Is absorbed, not refracted, by grey stone.
The dahlias sleep in the empty silence.
Wait for the early owl.

                    In that open field
If you do not come too close, if you do not come too
        close,
On a summer midnight, you can hear the music
Of the weak pipe and the little drum

And see them dancing around the bonfire
The association of man and woman
In daunsinge, signifying matrimonie—
A dignified and commodious sacrament.
Two and two, necessarye coniunction,
Holding eche other by the hand or the arm
Whiche betokeneth concorde. Round and round the
    fire
Leaping through the flames, or joined in circles,
Rustically solemn or in rustic laughter
Lifting heavy feet in clumsy shoes,
Earth feet, loam feet, lifted in country mirth
Mirth of those long since under earth
Nourishing the corn, Keeping time,
Keeping the rhythm in their dancing
As in their living in the living seasons
The time of the seasons and the constellations
The time of milking and the time of harvest
The time of the coupling of man and woman
And that of beasts. Feet rising and falling.
Eating and drinking. Dung and death.

Dawn points, and another day
Prepares for heat and silence. Out at sea the dawn
    wind
Wrinkles and slides. I am here
Or there, or elsewhere. In my beginning.

II

What is the late November doing
With the disturbance of the spring
And creatures of the summer heat,
And snowdrops writhing under feet
And hollyhocks that aim too high

T. S.   Red into grey and tumble down
ELIOT   Late roses filled with early snow?
        Thunder rolled by the rolling stars
        Simulates triumphal cars
        Deployed in constellated wars
        Scorpion fights against the Sun
        Until the Sun and Moon go down
        Comets weep and Leonids fly
        Hunt the heavens and the plains
        Whirled in a vortex that shall bring
        The world to that destructive fire
        Which burns before the ice-cap reigns.

        That was a way of putting it—not very satisfactory:
        A periphrastic study in a worn-out poetical fashion,
        Leaving one still with the intolerable wrestle
        With words and meanings. The poetry does not
                matter.
        It was not (to start again) what one had expected.
        What was to be the value of the long looked forward to,
        Long hoped for calm, the autumnal serenity
        And the wisdom of age? Had they deceived us
        Or deceived themselves, the quiet-voiced elders,
        Bequeathing us merely a receipt for deceit?
        The serenity only a deliberate hebetude,
        The wisdom only the knowledge of dead secrets
        Useless in the darkness into which they peered
        Or from which they turned their eyes. There is, it
                seems to us,
        At best, only a limited value
        In the knowledge derived from experience.
        The knowledge imposes a pattern, and falsifies,
        For the pattern is new in every moment
        And every moment is a new and shocking

Valuation of all we have been. We are only
    undeceived
Of that which, deceiving, could no longer harm.
In the middle, not only in the middle of the way
But all the way, in a dark wood, in a bramble,
On the edge of a grimpen, where there is no secure
    foothold,
And menaced by monsters, fancy lights,
Risking enchantment. Do not let me hear
Of the wisdom of old men, but rather of their folly,
Their fear of fear and frenzy, their fear of possession,
Of belonging to another, or to others, or to God.
The only wisdom we can hope to acquire
Is the wisdom of humility: humility is endless.

The houses are all gone under the sea.

The dancers are all gone under the hill.

III

O dark dark dark. They all go into the dark,
The vacant interstellar spaces, the vacant into the
    vacant,
The captains, merchant bankers, eminent men of
    letters,
The generous patrons of art, the statesmen and the
    rulers,
Distinguished civil servants, chairmen of many
    committees,
Industrial lords and petty contractors, all go into the
    dark,
And dark the Sun and Moon, and the Almanach de
    Gotha
And the Stock Exchange Gazette, the Directory of
    Directors,

T. S. And cold the sense and lost the motive of action.
ELIOT And we all go with them, into the silent funeral,
Nobody's funeral, for there is no one to bury.
I said to my soul, be still, and let the dark come upon
     you
Which shall be the darkness of God. As, in a theatre,
The lights are extinguished, for the scene to be
     changed
With a hollow rumble of wings, with a movement of
     darkness on darkness,
And we know that the hills and the trees, the distant
     panorama
And the bold imposing façade are all being rolled
     away—
Or as, when an underground train, in the tube, stops
     too long between stations
And the conversation rises and slowly fades into silence
And you see behind every face the mental emptiness
     deepen
Leaving only the growing terror of nothing to think
     about;
Or when, under ether, the mind is conscious but
     conscious of nothing—
I said to my soul, be still, and wait without hope
For hope would be hope for the wrong thing; wait
     without love
For love would be love of the wrong thing; there is
     yet faith
But the faith and the love and the hope are all in the
     waiting.
Wait without thought, for you are not ready for
     thought:
So the darkness shall be the light, and the stillness the
     dancing.

Whisper of running streams, and winter lightning.   T. S.
ELIOT
The wild thyme unseen and the wild strawberry,
The laughter in the garden, echoed ecstasy
Not lost, but requiring, pointing to the agony
Of death and birth.

                    You say I am repeating
Something I have said before. I shall say it again.
Shall I say it again? In order to arrive there,
To arrive where you are, to get from where you are
     not,
     You must go by a way wherein there is no ecstasy.
In order to arrive at what you do not know
     You must go by a way which is the way of ignorance.
In order to possess what you do not possess
     You must go by the way of dispossession.
In order to arrive at what you are not
     You must go through the way in which you are not.
And what you do not know is the only thing you know
And what you own is what you do not own
And where you are is where you are not.

IV

The wounded surgeon plies the steel
That questions the distempered part;
Beneath the bleeding hands we feel
The sharp compassion of the healer's art.
Resolving the enigma of the fever chart.

Our only health is the disease
If we obey the dying nurse
Whose constant care is not to please
But to remind of our, and Adam's curse,
And that, to be restored, our sickness must grow
     worse.

131

T. S. The whole earth is our hospital
ELIOT Endowed by the ruined millionaire,
      Wherein, if we do well, we shall
      Die of the absolute paternal care
      That will not leave us, but prevents us everywhere.

      The chill ascends from feet to knees,
      The fever sings in mental wires.
      If to be warmed, then I must freeze
      And quake in frigid purgatorial fires
      Of which the flame is roses, and the smoke is briars.

      The dripping blood our only drink,
      The bloody flesh our only food:
      In spite of which we like to think
      That we are sound, substantial flesh and blood—
      Again, in spite of that, we call this Friday good.

                      v

      So here I am, in the middle way, having had twenty
           years—
      Twenty years largely wasted, the years of l'entre
           deux guerres—
      Trying to learn to use words, and every attempt
      Is a wholly new start, and a different kind of failure
      Because one has only learnt to get the better of words
      For the thing one no longer has to say, or the way in
           which
      One is no longer disposed to say it. And so each venture
      Is a new beginning, a raid on the inarticulate
      With shabby equipment always deteriorating
      In the general mess of imprecision of feeling,
      Undisciplined squads of emotion. And what there
           is to conquer

By strength and submission, has already been discovered
Once or twice, or several times, by men whom one   ELIOT
    cannot hope
To emulate—but there is no competition—
There is only the fight to recover what has been lost
And found and lost again and again: and now, under
    conditions
That seem unpropitious. But perhaps neither gain
    nor loss.
For us, there is only the trying. The rest is not our
    business.

Home is where one starts from. As we grow older
The world becomes stranger, the pattern more
    complicated
Of dead and living. Not the intense moment
Isolated, with no before and after,
But a lifetime burning in every moment
And not the lifetime of one man only
But of old stones that cannot be deciphered.
There is a time for the evening under starlight,
A time for the evening under lamplight
(The evening with the photograph album).
Love is most nearly itself
When here and now cease to matter.
Old men ought to be explorers
Here and there does not matter
We must be still and still moving
Into another intensity
For a further union, a deeper communion
Through the dark cold and the empty desolation,
The wave cry, the wind cry, the vast waters
Of the petrel and the porpoise. In my end is my
    beginning.

HAROLD MONRO

LIVING

Slow bleak awakening from the morning dream
Brings me in contact with the sudden day.
I am alive—this I.
I let my fingers move along my body.
Realisation warns them, and my nerves
Prepare their rapid messages and signals.
While Memory begins recording, coding,
Repeating; all the time Imagination
Mutters: You'll only die.

Here's a new day. O Pendulum move slowly!
My usual clothes are waiting on their peg.
I am alive—this I.
And in a moment Habit, like a crane,
Will bow its neck and dip its pulleyed cable,
Gathering me, my body, and our garment,
And swing me forth, oblivious of my question,
Into the daylight—why?

I think of all the others who awaken,
And wonder if they go to meet the morning
More valiantly than I;
Nor asking of this Day they will be living:
What have I done that I should be alive?
O, can I not forget that I am living?
How shall I reconcile the two conditions:
Living, and yet—to die?

Between the curtains the autumnal sunlight
With lean and yellow finger points me out;

The clock moans: Why? Why? Why?
Heart, Brain and Body, and Imagination
All gather in tumultuous joy together,
Running like children down the path of morning
To fields where they can play without a quarrel:
A country I'd forgotten, but remember,
And welcome with a cry.

O cool glad pasture; living tree, tall corn,
Great cliff, or languid sloping sand, cold sea,
Waves; rivers curving: you, eternal flowers,
Give me content, while I can think of you:
Give me your living breath!
Back to your rampart, Death.

BITTER SANCTUARY

I

She lives in the porter's room; the plush is nicotined.
Clients have left their photos there to perish.
She watches through green shutters those who press
To reach unconsciousness.
She licks her varnished thin magenta lips,
She picks her foretooth with her finger nail,
She pokes her head out to greet new clients, or
To leave them (to what torture) waiting at the door.

II

Heat has locked the heavy earth,
Given strength to every sound.
He, where his life still holds him to the ground,
In anaesthesia, groaning for re-birth,

HAROLD Leans at the door.
MONRO From out the house there comes the dullest flutter;
       A lackey; and thin giggling from behind that shutter.

III

His lost eyes lean to find the number.
Follows his knuckled rap, and hesitating curse.
He cannot wake himself; he may not slumber;
While on the long white wall across the road
Drives the thin outline of a dwindling hearse.

IV

Now the door opens wide.

HE: 'Is there room inside?'
SHE: 'Are you past the bounds of pain?'
HE: 'May my body lie in vain
     Among the dreams I cannot keep!'
SHE: 'Let him drink the cup of sleep.'

V

Thin arms and ghostly hands; faint sky-blue eyes;
Long drooping lashes, lids like full-blown moons,
Clinging to any brink of floating skies:
What hope is there? What fear?—Unless to wake and
    see
Lingering flesh, or cold eternity.

O yet some face, half living, brings
Far gaze to him and croons—
SHE: 'You're white.   You are alone.
     Can you not approach my sphere?'
HE: 'I'm changing into stone.'
SHE: 'Would I were! Would *I* were!'
Then the white attendants fill the cup.

In the morning through the world,
Watch the flunkeys bring the coffee;
Watch the shepherds on the downs,
Lords and ladies at their toilet,
Farmers, merchants, frothing towns.

But look how he, unfortunate, now fumbles
Through unknown chambers, and unheedful stumbles.
Can he evade the overshadowing night?
Are there not somewhere chinks of braided light?

VII

How do they leave who once are in those rooms?
Some may be found, they say, deeply asleep
In ruined tombs.
Some in white beds, with faces round them. Some
Wander the world, and never find a home.

ELM ANGEL

O, why?—
Only a dove can venture that reply.

Large lawns were laid as far as eye could reach;
Ocean lolled inward on a cool long beach;
A tall town motionless and breathless gleamed;
The dead half-listened and their mind half-dreamed;
Wrecks trembled deep in their perpetual tomb;
A quiet drooped upon the summer room.
Now a blue hooded honeysuckle lane,
A garden built of roses on the wane,
Sahara buried under naked sand,
A boy with large eyes from an eastern land,

137

Muffled islands with hushed seas between
And one white temple glowing through the green;
Or, coming back, no place but only sound,
No elm that grew from any earthly ground,
But, heavenly throughout the atmosphere,
One ring dove cooing, crooning, cooing—Where?

CONRAD AIKEN

PRELUDE XXIX

What shall we do—what shall we think—what shall
    we say—?
Why, as the crocus does, on a March morning,
With just such shape and brightness; such fragility;
Such white and gold, and out of just such earth.
Or as the cloud does on the northeast wind—
Fluent and formless; or as the tree that withers.
What are we made of, strumpet, but of these?
Nothing. We are the sum of all these accidents—
Compounded all our days of idiot trifles,—
The this, the that, the other, and the next;
What x or y said, or old uncle thought;
Whether it rained or not, and at what hour;
Whether the pudding had two eggs or three,
And those we loved were ladies. . . . Were they
    ladies?
And did they read the proper books, and simper
With proper persons, at the proper teas?
O Christ and God and all deciduous things—
Let us void out this nonsense and be healed.

There is no doubt that we shall do, as always,
Just what the crocus does. There is no doubt
Your Helen of Troy is all that she has seen,—
All filth, all beauty, all honor and deceit.
The spider's web will hang in her bright mind,—
The dead fly die there doubly; and the rat
Find sewers to his liking. She will walk
In such a world as this alone could give—

CONRAD AIKEN This of the moment, this mad world of mirrors
And of corrosive memory. She will know
The lecheries of the cockroach and the worm,
The chemistry of the sunset, the foul seeds
Laid by the intellect in the simple heart. . . .
And knowing all these things, she will be she.

She will be also the sunrise on the grassblade—
But pay no heed to that. She will be also
The infinite tenderness of the voice of morning—
But pay no heed to that. She will be also
The grain of elmwood, and the ply of water,
Whirlings in sand and smoke, wind in the ferns,
The fixed bright eyes of dolls. . . . And this is all.

PRELUDE LVI

Rimbaud and Verlaine, precious pair of poets,
Genius in both (but what is genius?) playing
Chess on a marble table at an inn
With chestnut blossom falling in blond beer
And on their hair and between knight and bishop—
Sunlight squared between them on the chess-board
Cirrus in heaven, and a squeal of music
Blown from the leathern door of Ste. Sulpice—

Discussing, between moves, iamb and spondee
Anacoluthon and the open vowel
God the great peacock with his angel peacocks
And his dependent peacocks the bright stars:
Disputing too of fate as Plato loved it,
Or Sophocles, who hated and admired,
Or Socrates, who loved and was amused:

Verlaine puts down his pawn upon a leaf
And closes his long eyes, which are dishonest,
And says 'Rimbaud, there is one thing to do:
We must take rhetoric, and wring its neck! . . .'
Rimbaud considers gravely, moves his Queen;
And then removes himself to Timbuctoo.

And Verlaine dead,—with all his jades and mauves;
And Rimbaud dead in Marseilles with a vision,
His leg cut off, as once before his heart;
And all reported by a later lackey,
Whose virtue is his tardiness in time.

Let us describe the evening as it is:—
The stars disposed in heaven as they are:
Verlaine and Shakspere rotting, where they rot,
Rimbaud remembered, and too soon forgot;

Order in all things, logic in the dark;
Arrangement in the atom and the spark;
Time in the heart and sequence in the brain—

Such as destroyed Rimbaud and fooled Verlaine.
And let us then take godhead by the neck—

And strangle it, and with it, rhetoric.

FROM TIME IN THE ROCK: XCII AND XCIII

But no, the familiar symbol, as that the
curtain lifts on a current of air, the rain
drips at the window, the green leaves seen in the
lamplight are bright against the darkness, these
will no longer serve your appetite, you must have
something fresh, something sharp—

CONRAD The coarse grassblade, such as will cut
AIKEN a careless finger, the silver pencil
lying straight along the crack in the table
in its pure rondure a multitude of reflections
or else your own thumbnail suddenly seen
and as if for the first time

Strongly ridged, warm-coloured as flesh but cool,
the pale moon at the base, and the fleck of scar
which grows slowly towards the tip—you think of a
    river
down which a single dead leaf perhaps is carried
or you think of a glacier in which
an acorn has been frozen—

But these too are familiar, it is not these
which will say your thought, you lift desperately
your eyes to the wall—the smooth surface
awaits them as precisely and coldly
as the paper awaits the gleaming pencil, giving
nothing, not even a resistance—

Where will you turn now if not to the rain,
to the curtain in the wind, the leaf tapping the
    window,
these are the wilderness, these are beyond
your pencil with its reflections
your thumbnail with its suggestion of rivers and
    glaciers
now you must go abroad

To the wild night which everywhere awaits you
and the deep darkness full of sounds
to the deep terror in which shines for a moment

142

a single light, far-off, which is suddenly quenched
this is the meaning for which you seek a phrase
this is your phrase.

CONRAD
AIKEN

Or else, in an afternoon of minor reflection,
the savage sunset tamed, and in your garden
the bright stripes beneath your feet, fool
you think from footstep to footstep how easily
man's genius can compose an ode to death.
The honeysuckle puts down its tendrils from the wall
and seeks to embrace you, the seedlings
break the earth as you watch and seem to approach,
the thrush clings with cold claws of a serpent
to his favourite bough and sings. What can you say
that these have not said, are not saying,
you with your consciousness of time? time
swings with the tendril, sings in the birdsong, clings
with the bird-claw, it is time
which thrusts like the leaf's eye from the cold earth.
These already know death, in the mere adventure
in the mere going forth they know and seek it gladly,
they embrace it tightly, what can you say
that is not known to the cold claws of the thrush?
Your ode to death is not in a phrase,
nor in a hymn to darkness, nor in a knowledge
of timelessness, or the sad iteration
of time. Your ode to death is in the lifting
of a single eyelash. Lift it and see.

H. D.

EVENING

The light passes
from ridge to ridge,
from flower to flower—
the hepaticas, wide-spread
under the light
grow faint—
the petals reach inward,
the blue tips bend
toward the bluer heart
and the flowers are lost.

The cornel-buds are still white,
but shadows dart
from the cornel-roots—
black creeps from root to root
each leaf
cuts another leaf on the grass,
shadow seeks shadow,
then both leaf
and leaf-shadow are lost.

SEA ROSE

Rose, harsh rose,
marred and with stint of petals,
meagre flower, thin,
sparse of leaf,

144

more precious
than a wet rose
single on a stem—
you are caught in the drift.

Stunted, with small leaf,
you are flung on the sand,
you are lifted
in the crisp sand
that drives in the wind.

Can the spice-rose
drip such acrid fragrance
hardened in a leaf?

CHOROS FROM MORPHEUS

'Dream—dark-winged'

I

Give me your poppies,
poppies, one by one,
red poppies,
white ones,
red ones set by white;
I'm through with protestation;
my delight
knows nothing of the mind
or argument;
let me be done
with brain's intricacies;
your insight
has driven deeper
than the lordliest tome

H. D.   of Attic thought
or Cyrenian logic;
O strange, dark Morpheus,
covering me with wings,
you give the subtle fruit
Odysseus scorned
that left his townsmen fainting on the sands,
you bring the siren note,
the lotus-land;
O let me rest
at last,
at last,
at last;
your touch is sweeter
than the touch of Death;
O I am tired of measures
like deft oars;
the beat and ringing
of majestic song;
give me your poppies;
I would like along
hot rocks, listening;
still my ambition
that would rear and chafe
like chariot horses
waiting for the race;
let me forget
the spears of Marathon.

MARIANNE MOORE

THE STEEPLE-JACK

Dürer would have seen a reason for living
   in a town like this, with eight stranded whales
to look at; with the sweet sea air coming into your house
on a fine day, from water etched
   with waves as formal as the scales
on a fish.

One by one, in two's, in three's, the seagulls keep
   flying back and forth over the town clock,
or sailing around the lighthouse without moving the
      wings—
rising steadily with a slight
   quiver of the body—or flock
mewing where

a sea the purple of the peacock's neck is
   paled to greenish azure as Dürer changed
the pine green of the Tyrol to peacock blue and guinea
grey. You can see a twenty-five-
   pound lobster; and fishnets arranged
to dry. The

whirlwind fife-and-drum of the storm bends the salt
   marsh grass, disturbs stars in the sky and the
star on the steeple; it is a privilege to see so
much confusion. Disguised by what
   might seem austerity, the seaside flowers and

trees are favoured by the fog so that you have
   the tropics at first hand: the trumpet-vine,

MARI- fox-glove, giant snap-dragon, a salpiglossis that has
ANNE spots and stripes; morning-glories, gourds,
MOORE or moon-vines trained on fishing-twine
at the back

door. There are no banyans, frangipani, nor
jack-fruit trees; nor an exotic serpent
life. Ring lizard and snake-skin for the foot, or
crocodile;
but here they've cats, not cobras, to
keep down the rats. The diffident
little newt

with white pin-dots on black horizontal spaced
out bands lives here; yet there is nothing that
ambition can buy or take away. The college student
named Ambrose sits on the hill-side
with his not-native books and hat
and sees boats

at sea progress white and rigid as if in
a groove. Liking an elegance of which
the source is not bravado, he knows by heart the
antique
sugar-bowl-shaped summer-house of
interlacing slats, and the pitch
of the church

spire, not true, from which a man in scarlet lets
down a rope as a spider spins a thread;
he might be part of a novel, but on the sidewalk a
sign says C. J. Poole, Steeple Jack,
in black and white; and one in red
and white says

Danger. The church portico has four fluted
columns, each a single piece of stone, made

148

modester by white-wash. This would be a fit haven for MARI-
waifs, children, animals, prisoners, ANNE
   and presidents who have repaid MOORE
sin-driven

senators by not thinking about them. There
   are a school-house, a post-office in a
store, fish-houses, hen-houses, a three-masted
     schooner on
the stocks. The hero, the student,
   the steeple-jack, each in his way,
is at home.

It could not be dangerous to be living
   in a town like this, of simple people,
who have a steeple-jack placing danger signs by the
     church
while he is gilding the solid-
   pointed star, which on a steeple
stands for hope.

TO A SNAIL

If 'compression is the first grace of style',
you have it. Contractility is a virtue
as modesty is a virtue.
It is not the acquisition of any one thing
that is able to adorn,
or the incidental quality that occurs
as a concomitant of something well said.
that we value in style,
but the principle that is hid:
in the absence of feet, 'a method of conclusions';
'a knowledge of principles',
in the curious phenomenon of your occipital horn.

149

SILENCE

My father used to say,
'Superior people never make long visits,
have to be shown Longfellow's grave
or the glass flowers at Harvard.
Self-reliant like the cat—
that takes its prey to privacy,
the mouse's limp tail hanging like a shoelace from its
      mouth—
they sometimes enjoy solitude,
and can be robbed of speech
by speech which has delighted them.
The deepest feeling always shows itself in silence;
not in silence, but restraint'.
Nor was he insincere in saying, 'Make my house your
      inn'.
Inns are not residences.

THE PAPER NAUTILUS

For authorities whose hopes
are shaped by mercenaries?
    Writers entrapped by
    teatime fame and by
commuters' comforts? Not for these
    the paper nautilus
    constructs her thin glass shell.

    Giving her perishable
souvenir of hope, a dull
    white outside and smooth—
    edged inner surface
glossy as the sea, the watchful

maker of it guards it
day and night; she scarcely

eats until the eggs are hatched.
Buried eight-fold in her eight
   arms, for she is in
   a sense a devil-
fish, her glass ramshorn-cradled freight
   is hid but is not crushed.
   As Hercules, bitten

by a crab loyal to the hydra,
was hindered to succeed,
   the intensively
   watched eggs coming from
the shell free it when they are freed,—
   leaving its wasp-nest flaws
   of white on white, and close-

laid Ionic chiton-folds
like the lines in the mane of
   A Parthenon horse,
   round which the arms had
wound themselves as if they knew love
   is the only fortress
   strong enough to trust to.

ELEPHANTS

Uplifted and waved until immobilized
wistarialike, the opposing opposed
mouse-gray twined proboscises' trunk formed by two
trunks, fights itself to a spiraled inter-nosed

151

MARI- deadlock of dyke-enforced massiveness. It's a
ANNE knock-down drag-out fight that asks no quarter? Just
MOORE a pastime, as when the trunk rains on itself
the pool it siphoned up; or when—since each must

provide his forty-pound bough dinner—he broke
the leafy branches. These templars of the Tooth,
these matched intensities, take master care of
master tools. One, sleeping with the calm of youth,

at full length in the half dry sun-flecked stream-bed
rests his hunting-horn-curled trunk on shallowed stone.
The sloping hollow of the sleeper's body
cradles the gently breathing eminence's prone

mahout, asleep like a lifeless six-foot
frog, so feather light the elephant's stiff
ear's unconscious of the crossed feet's weight. And the
defenceless human thing sleeps as sound as if

incised with hard wrinkles, embossed with wide ears,
invincibly tusked, made safe by magic hairs!
As if, as if, it is all ifs; we are at
much unease. But magic's masterpiece is theirs,—

Houdini's serenity quelling his fears.
Elephant ear-witnesses-to-be of hymns
and glorias, these ministrants all gray or
gray with white on legs or trunk, are a pilgrims'

pattern of revery not reverence,—a
religious procession without any priests,
the centuries-old carefullest unrehearsed
play. Blessed by Buddha's Tooth, the obedient beasts

themselves as toothed temples blessing the streets, see MARI-
the white elephant carry the cushion that ANNE
carries the casket that carries the Tooth. MOORE
Amenable to what, matched with him, are gnat

trustees, he does not step on them as the white-
canopied blue-cushioned Tooth is augustly
and slowly returned to the shrine. Though white is
the colour of worship and of mourning, he

is not here to worship and he is too wise
to mourn,—a life-prisoner but reconciled,
With trunk tucked up compactly once—explicit
sign of defeat—he resisted, but is the child

of reason now. His straight trunk seems to say: when
what we hoped for came to nothing, we revived.
As loss could not ever alter Socrates'
tranquillity, equanimity is contrived

by the elephant. With the Socrates of
animals as with Sophocles the Bee, on whose
tombstone a hive was incised, sweetness tinctures
his gravity. His held up fore-leg for use

as a stair, to be climbed or descended with
the aid of his ear, expounds the brotherhood
of creatures to man the encroacher by the
small word with the dot, meaning know,—the verb
        bủd.

These knowers 'arouse the feeling that they are
allied to man' and can change roles with their
        trustees.

153

MARI- Hardship makes the soldier; then teachableness
ANNE makes him the philosopher—as Socrates,
MOORE

prudently testing the suspicious thing, knew
the wisest is he who's not sure that he knows.
Who rides on a tiger can never dismount;
asleep on an elephant, that is repose.

Note: For data incorporated in the above stanzas I am indebted
to a lecture-film entitled Ceylon, the Wondrous Isle, by Charles
Brooke Elliott. Deploring the sacrifice of elephants in the Roman
Games, Cicero said they 'aroused both pity and a feeling that the
elephant was somehow allied with man'—(p. 42 *Animals for Show
and Pleasure in Ancient Rome* by George Jennison).

WALLACE STEVENS

TWO AT NORFOLK

Mow the grass in the cemetery, darkies,
Study the symbols and the requiescats,
But leave a bed beneath the myrtles.
This skeleton had a daughter and that, a son.

In his time, this one had little to speak of,
The softest word went gurrituck in his skull.
For him the moon was always in Scandinavia
And his daughter was a foreign thing.

And that one was never a man of heart.
The making of his son was one more duty.
When the music of the boy fell like a fountain,
He praised Johann Sebastian, as he should.

The dark shadows of the funereal magnolias
Are full of the songs of Jamanda and Carlotta;
The son and the daughter, who come to the darkness,
He for her burning breast and she for his arms.

And these two never meet in the air so full of summer
And touch each other, even touching closely,
Without an escape in the lapses of their kisses.
Make a bed and leave the iris in it.

WALLACE STEVENS

TEA AT THE PALAZ OF HOON

Not less because in purple I descended
The western day through what you called
The loneliest air, not less was I myself.

What was the ointment sprinkled on my beard?
What were the hymns that buzzed beside my ears?
What was the sea whose tide swept through me there?

Out of my mind the golden ointment rained,
And my ears made the blowing hymns they heard.
I was myself the compass of that sea:

I was the world in which I walked, and what I saw
Or heard or felt came not but from myself;
And there I found myself more truly and more strange.

THE EMPEROR OF ICE-CREAM

Call the roller of big cigars,
The muscular one, and bid him whip
In kitchen cups concupiscent curds.
Let the wenches dawdle in such dress
As they are used to wear, and let the boys
Bring flowers in last month's newspapers.
Let be be finale of seem.
The only emperor is the emperor of ice-cream.

Take from the dresser of deal,
Lacking the three glass knobs, that sheet
On which she embroidered fantails once
And spread it so as to cover her face.
If her horny feet protrude, they come
To show how cold she is, and dumb.
Let the lamp affix its beam.
The only emperor is the emperor of ice-cream.

FROM 'ESTHETIQUE DU MAL'

WALLACE
STEVENS

How red the rose that is the soldier's wound,
The wounds of many soldiers, the wounds of all
The soldiers that have fallen, red in blood,
The soldier of time grown deathless in great size.

A mountain in which no ease is ever found,
Unless indifference to deeper death
Is ease, stands in the dark, a shadows' hill,
And there the soldier of time has deathless rest.

Concentric circles of shadows, motionless
Of their own part, yet moving on the wind,
Form mystical convolutions in the sleep
Of time's red soldier deathless on his bed.

The shadows of his fellows ring him round
In the high night, the summer breathes for them
Its fragrance, a heavy somnolence, and for him,
For the soldier of time, it breathes a summer sleep,

In which his wound is good because life was.
No part of him was ever part of death.
A woman smoothes her forehead with her hand
And the soldier of time lies calm beneath that stroke.

VACHEL LINDSAY

GENERAL WILLIAM BOOTH ENTERS INTO HEAVEN

Booth led boldly with his big bass drum.
(Are you washed in the blood of the Lamb?)
The Saints smiled gravely and they said: 'He's come.'
(Are you washed in the blood of the Lamb?)
Walking lepers following, rank on rank,
Lurching bravos from the ditches dank,
Drabs from the alleyways and drug fiends pale—
Minds still passion-ridden, soul-powers frail:
Vermin-eaten saints with moldy breath,
Unwashed legions with the ways of Death—
(Are you washed in the blood of the Lamb?)

Every slum had sent its half-a-score
The round world over. (Booth had groaned for more.)
Every banner that the wide world flies
Bloomed with glory and transcendent dyes.
Big-voiced lasses made their banjos bang,
Tranced, fanatical they shrieked and sang:
'Are you washed in the blood of the Lamb?'
Hallelujah! It was queer to see
Bull-necked convicts with that land make free.
Loons with trumpets blowed a blare, blare, blare
On, on upward thro' the golden air!
(Are you washed in the blood of the Lamb?)

Booth died blind and still by faith he trod,
Eyes still dazzled by the ways of God.
Booth led boldly, and he looked the chief

Eagle countenance in sharp relief,
Beard a-flying, air of high command
Unabated in that holy land.

Jesus came from out the court-house door,
Stretched his hands above the passing poor.
Booth saw not, but led his queer ones there
Round and round the mighty court-house square.
Then, in an instant all that blear review
Marched on spotless, clad in raiment new.
The lame were straightened, withered limbs uncurled
And blind eyes opened on a new, sweet world.

Drabs and vixens in a flash made whole!
Gone was the weasel-head, the snout, the jowl!
Sages and sibyls now, and athletes clean,
Rulers of empires, and of forests green!
The hosts were sandalled, and their wings were fire!
(Are you washed in the blood of the Lamb?)
But their noise played havoc with the angel-choir.
(Are you washed in the blood of the Lamb?)

Oh, shout Salvation! It was good to see
Kings and Princes by the Lamb set free.
The banjos rattled and the tambourines
Jing-jing-jingled in the hands of Queens.

And when Booth halted by the curb for prayer
He saw his Master thro' the flag-filled air.
Christ came gently with a robe and crown
For Booth the soldier, while the throng knelt down.
He saw King Jesus. They were face to face,
And he knelt a-weeping in that holy place.
Are you washed in the blood of the Lamb?

D. H. LAWRENCE

END OF ANOTHER HOME HOLIDAY

When shall I see the half-moon sink again
Behind the black sycamore at the end of the garden?
When will the scent of the dim white phlox
Creep up the wall to me, and in at my open window?

Why is it, the long, slow stroke of the midnight bell
    (Will it never finish the twelve?)
Falls again and again on my heart with a heavy
    reproach?

The moon-mist is over the village, out of the mist
    speaks the bell,
And all the little roofs of the village bow low, pitiful,
    beseeching, resigned.
—Speak, you my home! What is it I don't do well?

Ah home, suddenly I love you
As I hear the sharp clean trot of a pony down the road,
Succeeding sharp little sounds dropping into silence
Clear upon the long-drawn hoarseness of a train across
    the valley.

  .   .   .   .

The light has gone out, from under my mother's door.
    That she should love me so!—
    She, so lonely, greying now!
    And I leaving her,
    Bent on my pursuits!

        Love is the great Asker.
        The sun and the rain do not ask the secret

Of the time when the grain struggles down in the dark.
The moon walks her lonely way without anguish,
Because no-one grieves over her departure.

Forever, ever by my shoulder pitiful love will linger,
Crouching as little houses crouch under the mist when I turn.
Forever, out of the mist, the church lifts up a reproach-ful finger,
Pointing my eyes in wretched defiance where love hides her face to mourn.

Oh! but the rain creeps down to wet the grain
That struggles alone in the dark,
And asking nothing, patiently steals back again!
The moon sets forth o' nights
To walk the lonely, dusky heights
Serenely, with steps unswerving;
Pursued by no sigh of bereavement,
No tears of love unnerving
Her constant tread:
While ever at my side,
Frail and sad, with grey, bowed head,
The beggar-woman, the yearning-eyed
Inexorable love goes lagging.

The wild young heifer, glancing distraught,
With a strange new knocking of life at her side
Runs seeking a loneliness.
The little grain draws down the earth, to hide.
Nay, even the slumberous egg, as it labours under the shell

Patiently to divide and self-divide,
Asks to be hidden, and wishes nothing to tell.

But when I draw the scanty cloak of silence over my
eyes
Piteous love comes peering under the hood;
Touches the clasp with trembling fingers, and tries
To put her ear to the painful sob of my blood;
While her tears soak through to my breast,
Where they burn and cauterise.

. . . .

The moon lies back and reddens.
In the valley a corncrake calls
Monotonously,
With a plaintive, unalterable voice, that
deadens
My confident activity;
With a hoarse, insistent request that falls
Unweariedly, unweariedly,
Asking something more of me,
Yet more of me.

SONG OF A MAN WHO HAS COME
THROUGH

Not I, not I, but the wind that blows through me!
A fine wind is blowing the new direction of Time.
If only I let it bear me, carry me, if only it carry me!
If only I am sensitive, subtle, oh, delicate, a winged
gift!
If only, most lovely of all, I yield myself and am
borrowed

By the fine, fine wind that takes its course through the D. H.
    chaos of the world LAW-
Like a fine, an exquisite chisel, a wedge-blade RENCE
    inserted;
If only I am keen and hard like the sheer tip of a wedge
Driven by invisible blows,
The rock will split, we shall come at the wonder, we
    shall find the Hesperides.

Oh, for the wonder that bubbles into my soul,
I would be a good fountain, a good well-head,
Would blur no whisper, spoil no expression.

What is the knocking?
What is the knocking at the door in the night?
It is somebody wants to do us harm.

No, no, it is the three strange angels.
Admit them, admit them.

SNAKE

A snake came to my water-trough
On a hot, hot day, and I in pyjamas for the heat,
To drink there.

In the deep, strange-scented shade of the great dark
    carob-tree
I came down the steps with my pitcher
And must wait, must stand and wait, for there he was
    at the trough before me.

He reached down from a fissure in the earth-wall in the
    gloom
And trailed his yellow-brown slackness soft-bellied
    down, over the edge of the stone trough

163

And rested his throat upon the stone bottom,
And where the water had dripped from the tap, in a
    small clearness,
He sipped with his straight mouth,
Softly drank through his straight gums, into his slack
    long body,
Silently.

Someone was before me at my water-trough,
And I, like a second comer, waiting.

He lifted his head from his drinking, as cattle do,
And looked at me vaguely, as drinking cattle do,
And flickered his two-forked tongue from his lips, and
    mused a moment,
And stooped and drank a little more,
Being earth-brown, earth-golden from the burning
    bowels of the earth
On the day of Sicilian July, with Etna smoking.

The voice of my education said to me
He must be killed,
For in Sicily the black, black snakes are innocent, the
    gold are venomous.

And voices in me said, If you were a man
You would take a stick and break him now, and finish
    him off.

But must I confess how I liked him,
How glad I was he had come like a guest in quiet, to
    drink at my water-trough
And depart peaceful, pacified, and thankless,
Into the burning bowels of this earth?

Was it cowardice, that I dared not kill him?
Was it perversity, that I longed to talk to him?

Was it humility, to feel so honoured?
I felt so honoured.

And yet those voices:
If you were not afraid, you would kill him!

And truly I was afraid, I was most afraid,
But even so, honoured still more
That he should seek my hospitality
From out the dark door of the secret earth.

He drank enough
And lifted his head, dreamily, as one who has drunken,
And flickered his tongue like a forked night on the air, so
     black,
Seeming to lick his lips,
And looked around like a god, unseeing, into the air,
And slowly turned his head,
And slowly, very slowly, as if thrice adream,
Proceeded to draw his slow length curving round
And climb again the broken bank of my wall-face.

And as he put his head into that dreadful hole,
And as he slowly drew up, snake-easing his shoulders,
     and entered farther,
A sort of horror, a sort of protest against his with-
     drawing into that horrid black hole,
Deliberately going into the blackness, and slowly
     drawing himself after,
Overcame me now his back was turned.

I looked round, I put down my pitcher,
I picked up a clumsy log
And threw it at the water-trough with a clatter.

I think it did not hit him,
But suddenly that part of him that was left behind
     convulsed in undignified haste,

Writhed like lightning, and was gone
Into the black hole, the earth-lipped fissure in the
     wall-front,
At which, in the intense still noon, I stared with
     fascination.

And immediately I regretted it.
I thought how paltry, how vulgar, what a mean act!
I despised myself and the voices of my accursed human
     education.

And I thought of the albatross,
And I wished he would come back, my snake.

For he seemed to me again like a king,
Like a king in exile, uncrowned in the underworld,
Now due to be crowned again.

And so, I missed my chance with one of the lords
Of life.
And I have something to expiate;
A pettiness.

Taormina

BAVARIAN GENTIANS

Not every man has gentians in his house
in Soft September, at slow, Sad Michaelmas.

Bavarian gentians, big and dark, only dark
darkening the day-time torch-like with the smoking
     blueness of Pluto's gloom,
ribbed and torch-like, with their blaze of darkness
     spread blue
down flattening into points, flattened under the sweep
     of white day

166

torch-flower of the blue-smoking darkness, Pluto's
    dark-blue daze, D. H.
LAW-
RENCE
black lamps from the halls of Dio, burning dark blue,
giving off darkness, blue darkness, as Demeter's pale
    lamps give off light,
lead me then, lead me the way.

Reach me a gentian, give me a torch
let me guide myself with the blue, forked torch of this
    flower
down the darker and darker stairs, where blue is
    darkened on blueness.
even where Persephone goes, just now, from the
    frosted September
to the sightless realm where darkness is awake upon the
    dark
and Persephone herself is but a voice
or a darkness invisible enfolded in the deeper dark
of the arms Plutonic, and pierced with the passion of
    dense gloom,
among the splendour of torches of darkness, shedding
    darkness on the lost bride and her groom.

ISAAC ROSENBERG

RETURNING, WE HEAR THE LARKS

Sombre the night is:
And, though we have our lives, we know
What sinister threat lurks there.

Dragging these anguished limbs, we only know
This poison-blasted track opens on our camp—
On a little safe sleep.

But hark! Joy—joy—strange joy.
Lo! Heights of night ringing with unseen larks:
Music showering on our upturned listening faces.

Death could drop from the dark
As easily as song—
But song only dropped,
Like a blind man's dreams on the sand
By dangerous tides;
Like a girl's dark hair, for she dreams no ruin lies there,
Or her kisses where a serpent hides.

THE BURNING OF THE TEMPLE

Fierce wrath of Solomon,
Where sleepest thou? O see,
The fabric which thou won
Earth and ocean to give thee—
O look at the red skies.

Or hath the sun plunged down?
What is this molten gold—
These thundering fires blown
Through heaven, where the smoke rolled?
Again the great king dies.

His dreams go out in smoke.
His days he let not pass
And sculptured here are broke,
Are charred as the burnt grass,
Gone as his mouth's last sighs.

DEAD MAN'S DUMP

The plunging limbers over the shattered track
Racketed with their rusty freight,
Stuck out like many crowns of thorns,
And the rusty stakes like sceptres old
To stay the flood of brutish men
Upon our brothers dear.

The wheels lurched over sprawled dead
But pained them not, though their bones crunched;
Their shut mouths made no moan.
They lie there huddled, friend and foeman,
Man born of man, and born of woman;
And shells go crying over them
From night till night and now.

Earth has waited for them,
All the time of their growth
Fretting for their decay:
Now she has them at last!
In the strength of their strength
Suspended—stopped and held.

169

ISAAC What fierce imaginings their dark souls lit?
ROSEN- Earth! Have they gone into you?
BERG Somewhere they must have gone,
And flung on your hard back
Is their souls' sack,
Emptied of God-ancestralled essences.
Who hurled them out? Who hurled?

None saw their spirits' shadow shake the grass,
Or stood aside for the half used life to pass
Out of those doomed nostrils and the doomed mouth,
When the swift iron burning bee
Drained the wild honey of their youth.

What of us who, flung on the shrieking pyre,
Walk, our usual thoughts untouched,
Our lucky limbs as on ichor fed,
Immortal seeming ever?
Perhaps when the flames beat loud on us,
A fear may choke in our veins
And the startled blood may stop.

The air is loud with death,
The dark air spurts with fire,
The explosions ceaseless are.
Timelessly now, some minutes past,
These dead strode time with vigorous life,
Till the shrapnel called 'An end!'
But not to all. In bleeding pangs
Some borne on stretchers dreamed of home,
Dear things, war-blotted from their hearts.

A man's brains splattered on
A stretcher-bearer's face;
His shook shoulders slipped their load,
But when they bent to look again

The drowning soul was sunk too deep
For human tenderness.

They left this dead with the older dead,
Stretched at the cross roads.

Burnt black by strange decay
Their sinister faces lie,
The lid over each eye;
The grass and coloured clay
More motion have than they,
Joined to the great sunk silences.

Here is one not long dead.
His dark hearing caught our far wheels,
And the choked soul stretched weak hands
To reach the living word the far wheels said;
The blood-dazed intelligence beating for light,
Crying through the suspense of the far torturing
        wheels
Swift for the end to break
Or the wheels to break,
Cried as the tide of the world broke over his sight,
'Will they come? Will they ever come?'
Even as the mixed hoofs of the mules,
The quivering-bellied mules,
And the rushing wheels all mixed
With his tortured upturned sight.

So we crashed round the bend,
We heard his weak scream,
We heard his very last sound,
And our wheels grazed his dead face.

ISAAC
ROSEN-
BERG

BREAK OF DAY IN THE TRENCHES

The darkness crumbles away—
It is the same old druid Time as ever.
Only a live thing leaps my hand—
A queer sardonic rat—
As I pull the parapet's poppy
To stick behind my ear.
Droll rat, they would shoot you if they knew
Your cosmopolitan sympathies
(And God knows what antipathies).
Now you have touched this English hand
You will do the same to a German—
Soon, no doubt, if it be your pleasure
To cross the sleeping green between.
It seems you inwardly grin as you pass
Strong eyes, fine limbs, haughty athletes
Less chanced than you for life,
Bonds to the whims of murder,
Sprawled in the bowels of the earth,
The torn fields of France.
What do you see in our eyes
At the shrieking iron and flame
Hurled through still heavens?
What quaver—what heart aghast?
Poppies whose roots are in man's veins
Drop, and are ever dropping;
But mine in my ear is safe,
Just a little white with the dust.

From MOSES: A PLAY

ISAAC ROSEN- BERG

The Young Hebrew speaks:

Yesterday as I lay nigh dead with toil
Underneath the hurtling crane oiled with our blood,
Thinking to end all and let the crane crush me,
He came by and bore me into the shade:
O, what a furnace roaring in his blood
Thawed my congealed sinews and tingled my own
Raging through me like a strong cordial.
He spoke! Since yesterday
Am I not larger grown?
I've seen men hugely shapen in soul,
Of such unhuman shaggy male turbulence
They tower in foam miles from our neck-strained
        sight,
And to their shop only heroes come;
But all were cripples to this speed
Constrained to the stables of flesh.
I say there is a famine in ripe harvest
When hungry giants come as guests:
Come knead the hills and ocean into food,
There is none for him.
The streaming vigours of his blood erupting
From his halt tongue are like an anger thrust
Out of a madman's piteous craving for
A monstrous balked perfection.

WILFRED OWEN

FROM MY DIARY, JULY 1914

Leaves
  Murmuring by myriads in the shimmering trees.
Lives
  Wakening with wonder in the Pyrenees.
Birds
  Cheerily chirping in the early day.
Bards
  Singing of summer scything thro' the hay.
Bees
  Shaking the heavy dews from bloom and frond.
Boys
  Bursting the surface of the ebony pond.
Flashes
  Of swimmers carving thro' the sparkling cold.
Fleshes
  Gleaming with wetness to the morning gold.
A mead
  Bordered about with warbling water brooks.
A maid
  Laughing the love-laugh with me; proud of looks.
The heat
  Throbbing between the upland and the peak.
Her heart
  Quivering with passion to my pressed cheek.
Braiding
  Of floating flames across the mountain brow.
Brooding
  Of stillness; and a sighing of the bough.

Stirs
WILFRED
OWEN
    Of leaflets in the gloom; soft petal-showers;
Stars
    Expanding with the starr'd nocturnal flowers.

EXPOSURE

Our brains ache, in the merciless iced east winds that
    knive us . . .
Wearied we keep awake because the night is silent . . .
Low, drooping flares confuse our memory of the
    salient . . .
Worried by silence, sentries whisper, curious,
    nervous,
            But nothing happens.

Watching, we hear the mad gusts tugging on the wire,
Like twitching agonies of men among its brambles.
Northward, incessantly, the flickering gunnery
    rumbles,
Far off, like a dull rumour of some other war.
          What are we doing here?

The poignant misery of dawn begins to grow . . .
We only know war lasts, rain soaks, and clouds sag
    stormy.
Dawn massing in the east her melancholy army
Attacks once more in ranks on shivering ranks of gray,
          But nothing happens.

Sudden successive flights of bullets streak the silence.
Less deadly than the air that shudders black with snow,
With sidelong flowing flakes that flock, pause, and
    renew,

WILFRED
OWEN
We watch them wandering up and down the wind's
    nonchalance,
            But nothing happens.

Pale flakes with fingering stealth come feeling for our
    faces—
We cringe in holes, back on forgotten dreams, and
    stare, snow-dazed,
Deep into grassier ditches. So we drowse, sun-dozed,
Littered with blossoms trickling where the blackbird
    fusses.
            Is it that we are dying?

Slowly our ghosts drag home: glimpsing the sunk fires,
    glozed
With crusted dark-red jewels; crickets jingle there;
For hours the innocent mice rejoice: the house is
    theirs;
Shutters and doors, all closed: on us the doors are
    closed,—
            We turn back to our dying.

Since we believe not otherwise can kind fires burn;
Nor ever suns smile true on child, or field, or fruit.
For God's invincible spring our love is made afraid;
Therefore, not loath, we lie out here; therefore were
    born,
            For love of God seems dying.

To-night, His frost will fasten on this mud and us,
Shrivelling many hands, puckering foreheads crisp.
The burying-party, picks and shovels in their shaking
    grasp,
Pause over half-known faces. All their eyes are ice,
            But nothing happens.

GREATER LOVE

WILFRED
OWEN

Red lips are not so red
  As the stained stones kissed by the English dead.
Kindness of wooed and wooer
Seems shame to their love pure.
O Love, your eyes lose lure
  When I behold eyes blinded in my stead!

Your slender attitude
  Trembles not exquisite like limbs knife-skewed,
Rolling and rolling there
Where God seems not to care;
Till the fierce Love they bear
  Cramps them in death's extreme decrepitude.

Your voice sings not so soft,—
  Though even as wind murmuring through raftered
    loft,—
Your dear voice is not dear,
Gentle, and evening clear,
As theirs whom none now hear,
  Now earth has stopped their piteous mouths that
    coughed.

Heart, you were never hot,
  Nor large, nor full like hearts made great with shot;
And though your hand be pale,
Paler are all which trail
Your cross through flame and hail:
  Weep, you may weep, for you may touch them not

MENTAL CASES

Who are these? Why sit they here in twilight?
Wherefore rock they, purgatorial shadows,
Drooping tongues from jaws that slob their relish,
Baring teeth that leer like skulls' teeth wicked?
Stroke on stroke of pain,—but what slow panic,
Gouged these chasms round their fretted sockets?
Ever from their hair and through their hands' palms
Misery swelters. Surely we have perished
Sleeping, and walk hell; but who these hellish?

—These are men whose minds the Dead have ravished.
Memory fingers in their hair of murders,
Multitudinous murders they once witnessed.
Wading sloughs of flesh these helpless wander,
Treading blood from lungs that had loved laughter.
Always they must see these things and hear them,
Batter of guns and shatter of flying muscles,
Carnage incomparable, and human squander,
Rucked too thick for these men's extrication.

Therefore still their eyeballs shrink tormented
Back into their brains, because on their sense
Sunlight seems a blood-smear; night comes blood-
        black;
Dawn breaks open like a wound that bleeds afresh
—Thus their heads wear this hilarious, hideous,
Awful falseness of set-smiling corpses.
—Thus their hands are plucking at each other;
Picking at the rope-knouts of their scourging;
Snatching after us who smote them, brother,
Pawing us who dealt them war and madness.

FUTILITY

WILFRED
OWEN

Move him into the sun—
Gently its touch awoke him once,
At home, whispering of fields unsown.
Always it woke him, even in France,
Until this morning and this snow.
If anything might rouse him now
The kind old sun will know.

Think how it wakes the seeds,—
Woke, once, the clays of a cold star.
Are limbs, so dear-achieved, are sides,
Full-nerved—still warm—too hard to stir?
Was it for this the clay grew tall?
—O what made fatuous sunbeams toil
To break earth's sleep at all?

ANTHEM FOR DOOMED YOUTH

What passing-bells for these who die as cattle?
    Only the monstrous anger of the guns.
    Only the stuttering rifles' rapid rattle
Can patter out their hasty orisons.
No mockeries for them from prayers or bells,
    Nor any voice of mourning save the choirs,—
The shrill, demented choirs of wailing shells;
    And bugles calling for them from sad shires.

What candles may be held to speed them all?
    Not in the hands of boys, but in their eyes
Shall shine the holy glimmers of good-byes.
    The pallor of girls' brows shall be their pall;
Their flowers the tenderness of silent minds,
And each slow dusk a drawing-down of blinds.

STRANGE MEETING

It seemed that out of battle I escaped
Down some profound dull tunnel, long since scooped
Through granites which titanic wars had groined.
Yet also there encumbered sleepers groaned,
Too fast in thought or death to be bestirred.
Then, as I probed them, one sprang up, and stared
With piteous recognition in fixed eyes,
Lifting distressful hands as if to bless.
And by his smile, I knew that sullen hall,
By his dead smile I knew we stood in Hell.
With a thousand pains that vision's face was grained;
Yet no blood reached there from the upper ground,
And no guns thumped, or down the flues made moan.
'Strange friend', I said, 'here is no cause to mourn.'
'None', said the other, 'save the undone years,
The hopelessness. Whatever hope is yours,
Was my life also; I went hunting wild
After the wildest beauty in the world,
Which lies not calm in eyes, or braided hair,
But mocks the steady running of the hour,
And if it grieves, grieves richlier than here.
For by my glee might many men have laughed,
And of my weeping something had been left,
Which must die now. I mean the truth untold,
The pity of war, the pity war distilled.
Now men will go content with what we spoiled.
Or, discontent, boil bloody, and be spilled.
They will be swift with swiftness of the tigress,
None will break ranks, though nations trek from
        progress.
Courage was mine, and I had mystery,
Wisdom was mine, and I had mastery;

To miss the march of this retreating world   WILFRED
OWEN
Into vain citadels that are not walled.
Then, when much blood had clogged their chariot-
     wheels
I would go up and wash them from sweet wells,
Even with truths that lie too deep for taint.
I would hafe poured my spirit without stint
But not through wounds; not on the cess of war.
Foreheads of men have bled where no wounds were.
I am the enemy you killed, my friend.
I knew you in this dark; for so you frowned
Yesterday through me as you jabbed and killed.
I parried! but my hands were loath and cold.
Let us sleep now. . . .'

HERBERT READ

MY COMPANY

Foule ! Ton âme entière est debout
dans mon corps.

JULES ROMAINS

I

You became
In many acts and quiet observances
A body and a soul, entire.

I cannot tell
What time your life became mine :
Perhaps when one summer night
We halted on the roadside
In the starlight only,
And you sang your sad home-songs,
Dirges which I standing outside you
Coldly condemned.

Perhaps, one night, descending cold
When rum was mighty acceptable,
And my doling gave birth to sensual gratitude.

And then our fights: we've fought together
Compact, unanimous ;
And I have felt the pride of leadership.

In many acts and quiet observances
You absorbed me:
Until one day I stood eminent
And saw you gathered round me,
Uplooking,

182

And about you a radiance that seemed to beat
With variant glow and to give
Grace to our unity.

But, God! I know that I'll stand
Someday in the loneliest wilderness,
Someday my heart will cry
For the soul that has been, but that now
Is scattered with the winds,
Deceased and devoid.

I know that I'll wander with a cry:
'O beautiful men, O men I loved,
O whither are you gone, my company?'

2

My men go wearily
With their monstrous burdens.

They bear wooden planks
And iron sheeting
Through the area of death.

When a flare curves through the sky
They rest immobile.

Then on again,
Sweating and blaspheming—
'Oh, bloody Christ!'

My men, my modern Christs,
Your bloody agony confronts the world.

3

A man of mine
          lies on the wire.
It is death to fetch his soulless corpse.

A man of mine
            lies on the wire;
And he will rot
And first his lips
The worms will eat.

It is not thus I would have him kissed,
But with the warm passionate lips
Of his comrade here.

4

I can assume
A giant attitude and godlike mood,
And then detachedly regard
All riots, conflicts and collisions.

The men I've lived with
Lurch suddenly into a far perspective;
They distantly gather like a dark cloud of birds.
In the autumn sky.

Urged by some unanimous
Volition or fate,
Clouds clash in opposition;
The sky quivers, the dead descend;
Earth yawns.

They are all of one species.

From my giant attitude,
In godlike mood,
I laugh till space is filled
With hellish merriment.

Then again I assume
My human docility,
Bow my head
And share their doom.

CRANACH

But once upon a time
the oakleaves and the wild boars
Antonio Antonio
the old wound is bleeding.

We are in Silvertown
we have come here with a modest ambition
to know a little bit about the river
eating cheese and pickled onions on a terrace by the
          Thames.

Sweet Thames! the ferry glides across your bosom
like Leda's swan.
The factories ah slender graces
sly naked damsels nodding their downy plumes.

THE FALCON AND THE DOVE

I

This high-caught hooded Reason broods upon my
          wrist,
Fettered by a so tenuous leash of steel.
We are bound for the myrtle marshes, many leagues
          away,
And have a fair expectation of quarry.

185

Over the laggard dove, inclining to green boscage
Hovers this intentional doom—till the unsullied sky
   receives
A precipitation of shed feathers
And the swifter fall of wounded wings.

3

Will the plain aye echo with that loud *hullallo!*
Or retain an impress of our passage?
We have caught Beauty in a wild foray
And now the falcon is hooded and comforted away.

A NORTHERN LEGION

Bugle calls coiling through the rocky valley
have found echoes in the eagles' cries:
an outrage is done on anguished men
now men die and death is no deedful glory.

Eleven days this legion forced the ruined fields, the
burnt homesteads and empty garths, the broken arches
of bridges: desolation moving like a shadow before
   them, a
rain of ashes. Endless their anxiety

marching into a northern darkness: approaching
a narrow defile, the waters falling fearfully
the clotting menace of shadows and all the multiple
instruments of death in ambush against them.

The last of the vanguard sounds his doleful note
The legion now is lost. None will follow.

186

TIME REGAINED

HERBERT
READ

The limbs remember blood and fire:
a hurt that's done may in the mind
sink and lose identity;

for the mind has reasons of its own
for covering with an eyeless mask
marks of mortality.

The limbs remember fire and joy
and flesh to flesh is benison
of entity;

but the mind has reasons of its own
for circumventing life and love's
sodality.

THE SEVEN SLEEPERS

The seven sleepers ere they left
the light and colour of the earth
the seven sleepers they did cry
(banishing their final fears):

'Beauty will not ever fade.
To our cavern we retire
doomed to sleep ten thousand years.
Roll the rock across the gap

Then forget us; we are quiet:
stiff and cold our bodies lie;
Earth itself shall stir ere we
visit Earth's mortality.

Beauty when we wake will be
a solitude on land and sea.'

187

THE ANALYSIS OF LOVE

Else a great Prince in prison lies.

JOHN DONNE

1

I would have my own vision
    The world's vision:
The beauty settled in my mind
    A lamp in a busy street.

Yet these activities are too intimate,
    Made for a solitary sense:
However builded the emotion,
    The imagination's mute.

Could voice join mind's eye and scream
    Its vision out
Then the world would halt its toil,
    Passionless, time unreal.

2

Night palliates
    The ragged ridge of things;
The stars, however minute, are intense
    And pierce beyond the reckoning brain.

The stars and the dark palliation
    Are not indwelling
When driven lust has dark dominion
    In the mind's eclipse.

Yet sleep is relentless, extinguishing all
    Under its cone of annihilation;
And in the fresh and cool morning
    The lusting man is lost.

And lust is a finite thing,
  Deftly to be sized by the passionless mind.
Lust gone, other elements exist
  Wrought in the body's being.

The measuring mind can appraise
  An earthen grace;
The idiot's chatter
  Analyses into experience.

But your appeal is imperceptible
  As ultimate atoms
And the fast matrix
  Of all within the human universe.

4

There are moments when I see your mind
  Lapsed in your sex;
When one particular deployment
  Is the reflex of incomplete attainment.

These moments vanish
  Like lamps at daybreak:
The wide and even light
  Is kind and real.

And then you are universal;
  I too: our minds,
Not cramped by figured thought
  Unite in the impersonal beauty we possess.

5

Since you are finite you will never find
  The hidden source of the mind's emotion;

189

HERBERT It is a pool, secret in dusk and dawn,
READ   Deep in the chartless forest life has grown.

    Since you are blind you do not see
        The thirsting beasts peer from gnarled roots,
    And creep to the brink, at noon,
        To lap with rough tongues, rippling the burnished
           serenity.

    —This mind which is collected
        From many tricklings, of dew and rain,
    Of which you are the chief
        And freshest in its depths.

6

You will not drive me to the anguish of love
    By any torture of this faith,
Converting to the corrupted semblance of despair
    The still evidence of my look;

But by the triumph of those traits—
    Their multiplication to excess—
Which mark the frailties germinant
    In a mind emotion-bound.

Not that I fear your capture
    In human littlenesses;
These are drops we can absorb
    In the fount and flow of a passionless mood.

7

The teased fibrils of reason
    Weave vainly to dam
Some bank against the giant flood
    Of this emotion.

Waves' and winds' erosion
  Crumbles granitic cliffs,
Æonly obliterating
  The earth's known visage.

The multiple striving of the human race
  Wins slowly mind's conquest
Of brutal foes; or is the supreme foe
  This hope, deluding?

8

When you have totalled this life
  And got the vision complete:
When you have seen a central horror
  Blacking out the sun's gift—

Take me: englobe my soul
  And spin it on an axis;
Set about me ringed planets
  And diverse atmospheres.

And in that world
  Lacking the imperfections of this,
Live boldly, plant sapling trees,
  Expecting a burden of fruit.

9

You will say that I am in the scheme of things,
  A unit in the crumbling earth;
Trees are barren:
  Chance I'm a barren tree.

Link me with circumstances if you must,
  But live to triumph all the same:
We'll be insensate when the whirl
  Of circumstance is past.

You'll not avoid the avalanche;
    But parasitic on my soul
You run, beat, rebound and throb
    In world descent.

10

Nature has perpetual tears
    In drooping boughs,
And everywhere inanimate death
    Is immemorial.

But I have naught that will express
    The grief I feel
When men and moods combine to show
    The end of this—

This mental ecstasy all spent
    In disuniting death;
And the years that spread
    Oblivion on our zest.

THE CONTRARY EXPERIENCE

I

You cry as the gull cries
dipping low where the tide has ebbed
over the vapid reaches: your impulse
died in the second summer of the war.

The years dip their wings
brokenly over the uncovered springs.
Hands wasted for love and poetry
finger the hostile gunmetal.

192

Called to meaningless action
you hesitate
meditating faith to a conscience
more patently noble.

2

But even as you wait
like Arjuna in his chariot
the ancient wisdom whispers:
Live in action.

I do not forget the oath
taken one frosty dawn
when the shadows stretched
from horizon to horizon:

Not to repeat the false act
Not to inflict pain
To suffer, to hope, to build
To analyse the indulgent heart.

Wounds dried like sealing-wax
upon that bond
But time has broken
the proud mind.

No resolve can defeat suffering
no desire establish joy:
Beyond joy and suffering
is the equable heart

not indifferent to glory
if it lead to death
if it lead to the only life.

HERBERT
READ

Lybia, Egypt, Hellas
the same tide ebbing, the same gull crying
desolate shores and rocky deserts
hunger, thirst, death

the storm threatening and the air still
but other wings
librating in the ominous hush
and the ethereal voice

thrilling and clear.

Buffeted against the storm's sullen breath
the lark rises
over the grey dried grasses
rises and sings.

JOHN CROWE RANSOM

VISION BY SWEETWATER

Go and ask Robin to bring the girls over
To Sweetwater, said my Aunt; and that was why
It was like a dream of ladies sweeping by
The willows, clouds, deep meadowgrass, and the
    river.

Robin's sisters and my Aunt's lily daughter
Laughed and talked, and tinkled light as wrens
If there were a little colony all hens
To go walking by the steep turn of Sweetwater.

Let them alone, dear Aunt, just for one minute
Till I go fishing in the dark of my mind:
Where have I seen before, against the wind,
These bright virgins, robed and bare of bonnet,

Flowing with music of their strange quick tongue
And adventuring with delicate paces by the stream,—
Myself a child, old suddenly at the scream
From one of the white throats which it hid among?

CAPTAIN CARPENTER

Captain Carpenter rose up in his prime
Put on his pistols and went riding out
But had got well-nigh nowhere at that time
Till he fell in with ladies in a rout.

It was a pretty lady and all her train
That played with him so sweetly but before

An hour she'd taken a sword with all her main
And twined him of his nose for evermore.

Captain Carpenter mounted up one day
And rode straightway into a stranger rogue
That looked unchristian but be that as may
The Captain did not wait upon prologue.

But drew upon him out of his great heart
The other swung against him with a club
And cracked his two legs at the shinny part
And let him roll and stick like any tub.

Captain Carpenter rode many a time
From male and female took he sundry harms
He met the wife of Satan crying 'I'm
The she-wolf bids you shall bear no more arms'.

Their strokes and counters whistled in the wind
I wish he had delivered half his blows
But where she should have made off like a hind
The bitch bit off his arms at the elbows.

And Captain Carpenter parted with his ears
To a black devil that used him in this wise
O Jesus ere his threescore and ten years
Another had plucked out his sweet blue eyes.

Captain Carpenter got up on his roan
And sallied from the gate in hell's despite
I heard him asking in the grimmest tone
If any enemy yet there was to fight?

'To any adversary it is fame
If he risk to be wounded by my tongue
Or burnt in two beneath my red heart's flame
Such are the perils he is cast among.

'But if he can he has a pretty choice
From an anatomy with little to lose
Whether he cut my tongue and take my voice
Or whether it be my round red heart he choose.'

It was the neatest knave that ever was seen
Stepping in perfume from his lady's bower
Who at this word put in his merry mien
And fell on Captain Carpenter like a tower.

I would not knock old fellows in the dust
But there lay Captain Carpenter on his back
His weapons were the old heart in his bust
And a blade shook between rotten teeth alack.

The rogue in scarlet and gray soon knew his mind
He wished to get his trophy and depart
With gentle apology and touch refined
He pierced him and produced the Captain's heart.

God's mercy rest on Captain Carpenter now
I thought him Sirs an honest gentleman
Citizen husband soldier and scholar enow
Let jangling kites eat of him if they can.

But God's deep curses follow after those
That shore him of his goodly nose and ears
His legs and strong arms at the two elbows
And eyes that had not watered seventy years.

The curse of hell upon the sleek upstart
Who got the Captain finally on his back
And took the red red vitals of his heart
And made the kites to whet their beaks clack clack.

JUDITH OF BETHULIA

JOHN
CROWE
RANSOM

Beautiful as the flying legend of some leopard,
She had not yet chosen her great captain or prince
Depositary to her flesh, and our defence;
And a wandering beauty is a blade out of its scabbard.
You know how dangerous, gentlemen of three-score?
May you know it yet ten more.

Nor by process of veiling she grew the less fabulous.
Gray or blue veils, we were desperate to study
The invincible emanations of her white body,
And the winds at her ordered raiment were ominous.
Might she walk in the market, sit in the council of
    soldiers?
Only of the extreme elders.

But a rare chance was the girl's then, when the
    Invader
Trumpeted from the south, and rumbled from the
    north,
Beleaguered the city from four quarters of the earth,
Our soldiery too craven and sick to aid her—
Where were the arms could countervail his horde?
Her beauty was the sword.

She sat with the elders, and proved on their blear
    visage
How bright was the weapon unrusted in her keeping,
While he lay surfeiting on their harvest heaping,
Wasting the husbandry of their rarest vintage—
And dreaming of the broad-breasted dames for
    concubine?
These floated on his wine.

198

He was lapped with bay-leaves, and grass and fumiter JOHN
    weed, CROWE
And from under the wine-film encountered his mortal RANSOM
    vision.
For even within his tent she accomplished his derision;
She loosed one veil and another, standing unafraid;
And he perished.   Nor brushed her with even so much
    as a daisy?
She found his destruction easy.

The heathen are all perished. The victory was
    furnished,
We smote them hiding in our vineyards, barns,
    annexes,
And now their white bones clutter the holes of foxes,
And the chieftain's head, with grinning sockets, and
    varnished—
Is it hung on the sky with a hideous epitaphy?
No, the woman keeps the trophy.

May God send unto the virtuous lady her prince.
It is stated she went reluctant to that orgy,
Yet a madness fevers our young men, and not the
    clergy
Nor the elders have turned them unto modesty since.
Inflamed by the thought of her naked beauty with
    desire?
Yes, and chilled with fear and despair.

JOHN
CROWE
RANSOM

WHAT DUCKS REQUIRE

Ducks require no ship and sail
Bellied on the foamy skies,
Who scud north. Male and female
Make a slight nest to arise
Where they overtake the spring,
Which clogs with muddy going.

This zone is temperate. The pond,
Eye of a bleak Cyclops visage, catches
Such glints of hyacinth and bland
As bloom in aquarelles of ditches
On a cold spring ground, and render
A space supportable and a time tender.

The half-householders for estate
Beam their floor with ribs of grass,
Disdain your mortises and slate
And Lar who invalided lies,
Planting dangerous at the earth-heart
Where warm and cold precisely start.

Furled, then, the quadrate wing
From the lewd eye and fowler's gun
Till in that wet sequestering,
Webtoed, the progeny is done,
Cold-hatched, and from the blink of birth
Is native to the rhythmed earth.

Prodigious in his wide degrees
Who, as the winds and waters blow,
On raveling banks of fissured seas
In reeds nestles, or will rise and go
Where Capricornus dips his hooves
In the blue chasm of no wharves.

ALLEN TATE

HORATIAN EPODE
TO THE DUCHESS OF MALFI

DUCHESS: '*Who am I?*'
BOSOLA: '*Thou art a box of worm-seed, at best but a salvatory of green mummy.*'

The stage is about to be swept of corpses.
You have no more chance than an infusorian
Lodged in a hollow molar of an eohippus.
Come, now, no prattle of remergence with the
ὄντως ὄν.

. . . .

As (the form requires the myth)
A Greek girl stood once in the prytaneum
Of Carneades, hearing mouthings of Probability,
Then mindful of love dashed her brain on a megalith,

So you, O nameless Duchess who die young,
Meet death somewhat lovingly
And I am filled with a pity of beholding skulls.
There was no pride like yours.

Now considerations of the Void coming after,
Not changed by the strict gesture of your death,
Split the straight line of pessimism
Into two infinities.

It is moot whether there be divinities
As I finish this play by Webster:
The street cars are still running however
And the katharsis fades in the warm water of a yawn.

1922

IDIOT

The idiot greens the meadow with his eyes,
The meadow creeps, implacable and still;
A dog barks; the hammock swings; he lies.
One, two, three, the cows bulge on the hill.

Motion, which is not time, erects snowdrifts
While sister's hand sieves waterfalls of lace.
With a palm fan closer than death, he lifts
The Ozarks and tilted seas across his face.

In the long sunset where impatient sound
Strips niggers to a multiple of backs,
Flies yield their heat, magnolias drench the ground
With Appomattox! The shadows lie in stacks.

The julep glass weaves echoes in Jim's kinks
While ashy Jim puts murmurs in the day:
Now in the idiot's heart a chamber stinks
Of dead asters—as the potter's field, of May.

All evening the marsh is a slick pool
Where dream wild hares, witch hazel, pretty girls.
'Up from the important picnic of a fool
Those rotted asters!' Eddy on eddy swirls

The innocent mansion of a panther's heart!
It crumbles; tick-tick, time drags it in;
And now his arteries lag and now they start
Reverence with the frigid gusts of sin.

The stillness pelts the eye, assaults the hair;
A beech sticks out a branch to warn the stars;

A lightning-bug jerks angles in the air,
Diving. 'I am the captain of new wars!'

The dusk runs down the lane, driven like hail;
Far-off a precise whistle is escheat
To the dark; and then the towering weak and pale
Covers his eyes with memory like a sheet.

1926

THE MEDITERRANEAN

Quem das finem, rex magne, dolorum?

Where we went in the boat was a long bay
A slingshot wide walled in by towering stone,
Peaked margin of antiquity's delay—
And we went there out of time's monotone:

Where we went in the black hull no light moved
But a gull white-winged along the feckless wave;
The breeze, unseen but fierce as a body loved,
That boat drove onward like a willing slave;

Where we went in the small ship the seaweed
Parted and gave to us the murmuring shore
And we made feast and in our secret need
Devoured the very plates Aeneas bore:

Where derelict you see through the low twilight
The green coast that you thunder-tossed would win
Drop sail, and hastening to drink all night
Eat dish and bowl—to take the sweet land in!

Where we feasted and caroused on the sandless
Pebbles, affecting our day of piracy.

203

ALLEN What prophecy of eaten plates could landless
TATE Wanderers fulfil by the ancient sea?

We for that time might taste the famous age
Eternal here yet hidden from our eyes
When lust of power undid its stuffless rage;
They, in a wineskin, bore earth's paradise.

—Let us lie down once more by the breathing side
Of ocean, where our live forefathers sleep
As if the Known Sea still were a month wide—
Atlantis howls but is no longer steep!

What country shall we conquer, what fair land
Unman our conquest and locate our blood?
We've cracked the hemispheres with careless hand:
Now, from the Gates of Hercules we flood

Westward, westward till the barbarous brine
Whelms us to the tired world where tasseling corn,
Fat beans, grapes sweeter than muscadine
Rot on the vine: in that land were we born.

1932

ODE TO THE CONFEDERATE DEAD

Row after row with strict impunity
The headstones yield their names to the element,
The wind whirrs without recollection;
In the riven troughs the splayed leaves
Pile up, of nature the casual sacrament
To the seasonal eternity of death,
Then driven by the fierce scrutiny
Of heaven to their business in the vast breath,
They sough the rumour of mortality.

Autumn is desolation in the plot
Of a thousand acres, where these memories grow
From the inexhaustible bodies that are not
Dead, but feed the grass row after rich row:
Remember now the autumns that have gone—
Ambitious November with the humors of the year,
With a particular zeal for every slab,
Staining the uncomfortable angels that rot
On the slabs, a wing chipped here, an arm there:
The brute curiosity of an angel's stare
Turns you like them to stone,
Transforms the heaving air,
Till plunged to a heavier world below
You shift your sea-space blindly,
Heaving, turning like the blind crab.

        Dazed by the wind, only the wind
        The leaves flying, plunge

You know who have waited by the wall
The twilit certainty of an animal;
Those midnight restitutions of the blood
You know—the immitigable pines, the smoky frieze
Of the sky, the sudden call; you know the rage—
The cold pool left by the mounting flood—
The rage of Zeno and Parmenides.
You who have waited for the angry resolution
Of those desires that should be yours tomorrow,
You know the unimportant shrift of death
And praise the vision
And praise the arrogant circumstance
Of those who fall
Rank upon rank, hurried beyond decision—
Here by the sagging gate, stopped by the wall.

ALLEN   Seeing, seeing only the leaves
TATE   Flying, plunge and expire

Turn your eyes to the immoderate past
Turn to the inscrutable infantry rising
Demons out of the earth—they will not last.
Stonewall, Stonewall—and the sunken fields of hemp
Shiloh, Antietam, Malvern Hill, Bull Run.
Lost in that orient of the thick and fast
You will curse the setting sun.

Cursing only the leaves crying
Like an old man in a storm

You hear the shout—the crazy hemlocks point
With troubled fingers to the silence which
Smothers you, a mummy, in time. The hound bitch
Toothless and dying, in a musty cellar
Hears the wind only.

Now that the salt of their blood
Stiffens the saltier oblivion of the sea,
Seals the malignant purity of the flood,
What shall we, who count our days and bow
Our heads with a commemorial woe,
In the ribboned coats of grim felicity,
What shall we say of the bones, unclean—
Their verdurous anonymity will grow—
The ragged arms, the ragged heads and eyes
Lost in these acres of the insane green?
The grey lean spiders come; they come and go;
In a tangle of willows without light
The singular screech-owl's bright
Invisible lyric seeds the mind
With the furious murmur of their chivalry.

206

We shall say only, the leaves
Flying, plunge and expire

We shall say only, the leaves whispering
In the improbable mist of nightfall
That flies on multiple wing:
Night is the beginning and the end,
And in between the ends of distraction
Waits mute speculation, the patient curse
That stones the eyes, or like the jaguar leaps
For his own image in a jungle pool, his victim.

What shall we say who have knowledge
Carried to the heart? Shall we take the act
To the grave? Shall we, more hopeful, set up the grave
In the house? The ravenous grave?

Leave now
The turnstile and the old stone wall:
The gentle serpent, green in the mulberry bush,
Riots with his tongue through the hush—
Sentinel of the grave who counts us all!

1926-1930

THE TROUT MAP

The Management Area of Cherokee
National Forest, interested in fish,
Has mapped Tellico and Bald rivers
And North River, with the tributaries
Brookshire Branch and Sugar Cove Creek:
A fishy map for facile fishery

In Marvel's kind Ocean: drawn in two
Colours, blue and red—blue for the hue

207

ALLEN Of Europe (Tennessee water is green),
TATE Red lines by blue streams to warn
      The fancy-fishmen from protected fish;
      Black borders hold the Area in a cracked dish

      While other blacks, the dots and dashes, wire
      The fisher's will through classic laurel
      Over boar tracks to creamy pot-holes lying
      Under Bald falls that thump the shying
      Trout: we flew Professor, the Hackles, and Worms.
      (Tom Bagley and I were dotted and dashed wills.)

      Up Green Cove gap from Preacher Millsap's cabin
      We walked a confident hour of victory,
      Sloped to the west on a trail that led us
      To Bald River where map and scene were one
      In seen-identity. Eight trout is the story
      In three miles. We came to a rock-bridge

      On which the road went left around a hill,
      The river, right, tumbled into a cove;
      But the map dashed the road along the stream
      And we dotted man's fishiest enthymeme
      With jellied feet upon understanding love
      Of what eyes see not, that nourishes the will:

      We were fishers, weren't we? And tried to fish
      The egoed belly's dry cartograph—
      Which made the government fish lie down and laugh.
      (Tommy and I listened, we heard them shake
      Mountain and cove because the map was fake.)
      After eighteen miles our feet were clownish,

Then darkness took us into wheezing straits
Where coarse Magellan idling with his fates
Ran with the gulls for map around the Horn,
Or wheresoever the mind with tidy scorn
Revisits the world upon a dry sunbeam.
Now mapless the mountains were a dream.

HART CRANE

NORTH LABRADOR

A land of leaning ice
Hugged by plaster-grey arches of sky,
Flings itself silently
Into eternity.

'Has no one come here to win you,
Or left you with the faintest blush
Upon your glittering breasts?
Have you no memories, O Darkly Bright?'

Cold-hushed, there is only the shifting of moments
That journey toward no Spring—
No birth, no death, no time nor sun
In answer.

RECITATIVE

Regard the capture here, O Janus-faced,
As double as the hands that twist this glass.
Such eyes at search or rest you cannot see;
Reciting pain or glee, how can you bear!

Twin shadowed halves: the breaking second holds
In each the skin alone, and so it is
I crust a plate of vibrant mercury
Borne cleft to you, and brother in the half.

Inquire this much-exacting fragment smile,
Its drums and darkest blowing leaves ignore,—

Defer though, revocation of the tears
That yield attendance to one crucial sign.

Look steadily—how the wind feasts and spins
The brain's disk shivered against lust. Then watch
While darkness, like an ape's face, falls away,
And gradually white buildings answer day.

Let the same nameless gulf beleaguer us—
Alike suspend us from atrocious sums
Built floor by floor on shafts of steel that grant
The plummet heart, like Absalom, no stream.

The highest tower,—let her ribs palisade
Wrenched gold of Nineveh;—yet leave the tower.
The bridge swings over salvage, beyond wharves;
A wind abides the ensign of your will . . .

In alternating bells have you not heard
All hours clapped dense into a single stride?
Forgive me for an echo of these things,
And let us walk through time with equal pride.

FOR THE MARRIAGE OF FAUSTUS
AND HELEN

III

Capped arbiter of beauty in this street
That narrows darkly into motor dawn,—
You, here beside me, delicate ambassador
Of intricate slain numbers that arise
In whispers, naked of steel;

                              religious gunman!
Who faithfully, yourself, will fall too soon,
And in other ways than as the wind settles

HART On the sixteen thrifty bridges of the city:
CRANE Let us unbind our throats of fear and pity.

We even,

Who drove speediest destruction
In corymbulous formations of mechanics,—
Who hurried the hill breezes, spouting malice
Plangent over meadows, and looked down
On rifts of torn and empty houses
Like old women with teeth unjubilant
That waited faintly, briefly and in vain:

We know, eternal gunman, our flesh remembers
The tensile boughs, the nimble blue plateaus,
The mounted, yielding cities of the air!
That saddled sky that shook down vertical
Repeated play of fire—no hypogeum
Of wave or rock was good against one hour.
We did not ask for that, but have survived,
And will persist to speak again before
All stubble streets that have not curved
To memory, or known the ominous lifted arm
That lowers down the arc of Helen's brow
To saturate with blessing and dismay.

A goose, tobacco and cologne—
Three winged and gold-shod prophecies of heaven,
The lavish heart shall always have to leaven
And spread with bells and voices, and atone
The abating shadows of our conscript dust.

Anchises' navel, dripping of the sea,—
The hands Erasmus dipped in gleaming tides,
Gathered the voltage of blown blood and vine;
Delve upward for the new and scattered wine,

212

O brother-thief of time, that we recall.
Laugh out the meagre penance of their days
Who dare not share with us the breath released,
The substance drilled and spent beyond repair
For golden, or the shadow of gold hair.
Distinctly praise the years, whose volatile
Blamed bleeding hands extend and thresh the height
The imagination spans beyond despair,
Outpacing bargain, vocable and prayer.

CUTTY SARK

O, the navies old and oaken
O, the Temeraire no more!

MELVILLE

I met a man in South Street, tall—
a nervous shark tooth swung on his chain.
His eyes pressed through green grass
—green glasses, or bar lights made them
so—

     shine—

        GREEN—

               eyes—
stepped out—forgot to look at you
or left you several blocks away—

in the nickel-in-the-slot piano jogged
'Stamboul Nights'—weaving somebody's nickel—
    sang—

      O Stamboul Rose—dreams weave the rose!

      Murmurs of Leviathan he spoke,
      and rum was Plato in our heads . . .

213

HART 'It's S.S. *Ala*—Antwerp—now remember kid
CRANE to put me out at three she sails on time.
        I'm not much good at time any more keep
        weakeyed watches sometimes snooze—' his bony hands
        got to beating time . . . 'A whaler once—
        I ought to keep time and get over it—I'm a
        Democrat—I know what time it is—No
        I don't want to know what time it is—that
        damned white Arctic killed my time . . .'

           O Stamboul Rose—drums weave—

        'I ran a donkey engine down there on the Canal
        in Panama—got tired of that—
        then Yucatan selling kitchenware—beads—
        have you seen Popocatepetl—birdless mouth
        with ashes sifting down—?
                      and then the coast again . . .'

           Rose of Stamboul O coral Queen—
           teased remnants of the skeletons of cities—
           and galleries, galleries of watergutted lava
           snarling stone—green—drums—drown—

Sing!
    '—that spiracle!' he shot a finger out the door . . .
    'O life's a geyser—beautiful—my lungs—
    No—I can't live on land—!'

I saw the frontiers gleaming of his mind;
or are there frontiers—running sands sometimes
running sands—somewhere—sands running . . .
Or they may start some white machine that sings.
Then you may laugh and dance the axletree—
steel—silver—kick the traces—and know—

ATLANTIS ROSE drums wreathe the rose,
the star floats burning in a gulf of tears
and sleep another thousand—

                              interminably

long since somebody's nickel—stopped—
playing—

A wind worried those wicker-neat lapels, the
swinging summer entrances to cooler hells . . .
Outside a wharf truck nearly ran him down
—he lunged up Bowery way while the dawn
was putting the Statue of Liberty out—that
torch of hers you know—

I started walking home across the Bridge . . .
.   .   .   .

Blithe Yankee vanities, turreted sprites, winged
                    British repartees, skil-
ful savage sea-girls
that bloomed in the spring—Heave, weave
those bright designs the trade winds drive . . .

          Sweet opium and tea, Yo-ho!
          Pennies for porpoises that bank the keel!
          Fins whip the breeze around Japan!

Bright skysails ticketing the Line, wink round the
     Horn
to Frisco, Melbourne . . .
                    Pennants, parabolas—
clipper dreams indelible and ranging,
baronial white on lucky blue!

          Perennial-*Cutty*-trophied-*Sark!*

215

HART *Thermopylæ, Black Prince, Flying Cloud* through Sunda
CRANE —scarfed of foam, their bellies veered green
                    esplanades,
            locked in wind-humors, ran their eastings down;

                    at Java Head freshened the nip
                    (sweet opium and tea!)
                    and turned and left us on the lee . . .

        Buntlines tusselling (91 days, 20 hours and anchored!)
                            Rainbow, Leander
        (last trip a tragedy)—where can you be
        Nimbus? and you rivals two—

                    a long tack keeping—

                                    Taeping?
                                    Ariel?

216

E. E. CUMMINGS

ONE X

death is more than
certain a hundred these
sounds crowds odours it
is in a hurry
beyond that any this
taxi smile or angle we do

not sell and buy
things so necessary as
is death and unlike shirts
neckties trousers
we cannot wear it out

no sir which is why
granted who discovered
America ether the movies
may claim general importance

to me to you nothing is
what particularly
matters hence in a

little sunlight and less
moonlight ourselves against the worms

hate laugh shimmy

MY FATHER MOVED

my father moved through dooms of love
through sames of am through haves of give
singing each morning out of each night
my father moved through depths of height

this motionless forgetful where
turned at his glance to shining here;
that if (so timid air is firm)
under his eyes would stir and squirm

newly as from unburied which
floats the first who, his april touch
drove sleeping selves to swarm their fates
woke dreamers to their ghostly roots

and should some why completely weep
my father's fingers brought her sleep:
vainly no smallest voice might cry
for he could feel the mountains grow.

Lifting the valleys of the sea
my father moved through griefs of joy;
praising a forehead called the moon
singing desire into begin

joy was his song and joy so pure
a heart of star by him could steer
and pure so now and now so yes
the wrists of twilight would rejoice

keen as midsummer's keen beyond
conceiving mind of sun will stand,
so strictly (over utmost him
so hugely) stood my father's dream

his flesh was flesh his blood was blood:
no hungry man but wished him food;
no cripple wouldn't creep one mile
uphill to only see him smile.

E. E.
CUM-
MINGS

Scorning the pomp of must and shall
my father moved through dooms of feel;
his anger was as right as rain
his pity was as green as grain

septembering arms of year extend
less humbly wealth to foe and friend
than he to foolish and to wise
offered immeasurable is

proudly and (by octobering flame
beckoned) as earth will downward climb,
so naked for immortal work
his shoulders marched against the dark

his sorrow was as true as bread:
no liar looked him in the head;
if every friend became his foe
he'd laugh and build a world with snow.

My father moved through theys of we,
singing each new leaf out of each tree
(and every child was sure that spring
danced when she heard my father sing)

then let men kill which cannot share,
let blood and flesh be mud and mire,
scheming imagine, passion willed,
freedom a drug that's bought and sold

giving to steal and cruel kind,
a heart to fear, to doubt a mind,
to differ a disease of same,
conform the pinnacle of am

though dull were all we taste as bright,
bitter all utterly things sweet,
maggoty minus and dumb death
all we inherit, all bequeath

and nothing quite so least as truth
—i say though hate were why men breathe—
because my father lived his soul
love is the whole and more than all

LAURA RIDING

THE TILLAQUILS

Dancing lamely on a lacquered plain,
Never a Tillaquil murmurs for legs.
Embrace rustles a windy wistfulness,
But feels for no hands.
Scant stir of being, yet rather they
Unfulfilled unborn than failing alive,
Escaping the public shame of history.

Once only two Tillaquils nearly a man and woman
Violated a hopeless code with hope,
Slept a single dream seeming in time.
'Come,' he cried, coaxing her,
'Stairs stream upward not for rest at every step
But to reach the top always before Death.'
'Softly,' she whispered,
'Or two Tillaquils will wake.'

Death they passed always over and over,
Life grew always sooner and sooner.
But love like a grimace
Too real on Life's face
Smiled two terrified dreams of Tillaquils
Tremblingly down the falling flights;
Who saved themselves in waking
The waste of being something.
And danced traditionally
To nothingness and never;
With only a lost memory
Punishing this foolish pair
That nearly lived and loved
In one nightmare.

221

LAURA
RIDING

LUCRECE AND NARA

Astonished stood Lucrece and Nara,
Face flat to face, one sense and smoothness.
'Love, is this face or flesh,
Love, is this you?'
One breath drew the dear lips close and whispered,
'Nara, is there a miracle can last?'
'Lucrece, is there a simple thing can stay?'

Unnoticed as a single raindrop
Broke each dawn until
Blindness as the same day fell.
'How is the opalescence of my white hand, Nara?
Is it still pearly cool?'
'How is the faintness of my neck, Lucrece?
Is it blood shy with warmth, as always?'

Ghostly they clung and questioned
A thousand years, not yet eternal,
True to their fading,
Through their long watch defying
Time to make them whole, to part them.

A gentle clasp and fragrance played and hung
A thousand years and more
Around earth closely.
'Earth will be long enough,
Love has no elsewhere.'

And when earth ended, was devoured
One shivering midsummer
At the dissolving border,
A sound of light was felt.
'Nara, is it you, the dark?'
'Lucrece, is it you, the quiet?'

222

THE MAP OF PLACES

LAURA
RIDING

The map of places passes.
The reality of paper tears.
Land and water where they are
Are only where they were
When words read *here* and *here*
Before ships happened there.

Now on naked names feet stand,
No geographies in the hand,
And paper reads anciently,
And ships at sea
Turn round and round.
All is known, all is found.
Death meets itself everywhere.
Holes in maps look through to nowhere.

THE TIGER

The tiger in me I know late, not burning bright.
Of such women as I am, they say,
'Woman, many women in one,' winking.
Such women as I say, thinking,
'A procession of one, reiteration
Of blinking eyes and disentangled brains
Measuring their length in love.
A yard of thought marks the embrace.
To these I have charms.
Shame, century creature.'
To myself, hurrying, I whisper,
'The lechery of time greases their eyes.

223

LAURA
RIDING

Lust, earlier than time,
Unwinds their mind.
The green anatomy of desire
Plain as through glass
Quickens as I pass.'

Earlier than lust, not plain,
Behind a darkened face of memory,
My inner animal revives.
Beware, that I am tame.
Beware philosophies
Wherein I yield.

They cage me on three sides.
The fourth is glass.
Not to be image of the beast in me,
I press the tiger forward.
I crash through.
Now we are two.
One rides.

And now I know the tiger late,
And now they pursue:
'A woman in a skin, mad at her heels
With pride, pretending chariot wheels.
Fleeing our learned days,
She reassumes the brute.'

The first of the pursuers found me.
With lady-ears I listened.
'Dear face, to find you here
After such tiger-hunt and pressing of
Thick forest, to find you here
In high house in a jungle,
To brave as any room
The tiger-cave and as in any room

224

Find woman in the room
With dear face shaking her dress
To wave like any picture queen . . .'
'Dear pursuer, to find me thus
Belies no tiger. The tiger runs and rides,
But the lady is not venturous.

'Like any picture queen she hides
And is unhappy in her room,
Covering her eyes against the latest year,
Its learning of old queens,
Its death to queens and pictures,
Its lust of century creatures,
And century creatures as one woman,
Such a woman as I,
Mirage of all green forests—
The colour of the season always
When hope lives of abolished pleasures.'

So to the first pursuer I prolonged
Woman's histories and shames,
And yielded as became a queen
Picture-dreaming in a room
Among silk provinces where pain
Ruined her body without stain—
So white, so out of time, so story-like.
While woman's pride escaped
In tiger stripes.

Hymn to the hostage queen
And her debauched provinces.
Down fell her room,
Down fell her high couches.
The first pursuer rose from his hot cloak.
'Company,' he cried, 'the tiger made magic

LAURA
RIDING

While you slept and I dreamt of ravages
The queen was dust.'
And Queen, Queen, Queen
Crowded the Captain's brain.
And Queen, Queen, Queen
Spurred the whole train
With book-thoughts
And exploits of queen's armies
On gold and silver cloth.
Until they stumbled on their eyes,
Read the number of the year,
Remembered the fast tiger.

The tiger recalled man's fear
Of beast, in man-sweat they ran back,
Opened their books to the correct pages.
The chapter closed with queens and shepherdesses.
'Peace to their dim tresses,'
Chanted the pious sages.

And now the tiger in me I knew late.
'O pride,' I comforted, 'rest.
The mischief and the rape
Cannot come through.
We are in the time of never yet
Where bells peal backward,
Peal "forget, forget".'

Here am I found forgotten.
The sun is used. The men are in the book.
I, woman, have removed the window
And read in my high house in the dark,
Sitting long after reading, as before,
Waiting, as in the book, to hear the bell,
Though long since has fallen away the door,

Long since, when like a tiger I was pursued
And the first pursuer, at such and such a date,
Found how the tiger takes the lady
Far away where she is gentle.
In the high forest she is gentle.
She is patient in a high house.
Ah me, Ah me, says every lady in the end,
Putting the tiger in its cage
Inside her lofty head.
And weeps reading her own story.
And scarcely knows she weeps,
So loud the tiger roars.
Or thinks to close her eyes,
Though surely she must be sleeping,
To go on without knowing weeping,
Sleeping or not knowing,
Not knowing weeping,
Not knowing sleeping.

THE WIND SUFFERS

The wind suffers of blowing,
The sea suffers of water,
And fire suffers of burning,
And I of a living name.

As stone suffers of stoniness,
As light of its shiningness,
As birds of their wingedness,
So I of my whoness.

And what the cure of all this?
What the not and not suffering?
What the better and later of this?
What the more me of me?

How for the pain-world to be
More world and no pain?
How for the faithful rain to fall
More wet and more dry?

How for the wilful blood to run
More salt-red and sweet-white?
And how for me in my actualness
To more shriek and more smile?

By no other miracles,
By the same knowing poison,
By an improved anguish,
By my further dying.

THE FLOWERING URN

And every prodigal greatness
Must creep back into strange home,
Must fill the empty matrix of
The never-begotten perfect son
Who never can be born.

And every quavering littleness
Must pale more tinily than it knows
Into the giant hush whose sound
Reverberates within itself
As tenderest numbers cannot improve.

And from this jealous secrecy
Will rise itself, will flower up
The likeness kept against false seed:
When death-whole is the seed
And no new harvest will fraction sowing

228

Will rise the same peace that held
Before fertility's lie awoke
The virgin sleep of Mother All:
The same but for the way in flowering
It speaks of fruits that could not be

NOR IS IT WRITTEN

Nor is it written that you may not grieve.
There is no rule of joy, long may you dwell
Not smiling yet in that last pain,
On that last supper of the heart's palate.
It is not written that you must take joy
In that not thus again shall you sit down
To spread that mingled banquet
Which the deep larder of illusion spilled
Like ancient riches in time grown not astonishing.
Lean to the cloth awhile, and yet awhile,
And even may your eyes caress
Proudly the used abundance.
It is not written in what heart
You may not pass from ancient plenty
Into the straitened nowadays.
To each is given secrecy of heart,
To make himself what heart he please
In stirring up from that fond table
To sit him down at this sharp meal.
It shall not here be asked of him
'What thinks your heart?'
Long may you sorely to yourself accuse
This single bread and truth,
This disenchanted understanding.
It is not counted what loud passions
Your heart in ancient private keeps alive.
To each is given what defeat he will.

229

AUSPICE OF JEWELS

They have connived at those jewelled fascinations
That to our hands and arms and ears
And heads and necks and feet
And all the winding stalk
Extended the mute spell of the face.

They have endowed the whole of us
With such a solemn gleaming
As in the dark of flesh-love
But the face at first did have.
We are studded with wide brilliance
As the world with towns and cities—
The travelling look builds capitals
Where the evasive eye may rest
Safe from the too immediate lodgement.

Obscure and bright these forms
Which as the women of their lingering thought
In slow translucence we have worn.
And the silent given glitter locks us
In a not false unplainness:
Have we ourselves been sure
What steady countenance to turn them?

Until now—when this passionate neglect
Of theirs, and our twinkling reluctance,
Are like the reader and the book
Whose fingers and whose pages have confided
But whose sight and sense
Meet in a chilly time of strangeness;

And it is once more early, anxious,
And so late, it is intolerably the same
Not speaking coruscation

That both we and they made endless, dream-long,
Lest be cruel to so much love
The closer shine of waking,
And what be said sound colder
Than the ghastly love-lisp.

Until now—when to go jewelled
We must despoil the drowsy masquerade
Where gloom of silk and gold
And glossy dazed adornments
Kept safe from flagrant realness
The forgeries of ourselves we were—
When to be alive as love feigned us
We must steal death and its wan splendours
From the women of their sighs we were.

For we are now otherwise luminous.
The light which was spent in jewels
Has performed upon the face
A gradual eclipse of recognition.
We have passed from plaintive visibility
Into total rareness,
And from this reunion of ourselves and them
Under the snuffed lantern of time
Comes an astonished flash like truth
Or the unseen-unheard entrance of someone
Whom eyes and ears in their dotage
Have forgotten for dead or lost.

(And hurrying toward distracted glory,
Gemmed lady-pageants, bells on their hearts,
By restless knights attended
Whose maudlin plumes and pommels
Urge the adventure past return.)

ROBERT GRAVES

QUAYSIDE

And glad to find, on again looking at it,
It was not nearly so good as I had thought—
You know the ship is moving when you see
The boxes on the quayside sliding away
And growing smaller—and having real delight
When the port's cleared and the coast out of sight,
And ships are few, each on its proper course,
With no occasion for approach or discourse.

O LOVE IN ME

O love, be fed with apples while you may,
And feel the sun and go in royal array,
A smiling innocent on the heavenly causeway.

Though in what listening horror for the cry
That soars in outer blackness dismally,
The dumb blind beast, the paranoiac fury,

Be warm, enjoy the season, lift your head,
Exquisite in the pulse of tainted blood,
That shivering glory not to be despised.

Take your delight in momentariness,
Walk between dark and dark, a shining space
With the grave's narrowness, though not its peace.

LOST ACRES

ROBERT
GRAVES

These acres, always again lost
   By every new Ordnance-survey
And searched for at exhausting cost
   Of time and thought, are still away.

They have their paper-substitute—
   Intercalation of an inch
At the so many thousandth foot:
   And no one parish feels the pinch.

But lost they are, despite all care,
   So perhaps likeliest to be bound
Together in a piece somewhere,
   A plot of undiscovered ground.

Invisible, they have the spite
   To swerve the tautest measuring chain
And the exact theodolite
   Perched every side of them in vain.

Yet there's no scientific need
   To plot these acres of the mind
With prehistoric fern and reed
   And monsters such as heroes find.

They have, no doubt, their flowers, their birds,
   Their trees behind the phantom fence,
But of the substance of mere words:
   To walk there would be loss of sense.

THE BARDS

Their cheeks are blotched for shame, their running
            verse
Stumbles, with marrow-bones the drunken diners
Pelt them as they delay:
It is a something fearful in the song
Plagues them, an unknown grief that like a churl
Goes commonplace in cowskin
And bursts unheralded, crowing and coughing,
An unpilled holly-club twirled in his hand,
Into their many-shielded, samite-curtained
Jewel-bright hall where twelve kings sit at chess
Over the white-bronze pieces and the gold,
And by a gross enchantment
Flails down the rafters and leads off the queens—
The wild-swan-breasted, the rose-ruddy-cheeked
Raven-haired daughters of their admiration—
To stir his black pots and to bed on straw.

FLYING CROOKED

The butterfly, the cabbage-white,
(His honest idiocy of flight)
Will never now, it is too late,
Master the art of flying straight,
Yet has—who knows so well as I?—
A just sense of how not to fly:
He lurches here and here by guess
And God and hope and hopelessness
Even the aerobatic swift
Has not his flying-crooked gift.

TIME

ROBERT GRAVES

The vague sea thuds against the marble cliffs
And from their fragments age-long grinds
Pebbles like flowers.

Or the vague weather wanders in the fields,
When up spring flowers with coloured buds
Like marble pebbles.

The beauty of the flowers is Time, death-grieved:
The pebbles' beauty too is Time,
Life-weary.

It is all too easy to admire a flower
Or a smooth pebble flower-like freaked
By Time and vagueness.

Time is Time's ease and the sweet oil that coaxes
All obstinate locks and rusty hinges
To loving-kindness.

What monster's proof against that lovesome pair,
Old age and childhood, seals of Time,
His sorrowful vagueness?

Or will not render him the accustomed thanks,
Humouring age with filial flowers,
Childhood with pebbles?

OGRES AND PYGMIES

Those famous men of old, the Ogres—
They had long beards and stinking arm-pits.
They were wide-mouthed, long-yarded and great-
    bellied

ROBERT   Yet of not taller stature, Sirs, than you.
GRAVES   They lived on Ogre-Strand, which was no place
            But the churl's terror of their proud extent,
            Where every foot was three-and-thirty inches
            And every penny bought a whole sheep.
            Now of their company none survive, not one,
            The times being, thank God, unfavourable
            To all but nightmare memory of them.
            Their images stand howling in the waste,
            (The winds enforced against their wide mouths)
            Whose granite haunches king and priest must yearly
            Buss, and their cold knobbed knees.
            So many feats they did to admiration:
            With their enormous lips they sang louder
            Than ten cathedral choirs, with their grand yards
            Stormed the most rare and obstinate maidenheads,
            With their strong-gutted and capacious bellies
            Digested stones and glass like ostriches.
            They dug great pits and heaped great cairns,
            Deflected rivers, slew whole armies,
            And hammered judgements for posterity—
            For the sweet-cupid-lipped and tassel-yarded
            Delicate-stomached dwellers
            In Pygmy Alley, where with brooding on them
            A foot is shrunk to seven inches
            And twelve-pence will not buy a spare rib.
            And who would choose between Ogres and Pygmies—
            The thundering text, the snivelling commentary—
            Reading between such covers he will likely
            Prove his own disproportion and not laugh.

THE LEGS

ROBERT
GRAVES

There was this road,
And it led up-hill,
And it led down-hill,
And round and in and out.

And the traffic was legs,
Legs from the knees down,
Coming and going,
Never pausing.

And the gutters gurgled
With the rain's overflow,
And the sticks on the pavement
Blindly tapped and tapped.

What drew the legs along
Was the never-stopping,
And the senseless frightening
Fate of being legs.

Legs for the road,
The road for legs,
Resolutely nowhere
In both directions.

My legs at least
Were not in that rout,
On grass by the road-side
Entire I stood,

Watching the unstoppable
Legs go by
With never a stumble
Between step and step.

Though my smile was broad
The legs could not see,
Though my laugh was loud
The legs could not hear.

My head dizzied then:
I wondered suddenly,
Might I too be a walker
From the knees down?

Gently I touched my shins.
The doubt unchained them:
They had run in twenty puddles
Before I regained them.

TO WHOM ELSE?

To whom else other than,
To whom else not of man
Yet in human state,
Standing neither in stead
Of self nor idle godhead,
Should I, man in man bounded,
Myself dedicate?

To whom else momently,
To whom else endlessly,
But to you, I?
To you who only,
To you who mercilessly,
To you who lovingly,
Plucked out the lie?

To whom else less acquaint,
To whom else without taint
Of death, death-true?
With great astonishment
Thankfully I consent
To my estrangement
From me in you.

ON PORTENTS

If strange things happen where she is,
So that men say that graves open
And the dead walk, or that futurity
Becomes a womb and the unborn are shed,
Such portents are not to be wondered at,
Being tourbillions in Time made
By the strong pulling of her bladed mind
Through that ever-reluctant element.

TO BRING THE DEAD TO LIFE

To bring the dead to life
Is no great magic.
Few are wholly dead:
Blow on a dead man's embers
And a live flame will start.

Let his forgotten griefs be now,
And now his withered hopes;
Subject your pen to his handwriting
Until it prove as natural
To sign his name as yours.

Limp as he limped,
Swear by the oaths he swore;

239

If he wore black, affect the same;
If he had gouty fingers,
Be yours gouty too.

Assemble tokens intimate of him—
A ring, a purse, a chair:
Around these elements then build
A home familiar to
The greedy revenant.

So grant him life, but reckon
That the grave which housed him
May not be empty now:
You in his spotted garments
Must yourself lie wrapped.

TO JUAN AT THE WINTER SOLSTICE

There is one story and one story only
That will prove worth your telling,
Whether as learned bard or gifted child;
To it all lines or lesser gauds belong
That startle with their shining
Such common stories as they stray into.

Is it of trees you tell, their months and virtues,
Of strange beasts that beset you,
Of birds that croak at you the Triple will?
Or of the Zodiac and how slow it turns
Below the Boreal Crown,
Prison of all true kings that ever reigned?

Water to water, ark again to ark,
From woman back to woman:
So each new victim treads unfalteringly

The never altered circuit of his fate,
Bringing twelve peers as witness
Both to his starry rise and starry fall.

Or is it of the Virgin's silver beauty,
All fish below the thighs?
She in her left hand bears a leafy quince;
When with her right she crooks a finger, smiling,
How may the King hold back?
Royally then he barters life for love.

Or of the undying snake from chaos hatched,
Whose coils contain the ocean,
Into whose chops with naked sword he springs,
Then in black water, tangled by the reeds,
Battles three days and nights,
To be spewed up beside her scalloped shore?

Much snow is falling, winds roar hollowly,
The owl hoots from the elder,
Fear in your heart cries to the loving-cup:
Sorrow to sorrow as the sparks fly upward.
The log groans and confesses
There is one story and one story only.

Dwell on her graciousness, dwell on her smiling,
Do not forget what flowers
The great boar trampled down in ivy time.
Her brow was creamy as the long ninth wave,
Her sea-blue eyes were wild
But nothing promised that is not performed.

EDITH SITWELL

WHEN SIR BEELZEBUB

When
Sir
Beelzebub called for his syllabub in the hotel in Hell

      Where Proserpine first fell,

Blue as the gendarmerie were the waves of the sea,

      (Rocking and shocking the bar-maid).

Nobody comes to give him his rum but the
Rim of the sky hippopotamus-glum
Enhances the chances to bless with a benison
Alfred Lord Tennyson crossing the bar laid
With cold vegetation from pale deputations
Of temperance workers (all signed In Memoriam)
Hoping with glory to trip up the Laureate's feet,

      (Moving in classical metres) . . .

Like Balaclava, the lava came down from the
Roof, and the sea's blue wooden gendarmerie
Took them in charge while Beelzebub roared for his
    rum.
      . . . None of them come!

STILL FALLS THE RAIN

EDITH
SITWELL

The raids, 1940. *Night and Dawn*

Still falls the Rain—
Dark as the world of man, black as our loss—
Blind as the nineteen hundred and forty nails
Upon the Cross.

Still falls the Rain
With a sound like the pulse of the heart that is
    changed to the hammer-beat
In the Potter's Field, and the sound of the impious feet

On the Tomb:
         Still falls the Rain
In the Field of Blood where the small hopes breed
    and the human brain
Nurtures its greed, that worm with the brow of Cain.

Still falls the Rain
At the feet of the Starved Man hung upon the Cross.
Christ that each day, each night, nails there,
    have mercy on us—
On Dives and on Lazarus:
Under the Rain the sore and the gold are as one.

Still falls the Rain—
Still falls the Blood from the Starved Man's
    wounded Side:
He bears in His Heart all wounds,—those of the
    light that died,

The last faint spark
In the self-murdered heart, the wounds of the sad
    uncomprehending dark,

243

EDITH The wounds of the baited bear,—
SITWELL The blind and weeping bear whom the keepers beat
On his helpless flesh . . . the tears of the hunted hare.

Still falls the Rain—
Then—O Ile leape up to my God: who pulles me
    doune—
See, see where Christ's blood streames in the firmament:
It flows from the Brow we nailed upon the tree
Deep to the dying, to the thirsting heart
That holds the fires of the world,—dark-smirched
    with pain
As Caesar's laurel crown.

Then sounds the voice of One who like the heart
    of man
Was once a child who among beasts has lain—
'Still do I love, still shed my innocent light, my
    Blood, for thee.'

THE SWANS

In the green light of water, like the day
Under green boughs, the spray
And air-pale petals of the foam seem flowers,—
Dark-leaved arbutus blooms with wax-pale bells
And their faint honey-smells,
The velvety syringa with smooth leaves,
Gloxinia with a green shade in the snow,
Jasmine and moon-clear orange-blossoms and green
    blooms
Of the wild strawberries from the shade of woods.
Their showers
Pelt the white women under the green trees,

Venusia, Cosmopolita, Pistillarine—
White solar statues, white rose-trees in snow
Flowering for ever, child-women, half stars
Half flowers, waves of the sea, born of a dream.

Their laughter flying through the trees like doves,
These angels come to watch their whiter ghosts
In the air-pale water, archipelagos
Of stars and young thin moons from great wings falling
As ripples widen.
These are their ghosts, their own white angels these!
O great wings spreading—
Your bones are made of amber, smooth and thin
Grown from the amber dust that was a rose
Or nymph in swan-smooth waters.
                              But Time's winter falls
With snows as soft, as soundless . . . . Then, who
    knows
Rose-footed swan from snow, or girl from rose?

HYMN TO VENUS

An old Woman speaks:
'Lady, beside the great green wall of Sea
I kneel to make my plea

To you, great Rose of the world. . . . Beyond the
    seeds of petrifaction, Gorgon of itself,
Behind the face bright as the Rose—I pray
To the seeds of fire in the veins that should
Hold diamonds, iris, beryls for their blood,—

Since you are grown old too, and should be cold,
Although the heat of the air
Has the motion of fire

245

EDITH And light bears in its heart
SITWELL A cloud of colour . . . where

The great heap ripens in the mine
Of the body's earth, ruby, garnet, and almandine,

And in the dark cloud of the blood still grows
The rainbow, with the ruby and the rose.

Pity me then—a poor old woman who must wear a rag
Of Time's filth for a dress . . . .
O who would care to hold
That miserly rag now.

So I whose nights were violent as the buds
And roots of Spring, was taken by the Cold,

Have only the Cold for lover. Speak then to my dust!
Tell me that nothing dies
But only suffers change,—
And Folly may grow wise.

So we shall be transmuted—you who have grown
      chill, and I
Unto whose heart
My love preferred a heart like a winding-sheet of clay
—Fearing my fires would burn his body away!

Gone are your temples that were bright with heat.
But still I kneel at the feet
Of you who were built through aeons by a million
      lives,
Whispers and instincts, under the coralline light
That seems the great zone of sea-depths . . . .

In my blood grows
Like chlorophyll in the veins of the deep rose,

Our beauty's earthly dress
(Shrunk now to dust)—shall move through all degrees
Of Life, from mineral to plant, and from still rock to
        the green laughing seas;

From life's first trance, the mineral consciousness
That is deep blankness inside an invisible
And rigid box—defined, divisible

And separate from the sheath—(breathe not too deep
If you would know the mineral's trancèd sleep . . . .
So measure Time that you, too, are apart
And are not conscious of the living heart)—

To the plant that seeks the light that is its lover
And knows not separation between cover
And sentience. . . . The Sun's heat and the dew's
        chill
It knows in sleep with an undreaming thrill;

And colour breathes that is reflected light.
The ray and perfume of the Sun is white:
But when these intermingle as in love
With earth-bound things, the dream begins to move,

And colour that sleeps as in a dreamless cloud
Deep in the mineral trance within that shroud
Then to a fluid changes, grows
Deep in the stem and leaves of the dark rose.

So could the ruby, almandine and garnet move
From this great trance into a dreaming sleep,

EDITH They might become the rose whose perfume deep
SITWELL Grows in eternity, yet is
Still unawakened for its ephemeral hour
Beneath the great light's kiss;

The rose might seek the untamed rainbow through
The remembering Eden of a drop of dew;
Until at last in heavenly friendship grows
The ruby and the rainbow and the rose.
Nor will the one more precious than the other be—
Or make more rich the Shadow's treasury.

So, Lady, you and I,
And the other wrecks of the heart, left by the Lion
Of love, shall know all transmutations, each degree!
 Our apeish skeletons, clothed with rubies by the light
Are not less bright
In the Sun's eye than is the rose . . . and youth,
        and we,
Are but waves of Time's sea.

Folly and wisdom have dust equal-sweet,
And in the porphyry shade
Of this world's noon
The Poor seem Dives, burning in his robes bright as
        the rose
—Such transmutations even the brief moment made!'

SACHEVERELL SITWELL

THE FARNESE HERCULES

Heroes out of music born
March their glittering shades down myrtle alleys in the
     poet's wood
Breaking the rhymed lights of reason:
For these three lines of preface
The black cape of magic hides my head and hands
Till I fix the staring camera eye:
'Keep that position, gentlemen! keep it and look
     pleasant!'
The chattering agora, sudden camp of stalls,
Reaches to the statue's feet, to the platform for these
     stylites,
Who stand all day and night in rain's blue cage,   10
Fed with this water and the yellow bread of sun.

'It will make a very pretty water-colour.
Look how still he keeps. Tie your sandal to his ankle.'
He was one among a whole white wood of statues
In the market-place along a road of triumph,
Then moved with pulleys at the trumpet's sound
To the Baths of Caracalla where the rhymed lights of
     poetry
Bore the new Prometheus from the womb of that dead
     music.
Hercules lay broken in the heaped, dried dust;
His legs took twenty long years to find   20
So bitter had his fall been. To the roll of thunder
Fell he, or the red Goth's hand?

SACH- Now his dwelling is a dark museum,
EVERELL A dingy hotel dining-room with no food ever served,
SITWELL We'll forget that dreary future for his laboured past;
We will take him from the Thermae to his native land,
To the poplars and the caverns, to the hills of wild
    thyme,
Their limestone worn by rain's slow tide
In spires and guttering pinnacles;
No foot climbs to those towers but the bearded goat   30
Cropping the cold herb among the cactus swords,
While winds of prophecy in hollow caves foment
To break from the shepherd's lips, or speak by signs.

The agora, that platform for the quack and the actor,
For anyone swollen with the wind of talk,
Grew to a parliament of all the muses,
Till poetry and music, spawn of words, were born
And gods walked in the harvest, or among the grapes,
To choose a mirror of themselves in men;
They tired of immortal love and stole into the harvest
Hidden in wind's raiment, or at a tower of stone   41
Fell in a gold shower like sun with rain;
Such were the loves of gods who schemed in green
    barley
To snare the bowed reapers, or grape-gatherers on
    their ladders.

This talking, ceaseless talking, like a rookery in the
    elm's green roofs,
Cawed and chattered whilst they built with twigs,
Though here in the agora the twigs were beams of
    marble
And they worked like the rooks do by tradition and
    proportion;
Their temples were a shepherd's hut magnified

With ninepin pillars and a tilted roof
Walling in this open way a dark inner mystery.
Since the gods made a mirror of themselves in men,
Sculpture, a shepherd's craft—they carve in their
    waste-hours—
Copied like a camera this echoed immortality
And matched the mortal limbs of man against the
    deathless gods.

Then, the forests of white statues grew
And the gods and men among them only differed in
    their emblems;
The athlete oiled and slippery for wrestling
Stands by a god who treads the windy hills,
You could see this naked athlete in the stadium   60
And hear that god speaking in the groves of philosophy,
His limbs gleaming white from sharp edges of the
    myrtles
In the fainting sunset when the lengthened shades are
    lifted;
Then were those arsenals of legend stored,
The hills of thyme were the stepping-stones to heaven
And the wind spake in oracles from sacred woods.

The normal, the simple life was in the young, fresh air
With the shepherds sitting by their sticks of fire
Or the fisherman living by his nets of fortune
Throwing for fast silver in that tideless sea.   70
It was the Golden Age before the Age of Gold began;
How snow-soft were those legends falling every year
In a winter of white blossoms through the speaking
    trees,
For they formed, like the snow does, to the shapes they
    loved,
To a sliding gentle poetry that is made of nothing,

Though it lives by the body of its melted beauty,
In a sharp, deep river, or at a fountain in the rock.

The tumbrils slowly creaking under pyramids of grapes
That ran down their life-blood on these boards and on
    the oxen
Took home the husbandmen,   80
Maddened by these fumes and by the pulsing sun;
This shadow-life of drunkenness, this mocking of the
    fire of health,
Gave birth with its mirror to a world of ghosts,
The theatre and its actors began at that stained trestle
And masks to keep the mirror truth and hide the living
    difference
Were born in that blue autumn. The mock children
Of fine shepherds and their bearded goats were shown;
And the goat-god in dark rocks once seen.

Where the tumbril waited in the pine-tree shade
They made a trodden dancing-floor,   90
This grew into a half-moon of rough-hewn stone,
To the theatre of mock death and laughter;
There did these ghosts stalk on stilt-like pattens
And thunder the heroic verse through mouths of brass.
In the dun twilight other shadows creep,
While this first giant art is born out of rolling high
    speeches;
Other shadows creep between the syllables
In chequers so that light or shade can hide them,
And Harlequin's wand becomes a thyrsus in the grape-
    harvest.

Thus was the camera eye tricked and cheated,   100
For these ghosts with their masks and stilts were out-
    side life.

Was ever death so cold as this, or love so fiery?   SACH-
Those armoured gods, those women calm as oxen,   EVERELL
In the cold heroic mazes, in sacred families of tragedy,   SITWELL
Move to their destiny. The beardless ephebus
Comes through the flower-thickets, stands naked in full
     light of day,
For he was the vehicle of their strange loves;
So to those legends we have giant stilted shades,
Ox-eyed women, and young naked limbs
That will tear on a rose-bush, or stain with the grape.

He was born, our Hercules, in the yard of a stone-
     mason,   III
Dragged in his matrix by a team of oxen
And tilted with a lever to that ground thick with
     statues,
There he stands rough and clumsy like a boy on his first
     school day
Waiting for the chisel and the cold eye to study him.
Tie your sandal to his ankle! Tease him like a bear!
Though who can the gipsy be who leads him, ring in
     nose,
By green hedges, his rough bed at night,
To the crowded, noisy agora,
To that theatre where the gipsy's horn   120
Sounds among the shadows that the statues throw?

Twelve labours, twelve slow tours on foot,
Has he who made the beetle walk laid out before him,
Though the labours of Hercules are tasks he can't
     avoid,
He is carried there by instinct like dogs to a dog-fight.
Instinct, little voice, scarce seen, scarce felt,
Like the Indian on his elephant who guides it with a
     whisper

And can ride in a castle on that patient wave-back
Through green waters of the Indian bright boughs;
So, turned gipsy to our Hercules   130
　　　　　We will walk in the dew-deep orchard
　　　　　Tasting apples of Hesperides.

　　　　　Tie your sandal to his ankle! He will be your winged
　　　　　　　Mercury
　　　　　To run before you. Won't he move? Won't he stir?
　　　　　He is dank, cold, and dewy like mushrooms of the
　　　　　　　night
　　　　　Spawned in summer showers from goatskins of the
　　　　　　　rain;
　　　　　He leans on his truncheon like a great policeman.
　　　　　Glycon was his sculptor, and Lysippus before him
　　　　　Had planned this demi-god leaning weary on his club;
　　　　　Lysippus of Sicyon with his fifteen hundred shapes of
　　　　　　　stone   140
　　　　　Who wrought his white nightmares like the sculptors
　　　　　　　of Carrara
　　　　　From the salt-white quarries;—
　　　　　While Glycon had the Romans for his Yankee patrons.

　　　　　At least there was never such a gladiator:—
　　　　　Or there'd be no audience in the Roman theatre;
　　　　　He'd eat them up like paper!
　　　　　No hero on wars of love in the wood's green tent
　　　　　Ever heard the nightingales, bright stars to such an
　　　　　　　armour;
　　　　　Had he lulled, my Hercules, below these lights
　　　　　That sang in wan air   150
　　　　　Before the moon in green tree-windows,
　　　　　The glitter, while he slept, that should have touched
　　　　　　　his steel

Would lie on no armour but his heaped rings of
    muscle,
Rocks deep-hidden in a sea of smooth skin.

He should be the sentinel on cyclopaean walls
Guarding a megalithic rock-hewn town
And moved to ram's-horn trumpet, blown
At the tomb-mouth lintel of that city-gate;
He is watching the flocks of sheep, dropped petals from
    the clouds
That move with shadow-stilts along the hill's green
    sides,   160
Or he guards the hayricks, honeystacks of grass,
That are pitched like a shepherd's hut with high,
    sloped roof
And yet are combs of honey that are cut for the cattle,
For they store all the yellow light that fed the grass
And hold sun and rain within their golden straws.

These villages of giant stone spread like a fashion
From mouth to mouth of shepherds
As by beacons on high, lonely hills;
Temples like giant hearthstones are built on the bare
    plains
And they save up their captives for the sacrifice of fire
When they burn a wicker tower of them above the
    stones.   171
That was a Golden Age for Hercules,
On wrestling ground, or at rough bed of leaves,
In fleecy nights of winter
Wrapped in woven wool as white as they,
When breath turns to smoke.

See him throw stones to keep the rooks off the barley!
They start quite low and rise on a parabola,

They blossom at their zenith, shut their wings into a
      meteor,
And fall like an anchor out of the clouds among the
      rooks.   180
See him run to turn the drove of horses!
He can blow in a corner of the barley
And bend that sunny hair against the wind,
So the reaper with his sickle cuts two sheaves for one;
Those horses that he turned and headed
Gallop in front of Hercules like a drum shower of the
      rain
Falling on loud leaves and the thatched hair of houses.

Hercules as husbandman is in the grapes,
He pulls the blue bunches from their roof of leaves
To fill the wicker baskets that the women hold   190
And they spill them into a pyramid in a space between
      the vines:
It towers like a summer wave full of the sun,
Could this be still and frozen for a word to break;
Then into that deep sea of sun and summer rain
He wades and treads until its fire is loosed;
The rocks and hollow hills echo with his laughter,
Rocks that are the cold bed for goat-foot gods,
And caves, old mirrors for their sighs and loves.

The kneeling, fainting cherry trees,
So deep their green sails and their mouths of fire   200
That they burn like a galleon to the water-line,
Kiss with red lips his hands
That feel among the apple-trees
To their branches heavy with those sweets of rain.
Who knows what voices rang among the boughs
When limbs, so light they were like the wind between
      the leaves,

Climbed from cool water,
And the orchard, one green tree of birds,
Sang from every window in its sunny leaves?

Cunning or big muscle were the ways to power,   210
To the Emperor lifted on a shield in the camp,
Till the Hebrew prophet and the fishermen;—
Then the men of destiny like old idols were thrown
      down
And the trumpets of triumph became horns at the
      tournament;
The walls of the castle like white cliffs of chalk
Stood like bulwarks to the green sea of time:
Long Gothic faces of the fair-haired warriors
Showed from beetle armour for those glitters down the
      myrtle glade:
Those ancient heroes to long trees of birth
Surrendered, and the herald's horns.   220

Now there'd be no use for him, no work for Hercules,
Unless he turned policeman
And joined the Irish bullies on loud Broadway;
He could part the streams of traffic with a white-gloved
      hand
And snare the gunmen in their stolen motor;
Glycon and Lysippus would be sad to see him
With his fugal muscles in neat armour of blue cloth.
Away with him! Roll him to the drab museum,
To the stone companionship of other shades:
Let there be a banquet of the gods   230
On tired air through tangled, cobweb windows!

He lives again in thin shade of the olive-trees
At a cold fountain in the rocks
Watering his oxen;

SACH-   From the orchard walled with river stones
EVERELL   Apples of sweet rain hang forth
SITWELL   While kneeling, fainting cherry trees bleed fire on to
                the grass:
           Let those green wings of the wind, sharp leaves,
           Give him music for his feasting,
           While fine nymphs of the river from their sighing
                brakes   240
           Climb into the orchard, where great Hercules
           Sleeps by sweet rain boughs and by cherry mouths of
                fire.

RICHARD EBERHART

THE GROUNDHOG

In June, amid the golden fields,
I saw a groundhog lying dead.
Dead lay he; my senses shook,
And mind outshot our naked frailty.
There lowly in the vigorous summer
His form began its senseless change,
And made my senses waver dim
Seeing nature ferocious in him.
Inspecting close his maggot's might
And seething cauldron of his being,
Half with loathing, half with a strange love,
I poked him with an angry stick.
The fever arose, became a frame
And Vigour circumscribed the skies,
Immense energy in the sun,
And through my frame a sunless trembling.
My stick had done nor good nor harm.
Then stood I silent in the day
Watching the object, as before;
And kept my reverence for knowledge
Trying for control, to be still,
To quell the passion of the blood;
Until I had bent down on my knees
Praying for joy in the sight of decay.
And so I left; and I returned
In Autumn strict of eye, to see
The sap gone out of the groundhog,
But the bony sodden hulk remained.
But the year had lost its meaning,

RICHARD And in intellectual chains
EBERHART I lost both love and loathing,
Mured up in the wall of wisdom.
Another summer took the fields again
Massive and burning, full of life,
But when I chanced upon the spot
There was only a little hair left,
And bones bleaching in the sunlight
Beautiful as architecture;
I watched them like a geometer,
And cut a walking stick from a birch.
It has been three years, now.
There is no sign of the groundhog.
I stood there in the whirling summer,
My hand capped a withered heart,
And thought of China and of Greece,
Of Alexander in his tent;
Of Montaigne in his tower,
Of Saint Theresa in her wild lament.

PETER QUENNELL

HERO ENTOMBED (I)

My lamp, full charged with its sweet oil, still burns,
Has burned a whole year and it shows no check.
My cerements there
Lie where I rolled them off,
The death odours within them,
Harshly composed, coiled up in marble fold.

This tent of white translucent stone, my tomb,
Lets through its panel such a ray of light,
Blind and refracted,
As a calm sea might do
Through its tough warping lens
From the ascendant moon at its highest step.

Some have complained the gentleness of the sea,
Stagnantly streaming, in quick ebb withdrawing
Along the tideless South,
Thus sound to me,
And like its noonday hiss
Wheels, voices, music, thunder, the trumpet at dawn.

You must not think my entertainment slight
In the close prison where I walk all day.
'And yet, entombed,
Do not your thoughts oppressed
Pluck off the bandage from your sores,
From arrow wound and from ulcered armour-gall?'

My wounds are dried already to pale weals,
I did not fall in battle as you think,

PETER   On Epipolae
QUEN-   Dashed from the rock head down,
 NELL   Or in the quarries stifle,
         But stoned by words and pierced with beams of eyes.

         So, patient, not regretful, self consoling
         I walk, touching the tomb wall with my fingers,
         In silent entertainment.
         On the smooth floor
         The stirred dust ankle deep
         Steams up languid, to clog the struggling lamp flame.
         Syracuse

PROCNE

So she became a bird and bird-like danced
On a long sloe-bough, treading the silver blossom
With a bird's lovely feet,
And shaken blossoms fell into the hands
Of sunlight, and he held them for a moment
And let them drop.
And in the autumn Procne came again
And leapt upon the crooked sloe-bough singing
And the dark berries winked like earth-dimmed beads,
As the branch swung beneath her dancing feet.

WILLIAM EMPSON

INVITATION TO JUNO

Lucretius could not credit centaurs;
Such bicycle he deemed asynchronous.
'Man superannuates the horse;
Horse pulses will not gear with ours.'

Johnson could see no bicycle would go;
'You bear yourself, and the machine as well.'
Gennets for germans sprang not from Othello,
And Ixion rides upon a single wheel.

Courage. Weren't strips of heart culture seen
Of late mating two periodicities?
Could not Professor Charles Darwin
Graft annual upon perennial trees?

CAMPING OUT

And now she cleans her teeth into the lake:
Gives it (God's grace) for her own bounty's sake
What morning's pale and the crisp mist debars:
Its glass of the divine (that Will could break)
Restores, beyond Nature: or lets Heaven take
(Itself being dimmed) her pattern, who half awake
Milks between rocks a straddled sky of stars.

Soap tension the star pattern magnifies.
Smoothly Madonna through-assumes the skies
Whose vaults are opened to achieve the Lord.

No, it is we soaring explore galaxies,
Our bullet boat light's speed by thousands flies.
Who moves so among stars their frame unties;
See where they blur, and die, and are outsoared.

LEGAL FICTION

Law makes long spokes of the short stakes of men.
Your well fenced out real estate of mind
No high flat of the nomad citizen
Looks over, or train leaves behind.

Your rights extend under and above your claim
Without bound; you own land in Heaven and Hell;
Your part of earth's surface and mass the same,
Of all cosmos' volume, and all stars as well.

Your rights reach down where all owners meet, in
    Hell's
Pointed exclusive conclave, at earth's centre
(Your spun farm's root still on that axis dwells);
And up, through galaxies, a growing sector.

You are nomad yet; the lighthouse beam you own
Flashes, like Lucifer, through the firmament.
Earth's axis varies; your dark central cone
Wavers, a candle's shadow, at the end.

264

THIS LAST PAIN

WILLIAM
EMPSON

This last pain for the damned the Fathers found:
'They knew the bliss with which they were not
     crowned.'
    Such, but on earth, let me foretell,
    Is all, of heaven or of hell.

Man, as the prying housemaid of the soul,
May know her happiness by eye to hole:
    He's safe; the key is lost; he knows
    Door will not open, nor hole close.

'What is conceivable can happen too,'
Said Wittgenstein, who had not dreamt of you;
    But wisely; if we worked it long
    We should forget where it was wrong:

Those thorns are crowns which, woven into knots,
Crackle under and soon boil fools' pots;
    And no man's watching, wise and long,
    Would ever stare them into song.

Thorns burn to a consistent ash, like man;
A splendid cleanser for the frying-pan:
    And those who leap from pan to fire
    Should this brave opposite admire.

All those large dreams by which men long live well
Are magic-lanterned on the smoke of hell;
    This then is real, I have implied,
    A painted, small, transparent slide.

These the inventive can hand-paint at leisure,
Or most emporia would stock our measure;
    And feasting in their dappled shade
    We should forget how they were made.

WILLIAM
EMPSON Feign then what's by a decent tact believed
And act that state is only so conceived,
And build an edifice of form
For house where phantoms may keep warm.

Imagine, then, by miracle, with me,
(Ambiguous gifts, as what gods give must be)
What could not possibly be there,
And learn a style from a despair.

HOMAGE TO THE BRITISH MUSEUM

There is a supreme God in the ethnological section;
A hollow toad shape, faced with a blank shield.
He needs his belly to include the Pantheon,
Which is inserted through a hole behind.
At the navel, at the points formally stressed, at the
        organs of sense,
Lice glue themselves, dolls, local deities,
His smooth wood creeps with all the creeds of the
        world.

Attending there let us absorb the cultures of nations
And dissolve into our judgement all their codes.
Then, being clogged with a natural hesitation
(People are continually asking one the way out),
Let us stand here and admit that we have no road.
Being everything, let us admit that is to be something,
Or give ourselves the benefit of the doubt;
Let us offer our pinch of dust all to this God,
And grant his reign over the entire building.

NOTE ON LOCAL FLORA

WILLIAM
EMPSON

There is a tree native in Turkestan,
Or further east towards the Tree of Heaven,
Whose hard cold cones, not being wards to time,
Will leave their mother only for good cause;
Will ripen only in a forest fire;
Wait, to be fathered as was Bacchus once,
Through men's long lives, that image of time's end.
I knew the Phœnix was a vegetable.
So Semele desired her deity
As this in Kew thirsts for the Red Dawn.

MISSING DATES

Slowly the poison the whole blood stream fills.
It is not the effort nor the failure tires.
The waste remains, the waste remains and kills.

It is not your system or clear sight that mills
Down small to the consequence a life requires;
Slowly the poison the whole blood stream fills.

They bled an old dog dry yet the exchange rills
Of young dog blood gave but a month's desires;
The waste remains, the waste remains and kills.

It is the Chinese tombs and the slag hills
Usurp the soil, and not the soil retires.
Slowly the poison the whole blood stream fills.

Not to have fire is to be a skin that shrills.
The complete fire is death. From partial fires
The waste remains, the waste remains and kills.

It is the poems you have lost, the ills
From missing dates, at which the heart expires.
Slowly the poison the whole blood stream fills.
The waste remains, the waste remains and kills.

C. DAY LEWIS

'AS ONE WHO WANDERS INTO OLD WORKINGS'

As one who wanders into old workings
Dazed by the noonday, desiring coolness,
Has found retreat barred by fall of rockface;
Gropes through galleries where granite bruises
Taut palm and panic patters close at heel;
Must move forward as tide to the moon's nod,
As mouth to breast in blindness is beckoned.
Nightmare nags at his elbow and narrows
Horizon to pinpoint, hope to hand's breadth.
Slow drip the seconds, time is stalactite,
For nothing intrudes here to tell the time,
Sun marches not, nor moon with muffled step.
He wants an opening,—only to break out,
To see the dark glass cut by day's diamond,
To relax again in the lap of light.

But we seek a new world through old workings,
Whose hope lies like seed in the loins of earth,
Whose dawn draws gold from the roots of darkness.
Not shy of light nor shrinking from shadow
Like Jesuits in jungle we journey
Deliberately bearing to brutish tribes
Christ's assurance, arts of agriculture.
As a train that travels underground track
Feels current flashed from far-off dynamos,
Our wheels whirling with impetus elsewhere
Generated we run, are ruled by rails.
Train shall spring from tunnel to terminus,

Out on to plain shall the pioneer plunge,
Earth reveal what veins fed, what hill covered.
Lovely the leap, explosion into light.

C. DAY
LEWIS

'YOU THAT LOVE ENGLAND'

You that love England, who have an ear for her music,
The slow movement of clouds in benediction,
Clear arias of light thrilling over her uplands,
Over the chords of summer sustained peacefully;
Ceaseless the leaves' counterpoint in a west wind
      lively,
Blossom and river rippling loveliest allegro,
And the storms of wood strings brass at year's finale:
Listen. Can you not hear the entrance of a new theme?

You who go out alone, on tandem or on pillion,
Down arterial roads riding in April,
Or sad beside lakes where hill-slopes are reflected
Making fires of leaves, your high hopes fallen:
Cyclists and hikers in company, day excursionists,
Refugees from cursed towns and devastated areas;
Know you seek a new world, a saviour to establish
Long-lost kinship and restore the blood's fulfilment.

You who like peace, good sticks, happy in a small way
Watching birds or playing cricket with schoolboys,
Who pay for drinks all round, whom disaster chose
      not:
Yet passing derelict mills and barns roof-rent
Where despair has burnt itself out—hearts at a stand-
      still,
Who suffer loss, aware of lowered vitality;
We can tell you a secret, offer a tonic; only
Submit to the visiting angel, the strange new healer.

269

C. Day You above all who have come to the far end, victims
Lewis Of a run-down machine, who can bear it no longer;
Whether in easy chairs chafing at impotence
Or against hunger, bullies and spies preserving
The nerve for action, the spark of indignation—
Need fight in the dark no more, you know your
enemies.
You shall be leaders when zero hour is signalled,
Wielders of power and welders of a new world.

THE CONFLICT

I sang as one
Who on a tilting deck sings
To keep their courage up, though the wave hangs
That shall cut off their sun.

As storm-cocks sing,
Flinging their natural answer in the wind's teeth,
And care not if it is waste of breath
Or birth-carol of spring.

As ocean-flyer clings
To height, to the last drop of spirit driving on
While yet ahead is land to be won
And work for wings.

Singing I was at peace,
Above the clouds, outside the ring:
For sorrow finds a swift release in song
And pride its poise.

Yet living here,
As one between two massing powers I live
Whom neutrality cannot save
Nor occupation cheer.

None such shall be left alive:
The innocent wing is soon shot down,
And private stars fade in the blood-red dawn
Where two worlds strive.

The red advance of life
Contracts pride, calls out the common blood,
Beats song into a single blade,
Makes a depth-charge of grief.

Move then with new desires,
For where we used to build and love
Is no man's land, and only ghosts can live
Between two fires.

A TIME TO DANCE

For those who had the power
    of the forest fires that burn
Leaving their source in ashes
    to flush the sky with fire:
Those whom a famous urn
    could not contain, whose passion
Brimmed over the deep grave
    and dazzled epitaphs:
For all that have won us wings
    to clear the tops of grief,
My friend who within me laughs
    bids you dance and sing.

Some set out to explore
    earth's limit, and little they recked if
Never their feet came near it
    outgrowing the need for glory:
Some aimed at a small objective
    but the fierce updraught of their spirit

271

Forced them to the stars.
    Are honoured in public who built
The dam that tamed a river;
    or holding the salient for hours
Against odds, cut off and killed,
    are remembered by one survivor.

All these. But most for those
    whom accident made great,
As a radiant chance encounter
    of cloud and sunlight grows
Immortal on the heart:
    whose gift was the sudden bounty
Of a passing moment, enriches
    the fulfilled eye for ever.
Their spirits float serene
    above time's roughest reaches,
But their seed is in us and over
    our lives they are evergreen.

From THE FLIGHT

(*'Sing we the two Lieutenants, Parer and M'Intosh'*)

And now the earth they had spurned rose up against
    them in anger,
Tier upon tier it towered, the terrible Apennines:
No sanctuary there for wings, not flares nor landing-
    lines,
No hope of floor and hangar.
Yet those ice-tipped spears that disputed the passage set
    spurs
To their two hundred and forty horse power; grimly
    they gained

Altitude, though the hand of heaven was heavy upon
    them,
The downdraught from the mountains: though
    desperate eddies spun them
Like a coin, yet unkindly tossed their luck came upper-
    most
And mastery remained.

Air was all ambushes round them, was avalanche earth-
    quake
Quicksand, a funnel deep as doom, till climbing steep
They crawled like a fly up the face of perpendicular
    night
And levelled, finding a break
At fourteen thousand feet. Here earth is shorn from
    sight:
Deadweight a darkness hangs on their eyelids, and they
    bruise
Their eyes against a void: vindictive the cold airs close
Down like a trap of steel and numb them from head to
    heel;
Yet they kept an even keel,
For their spirit reached forward and took the controls
    while their fingers froze.

They had not heard the last of death. When the
    mountains were passed,
He raised another crest, the long crescendo of pain
Kindled to climax, the plane
Took fire. Alone in the sky with the breath of their
    enemy
Hot in their face they fought: from three thousand feet
    they tilted
Over, side-slipped away—a trick for an ace, a race

C. DAY   And running duel with death: flame streamed out
LEWIS   behind,
A crimson scarf of, as life-blood out of a wound, but
        the wind
Of their downfall staunched it; death wilted,
Lagged and died out in smoke—he could not stay their
        pace.

A lull for a while. The powers of hell rallied their
        legions.
On Parer now fell the stress of the flight; for the plane
        had been bumped,
Buffeted, thrashed by the air almost beyond repair:
But he tinkered and coaxed, and they limped
Over the Adriatic on into warmer regions.
Erratic their course to Athens, to Crete: coolly they
        rode her
Like a tired horse at the water-jumps, they jockeyed
        her over seas,
Till they came at last to a land whose dynasties of sand
Had seen Alexander, Napoleon, many a straddling
        invader,
But never none like these.

England to Cairo, a joy-ride, a forty-hour journey at
        most,
Had cost them forty-four days. What centuried strata
        of life
Fuelled the fire that haled them to heaven, the power
        that held them
Aloft? For their plane was a laugh,
A patch, brittle as matchstick, a bubble, a lift for a
        ghost:
Bolts always working loose of propeller, cylinder,
        bearer;

274

Instruments faulty; filter, magneto, each strut
    unsound.
Yet after four days, though we swore she never could
    leave the ground,
We saw her in headstrong haste diminish towards the
    east—
That makeshift, mad sky-farer.

Aimed they now for Baghdad, unwritten in air's annals
A voyage. But theirs the fate all flights of logic to
    refute,
Who obeyed no average law, who buoyed the viewless
    channels
Of sky with a courage steadfast, luminous. Safe they
    crossed
Sinai's desert, and daring
The Nejd, the unneighbourly waste of Arabia, yet
    higher soaring
(Final a fall there for birds of passage, limed and lost
In shifty the sand's embrace) all day they strove to
    climb
Through stormy rain: but they felt her shorten her
    stride and falter,
And they fell at evening time.

Slept that night beside their machine, and the next
    morning
Raider Arabs appeared reckoning this stranded bird
A gift: like cobras they struck, and their gliding
    shadows athwart
The sand were all their warning.
But the aeronauts, knowing iron the coinage here, had
    brought
Mills bombs and revolvers, and M'Intosh held them off

C. DAY While Parer fought for life—
  LEWIS A spark, the mechanic's right answer, and finally
             wrought
           A miracle, for the dumb engine spoke and they rose
           Convulsively out of the clutch of the desert, the clench
             of their foes.

           .   .   .   .

           And they picked her up out of it somehow and put her
             at the air, a
           Sorry hack for such steeplechasing, to leap the sky.
           'We'll fly this bloody crate till it falls to bits at our
             feet,'
           Said the mechanic Parer.
           And at Moulmein soon they crashed; and the plane by
             their spirit's high
           Tension long pinned, girded and guarded from dis-
             solution,
           Fell to bits at their feet. Wrecked was the under-
             carriage,
           Radiator cracked, in pieces, compasses crocked;
           Fallen all to confusion.
           Their winged hope was a heap of scrap, but un-
             splintered their courage.

           Six weeks they worked in sun-glare and jungle damps,
             assembling
           Fragments to make airworthy what was worth not its
             weight in air.
           As a surgeon, grafter of skin, as a setter of bones
             tumbling
           Apart, they had power to repair
           This good for naught but the grave: they livened her
             engine and gave

           276

Fuselage faith to rise rejuvenated from ruin.
Went with them stowaways, not knowing what hazard
    they flew in—
Bear-cubs, a baby alligator, lizards and snakes galore;
Mascots maybe, for the plane though twice she was
    floored again
Always came up for more.

C. DAY
LEWIS

Till they came to the pitiless mountains of Timor. Yet
    these, untamed,
Not timorous, against the gradient and Niagara of air
    they climbed
Scarce-skimming the summits; and over the shark-
    toothed Timor sea
Lost their bearings, but shirked not the odds, the
    deaths that lurked
A million to one on their trail:
They reached out to the horizon and plucked their
    destiny.
On for eight hours they flew blindfold against the
    unknown,
And the oil began to fail
And their flying spirit waned—one pint of petrol
    remained
When the land stood up to meet them and they came
    into their own.

Southward still to Melbourne, the bourn of their
    flight, they pressed
Till at last near Culcairn, like a last fretted leaf
Falling from brave autumn into earth's breast,
D.H. nine, their friend that had seen them to the end,
Gave up her airy life.

The Southern Cross was splendid above the spot where
she fell,
The end of her rainbow curve over our weeping day:
And the flyers, glad to be home, unharmed by that
dizzy fall,
Dazed as the dead awoken from death, stepped out of
the broken
Body and went away.

MAPLE AND SUMACH

Maple and sumach down this autumn ride—
Look, in what scarlet character they speak!
For this their russet and rejoicing week
Trees spend a year of sunsets on their pride.
You leaves drenched with the lifeblood of the year—
What flamingo dawns have wavered from the east,
What eves have crimsoned to their toppling crest
To give the fame and transience that you wear!
Leaf-low he shall lie soon: but no such blaze
Briefly can cheer man's ashen, harsh decline;
His fall is short of pride, he bleeds within
And paler creeps to the dead end of his days.
O light's abandon and the fire-crest sky
Speak in me now for all who are to die!

IN THE HEART OF CONTEMPLATION

In the heart of contemplation—
Admiring, say, the frost-flowers of the white lilac,
Or lark's song busily sifting like sand-crystals
Through the pleased hourglass an afternoon of summer,

Or your beauty, dearer to me than these—
Discreetly a whisper in the ear,
The glance of one passing my window recall me
From lark, lilac, you, grown suddenly strangers.

C. DAY
LEWIS

In the plump and pastoral valley
Of a leisure time, among the trees like seabirds
Asleep on a glass calm, one shadow moves—
The sly reminder of the forgotten appointment.
All the shining pleasures, born to be innocent,
Grow dark with a truant's guilt:
The day's high heart falls flat, the oaks tremble,
And the shadow sliding over your face divides us.

In the act of decision only,
In the hearts cleared for action like lovers naked
For love, this shadow vanishes: there alone
There is nothing between our lives for it to thrive on.
You and I with lilac, lark and oak-leafed
Valley are bound together
As in the astounded clarity before death.
Nothing is innocent now but to act for life's sake.

THE SITTING

(*for Laurence Gowing*)

So like a god I sit here,
One of those stone dreamers quarried from solitude,
A genius—if ever there was one—of the place:
The mountain's only child, lips aloof as a snow line,
Forearms impassive along the cloud-base of aeons,
Eyes heavy on distance—
Graven eyes that flinch not, flash not, if eagles
Clap their wings in my face.

279

C. DAY With hieratic gestures
  LEWIS He the suppliant, priest, interpreter, subtly
         Wooing my virtue, officiates by the throne.
         I know the curious hands are shaping, reshaping the
              image
         Of what is only an image of things impalpable.
         I feel how the eyes strain
         To catch a truth behind the oracular presence—
         Eyes that augur through stone.

         And the god asks, 'What have I for you
         But the lichenous shadow of thought veiling my
              temple,
         The runnels a million time-drops have chased on my
              cheek?'
         And the man replies, 'I will show you the creed of
              your bone, I'll draw you
         The shape of solitude to which you were born.'
         And the god cries, 'I am meek,
         Brushed by an eagle's wing; and a voice bids me
         Speak. But I cannot speak.'

         The god thinks, Let him project, if
         He must, his passionate shapings on my stone heart,
         Wrestle over my body with his sprite,
         Through these blind eyes imagine a skin-deep world
              in perspective:
         Let him make, if he will, the crypt of my holy
              mountain
         His own: let even the light
         That bathes my temple become as it were an active
         Property of his sight.

O man, O innocent artist
Who paint me with green of your fields, with
    amber or yellow
Of love's hair, red of the heart's blood, eyebright
    blue,
Conjuring forms and rainbows out of an empty mist—
Your hand is upon me, as even now you follow
Up the immortal clue
Threading my veins of emerald, topaz, amethyst,
And know not it ends in you.

ALL GONE

The sea drained off, my poverty's uncovered—
Sand, sand, a rusted anchor, broken glass,
The listless sediment of sparkling days
When through a paradise of weed joy wavered.

The sea rolled up like a blind, oh pitiless light
Revealing, shrivelling all! Lacklustre weeds
My hours, my truth a salt-lick. Love recedes
From rippled flesh bared without appetite.

A stranded time, neap and annihilation
Of spirit. Gasping on the inglorious rock,
I pray the sea return, even though its calm
Be treachery, its virtue a delusion.

Put forth upon my sands, whether to mock,
Revive or drown, a liberating arm!

W. H. AUDEN

PROLOGUE

O love, the interest itself in thoughtless Heaven
Make simpler daily the beating of man's heart; within
There in the ring where name and image meet

Inspire them with such a longing as will make his
    thought
Alive like patterns a murmuration of starlings
Rising in joy over wolds unwittingly weave;

Here too on our little reef display your power,
This fortress perched on the edge of the Atlantic scarp
The mole between all Europe and the exile-crowded
    sea;

And make us as Newton was who in his garden watch-
    ing
The apple falling towards England became aware
Between himself and her of an eternal tie.

For now that dream which so long has contented our
    will,
I mean, of uniting the dead into a splendid empire,
Under whose fertilising flood the Lancashire moss

Sprouted up chimneys and Glamorgan hid a life
Grim as a tidal rock-pool's in its glove-shaped valleys,
Is already retreating into her maternal shadow;

Leaving the furnaces gasping in the impossible air
The flotsam at which Dumbarton gapes and hungers,
While upon wind-loved Rowley no hammer shakes

The cluster of mounds like a midget golf course,
     graves
Of some who created these intelligible dangerous
     marvels;
Affectionate people, but crude their sense of glory.

W. H.
AUDEN

Far-sighted as falcons, they looked down another
     future.
For the seed in their loins were hostile, though afraid
     of their pride,
And tall with a shadow now, inertly wait

In bar, in netted chicken-farm, in lighthouse,
Standing on these impoverished constricting acres,
The ladies and gentlemen apart, too much alone.

Consider the years of the measured world begun,
The barren spiritual marriage of stone and water.
Yet, O, at this very moment of our hopeless sigh

When inland they are thinking their thoughts but are
     watching these islands
As children in Chester look to Moel Fammau to decide
On picnics by the clearness or withdrawal of her tree-
     less crown,

Some dream, say yes, long coiled in the ammonite's
     slumber
Is uncurling, prepared to lay on our talk and kindness
Its military silence, its surgeon's idea of pain.

And called out of tideless peace by a living sun
As when Merlin, tamer of horses, and his lords to
     whom
Stonehenge was still a thought, the Pillars passed

283

And into the undared ocean swung north their prow,
Drives through the night and star-concealing dawn
For the virgin roadsteads of our hearts an unwavering
keel.

'WATCH ANY DAY'

Watch any day his nonchalant pauses, see
His dextrous handling of a wrap as he
Steps after into cars, the beggar's envy.

'There is a free one' many say, but err.
He is not that returning conqueror,
Nor ever the poles' circumnavigator.

But poised between shocking falls on razor-edge
Has taught himself this balancing subterfuge
Of the accosting profile, the erect carriage.

The song, the varied action of the blood
Would drown the warning from the iron wood
Would cancel the inertia of the buried:

Travelling by daylight on from house to house
The longest way to the intrinsic peace,
With love's fidelity and with love's weakness.

'TALLER TO-DAY, WE REMEMBER'

Taller to-day, we remember similar evenings,
Walking together in the windless orchard
Where the brook runs over the gravel, far from the
glacier.

284

Again in the room with the sofa hiding the grate,
Look down to the river when the rain is over,
See him turn to the window, hearing our last
Of Captain Ferguson.

It is seen how excellent hands have turned to
     commonness.
One staring too long, went blind in a tower,
One sold all his manors to fight, broke through, and
     faltered.

Nights come bringing the snow, and the dead howl
Under the headlands in their windy dwelling
Because the Adversary put too easy questions
On lonely roads.

But happy now, though no nearer each other,
We see the farms lighted all along the valley;
Down at the mill-shed the hammering stops
And men go home.

Noises at dawn will bring
Freedom for some, but not this peace
No bird can contradict: passing, but is sufficient now
For something fulfilled this hour, loved or endured.

'SIR, NO MAN'S ENEMY'

Sir, no man's enemy, forgiving all
But will his negative inversion, be prodigal:
Send to us power and light, a sovereign touch
Curing the intolerable neural itch,
The exhaustion of weaning, the liar's quinsy,
And the distortions of ingrown virginity.
Prohibit sharply the rehearsed response

And gradually correct the coward's stance;
Cover in time with beams those in retreat
That, spotted, they turn though the reverse were great;
Publish each healer that in city lives
Or country houses at the end of drives;
Harrow the house of the dead; look shining at
New styles of architecture, a change of heart.

A BRIDE IN THE '30'S

(For Madame Mangeot)

Easily, my dear, you move, easily your head
And easily as through leaves of a photograph album I'm
    led
Through the night's delights and the day's impressions
Past the tall tenements and the trees in the wood
Though sombre the sixteen skies of Europe
           And the Danube flood.

Looking and loving our behaviours pass
The stones the steels and the polished glass;
Lucky to love the new pansy railway
The sterile farms where his looks are fed,
And in the policed unlucky city
           Lucky his bed.

He from these lands of terrifying mottoes
Makes worlds as innocent as Beatrix Potter's;
Through bankrupt countries where they mend the
    roads
Along the endless plains his will is
Intent as a collector to pursue
           His greens and lilies.

Easy for him to find in your face
The pool of silence and the tower of grace
To conjure a camera into a wishing rose
Simple to excite in the air from a glance
The horses, the fountains, the sidedrum, the trombone
                    And the dance, the dance.

Summoned by such a music from our time
Such images to audience come
As vanity cannot dispel nor bless:
Hunger and love in their variations
Grouped invalids watching the flight of the birds
                    And single assassins.

Ten thousand of the desperate marching by
Five feet, six feet, seven feet high:
Hitler and Mussolini in their wooing poses
Churchill acknowledging the voter's greeting
Roosevelt at the microphone, Van Lubbe laughing
                    And our first meeting.

But love except at our proposal
Will do no trick at his disposal;
Without opinions of his own performs
The programme that we think of merit,
And through our private stuff must work
                    His public spirit.

Certain it became while we were still incomplete
There were certain prizes for which we would never
        compete;
A choice was killed by every childish illness,
The boiling tears among the hothouse plants,
The rigid promise fractured in the garden,
                    And the long aunts.

W. H. And every day there bolted from the field
AUDEN Desires to which we could not yield;
Fewer and clearer grew the plans,
Schemes for a life and sketches for a hatred,
And early among my interesting scrawls
Appeared your portrait.

You stand now before me, flesh and bone
These ghosts would like to make their own.
Are they your choices? O, be deaf
To hatred proffering immediate pleasure
Glory to swap her fascinating rubbish
For your one treasure.

Be deaf too standing uncertain now,
A pine tree shadow across your brow,
To what I hear and wish I did not,
The voice of love saying lightly, brightly
'Be Lubbe, Be Hitler, but be my good
Daily, nightly'.

The power which corrupts, that power to excess
The beautiful quite naturally possess:
To them the fathers and the children turn
And all who long for their destruction
The arrogant and self-insulted wait
The looked instruction.

Shall idleness ring then your eyes like the pest?
O will you unnoticed and mildly like the rest,
Will you join the lost in their sneering circles,
Forfeit the beautiful interest and fall
Where the engaging face is the face of the betrayer
And the pang is all?

Wind shakes the tree; the mountains darken: W. H.
And the heart repeats though we would not hearken;   AUDEN
'Yours the choice to whom the gods awarded
The language of learning and the language of love
Crooked to move as a moneybug or a cancer
      Or straight as a dove'.

SONG

Warm are the still and lucky miles,
White shores of longing stretch away,
The light of recognition fills
   The whole great day, and bright
The tiny world of lovers' arms.

Silence invades the breathing wood
Where drowsy limbs a treasure keep,
Now greenly falls the learned shade
   Across the sleeping brows
And stirs their secret to a smile.

Restored! Returned! The lost are borne
On seas of shipwreck home at last:
See! In the fire of praising burns
   The dry dumb past, and we
The life-day long shall part no more.

IN MEMORY OF SIGMUND FREUD
(d. September 1939)

When there are so many we shall have to mourn,
When grief has been made so public, and exposed
   To the critique of a whole epoch
   The frailty of our conscience and anguish,

W. H. AUDEN

Of whom shall we speak? For every day they die
Among us, those who were doing us some good,
         And knew it was never enough but
         Hoped to improve a little by living.

Such was this doctor: still at eighty he wished
To think of our life, from whose unruliness
         So many plausible young futures
         With threats or flattery ask obedience.

But his wish was denied him; he closed his eyes
Upon that last picture common to us all,
         Of problems like relatives standing
         Puzzled and jealous about our dying.

For about him at the very end were still
Those he had studied, the nervous and the nights,
         And shades that still waited to enter
         The bright circle of his recognition

Turned elsewhere with their disappointment as he
Was taken away from his old interest
         To go back to the earth in London
         An important Jew who died in exile.

Only Hate was happy, hoping to augment
His practice now, and his shabby clientèle
         Who think they can be cured by killing
         And covering the gardens with ashes.

They are still alive but in a world he changed
Simply by looking back with no false regrets;
         All that he did was to remember
         Like the old and be honest like children.

He wasn't clever at all: he merely told
The unhappy Present to recite the Past
      Like a poetry lesson till sooner
      Or later it faltered at the line where

W. H.
AUDEN

Long ago the accusations had begun,
And suddenly knew by whom it had been judged,
      How rich life had been and how silly,
      And was life-forgiven and more humble.

Able to approach the Future as a friend
Without a wardrobe of excuses, without
      A set mask of rectitude or an
      Embarrassing over-familiar gesture.

No wonder the ancient cultures of conceit
In his technique of unsettlement foresaw
      The fall of princes, the collapse of
      Their lucrative patterns of frustration.

If he succeeded, why, the Generalized Life
Would become impossible, the monolith
      Of State be broken and prevented
      The co-operation of avengers.

Of course they called on God: but he went his way,
Down among the Lost People like Dante, down
      To the stinking fosse where the injured
      Lead the ugly life of the rejected.

And showed us what evil is: not as we thought
Deeds that must be punished, but our lack of faith,
      Our dishonest mood of denial,
      The concupiscence of the oppressor.

W. H. And if something of the autocratic pose,
AUDEN The paternal strictness he distrusted, still
            Clung to his utterance and features,
            It was a protective imitation

      For one who lived among enemies so long;
      If often he was wrong and at times absurd,
            To us he is no more a person
            Now but a whole climate of opinion,

      Under whom we conduct our differing lives:
      Like weather he can only hinder or help,
            The proud can still be proud but find it
            A little harder, and the tyrant tries

      To make him do but doesn't care for him much.
      He quietly surrounds all our habits of growth;
            He extends, till the tired in even
            The remotest most miserable duchy

      Have felt the change in their bones and are cheered,
      And the child unlucky in his little State,
            Some hearth where freedom is excluded,
            A hive whose honey is fear and worry,

      Feels calmer now and somehow assured of escape;
      While as they lie in the grass of our neglect,
            So many long-forgotten objects
            Revealed by his undiscouraged shining

      Are returned to us and made precious again;
      Games we had thought we must drop as we grew up,
            Little noises we dared not laugh at,
            Faces we made when no one was looking.

292

But he wishes us more than this: to be free
Is often to be lonely; he would unite
      The unequal moieties fractured
      By our own well-meaning sense of justice.

Would restore to the larger the wit and will
The smaller possesses but can only use
      For arid disputes, would give back to
      The son the mother's richness of feeling.

But he would have us remember most of all
To be enthusiastic over the night
      Not only for the sense of wonder
      It alone has to offer, but also

Because it needs our love: for with sad eyes
Its delectable creatures look up and beg
      Us dumbly to ask them to follow;
      They are exiles who long for the future

That lies in our power. They too would rejoice
If allowed to serve enlightenment like him,
      Even to bear our cry of 'Judas'.
      As he did and all must bear who serve it.

One rational voice is dumb: over a grave
The household of Impulse mourns one dearly loved.
      Sad is Eros, builder of cities,
      And weeping anarchic Aphrodite.

W. H.
AUDEN

W. H.
AUDEN

MIRANDA'S SONG

My Dear One is mine as mirrors are lonely,
As the poor and sad are real to the good king,
And the high green hill sits always by the sea.

Up jumped the Black Man behind the elder tree,
Turned a somersault and ran away waving;
My Dear One is mine as mirrors are lonely.

The Witch gave a squawk: her venomous body
Melted into light as water leaves a spring
And the high green hill sits always by the sea.

At his crossroads, too, the Ancient prayed for me;
Down his wasted cheeks tears of joy were running:
My Dear One is mine as mirrors are lonely.

He kissed me awake, and no one was sorry;
The sun shone on sails, eyes, pebbles, anything,
And the high green hill sits always by the sea.

So, to remember our changing garden, we
Are linked as children in a circle dancing:
My Dear One is mine as mirrors are lonely,
And the high green hill sits always by the sea.

THE LESSON

The first time that I dreamed, we were in flight,
And fagged with running; there was civil war,
A valley full of thieves and wounded bears.

Farms blazed behind us; turning to the right,
We came at once to a tall house, its door
Wide open, waiting for its long-lost heirs.

An elderly clerk sat on the bedroom stairs
Writing; but we had tiptoed past him when
He raised his head and stuttered—'Go away'.
We wept and begged to stay:
He wiped his pince-nez, hesitated, then
Said no, he had no power to give us leave;
Our lives were not in order; we must leave.

W. H.
AUDEN

*   *   *

The second dream began in a May wood;
We had been laughing; your blue eyes were kind,
Your excellent nakedness without disdain.
Our lips met, wishing universal good;
But on their impact sudden flame and wind
Fetched you away and turned me loose again

To make a focus for a wide wild plain,
Dead level and dead silent and bone dry,
Where nothing could have suffered, sinned, or grown.
On a high chair alone
I sat, my little master, asking why
The cold and solid object in my hands
Should be a human hand, one of your hands.

*   *   *

And the last dream was this: we were to go
To a great banquet and a Victory Ball
After some tournament or dangerous test.

Only our seats had velvet cushions, so
We must have won; though there were crowns for all,
Ours were of gold, of paper all the rest.

W. H. O fair or funny was each famous guest.
AUDEN Love smiled at Courage over priceless glass,
And rockets died in hundreds to express
Our learned carelessness.
A band struck up; all over the green grass
A sea of paper crowns rose up to dance:
Ours were too heavy; we did not dance.

*   *   *

I woke. You were not there. But as I dressed
Anxiety turned to shame, feeling all three
Intended one rebuke. For had not each
In its own way tried to teach
My will to love you that it cannot be,
As I think, of such consequence to want
What anyone is given, if they want?

LOUIS MACNEICE

AN ECLOGUE FOR CHRISTMAS

A. I meet you in an evil time.

B.   The evil bells
    Put out of our heads, I think, the thought of every-
          thing else.

A. The jaded calender revolves,
    Its nuts need oil, carbon chokes the valves,
    The excess sugar of a diabetic culture
    Rotting the nerve of life and literature;
    Therefore when we bring out the old tinsel and
          frills
    To announce that Christ is born among the barbar-
          ous hills
    I turn to you whom a morose routine
    Saves from the mad vertigo of being what has been.

B. Analogue of me, you are wrong to turn to me,
    My country will not yield you any sanctuary,
    There is no pinpoint in any of the ordnance maps
    To save you when your towns and town-bred
          thoughts collapse,
    It is better to die *in situ* as I shall,
    One place is as bad as another. Go back where your
          instincts call
    And listen to the crying of the town-cats and the
          taxis again,
    Or wind your gramophone and eavesdrop on great
          men.

LOUIS
MAC-
NEICE
A. Jazz-weary of years of drums and Hawaian guitar,
Pivoting on the parquet I seem to have moved far
From bombs and mud and gas, have stuttered on my
    feet
Clinched to the streamlined and butter-smooth
    trulls of the élite,
The lights irritating and gyrating and rotating in
    gauze—
Pomade-dazzle, a slick beauty of gewgaws—
I who was Harlequin in the childhood of the
    century,
Posed by Picasso beside an endless opaque sea,
Have seen myself sifted and splintered in broken
    facets,
Tentative pencillings, endless liabilities, no assets,
Abstractions scalpelled with a palette-knife
Without reference to this particular life,
And so it has gone on; I have not been allowed to be
Myself in flesh or face, but abstracting and dissecting
    me
They have made of me pure form, a symbol or a
    pastiche,
Stylised profile, anything but soul and flesh:
And that is why I turn this jaded music on
To forswear thought and become an automaton.

B. There are in the country also of whom I am afraid—
Men who put beer into a belly that is dead,
Women in the forties with terrier and setter who
    whistle and swank
Over down and plough and Roman road and daisied
    bank,
Half-conscious that these barriers over which they
    stride

Are nothing to the barbed wire that has grown
    round their pride.

LOUIS
MAC-
NEICE

A. And two there are, as I drive in the city, who
        suddenly perturb—
  The one sirening me to draw up by the kerb
  The other, as I lean back, my right leg stretched
        creating speed,
  Making me catch and stamp, the brakes shrieking,
        pull up dead:
  She wears silk stockings taunting the winter wind,
  He carries a white stick to mark that he is blind.

B. In the country they are still hunting, in the heavy
        shires
  Greyness is on the fields and sunset like a line of
        pyres
  Of barbarous heroes smoulders through the ancient
        air
  Hazed with factory dust and, orange opposite, the
        moon's glare,
  Goggling yokel-stubborn through the iron trees,
  Jeers at the end of us, our bland ancestral ease;
  We shall go down like palaeolithic man
  Before some new Ice Age or Genghiz Khan.

A. It is time for some new coinage, people have got so
        old,
  Hacked and handled and shiny from pocketing they
        have made bold
  To think that each is himself through these
        accidents, being blind
  To the fact that they are merely the counters of an
        unknown Mind.

LOUIS
MAC-
NEICE

B. A Mind that does not think, if such a thing can be,
Mechanical Reason, capricious Identity.
That I could be able to face this domination nor
flinch—

A. The tin toys of the hawker move on the pavement
inch by inch
Not knowing that they are wound up; it is better to
be so
Than to be, like us, wound up and while running
down to know—

B. But everywhere the pretence of individuality
recurs—

A. Old faces frosted with powder and choked in furs.

B. The jutlipped farmer gazing over the humpbacked
wall.

A. The commercial traveller joking in the urinal.

B. I think things draw to an end, the soil is stale.

A. And over-elaboration will nothing now avail,
The street is up again, gas, electricity or drains,
Ever-changing conveniences, nothing comfortable
remains
Un-improved, as flagging Rome improved villa and
sewer
(A sound-proof library and a stable temperature).
Our street is up, red lights sullenly mark
The long trench of pipes, iron guts in the dark,
And not till the Goths again come swarming down
the hill
Will cease the clangour of the electric drill.
But yet there is beauty narcotic and deciduous
In this vast organism grown out of us:

On all the traffic islands stand white globes like LOUIS MAC-NEICE
    moons,
The city's haze is clouded amber that purrs and
    croons,
And tilting by the noble curve bus after tall bus
    comes
With an osculation of yellow light, with a glory like
    chrysanthemums.

B. The country gentry cannot change, they will die in
    their shoes
From angry circumstance and moral self-abuse,
Dying with a paltry fizzle they will prove their lives
    to be
An ever-diluted drug, a spiritual tautology.
They cannot live once their idols are turned out,
None of them can endure, for how could they,
    possibly, without
The flotsam of private property, pekingese and
    polyanthus,
The good things which in the end turn to poison
    and pus,
Without the bandy chairs and the sugar in the silver
    tongs
And the inter-ripple and resonance of years of
    dinner-gongs?
Or if they could find no more that cumulative proof
In the rain dripping off the conservatory roof?
What will happen when the only sanction the
    country-dweller has—

A. What will happen to us, planked and panelled with
    jazz?
Who go to the theatre where a black man dances
    like an eel,

Where pink thighs flash like the spokes of a wheel,
        where we feel
That we know in advance all the jogtrot and the cake-
    walk jokes,
        All the bumfun and the gags of the comedians in
            boaters and toques,
        All the tricks of the virtuosos who invert the
            usual—

B. What will happen to us when the State takes down
        the manor wall,
    When there is no more private shooting or fishing,
        when the trees are all cut down,
    When faces are all dials and cannot smile or
        frown—

A. What will happen when the sniggering machine-
        guns in the hands of the young men
    Are trained on every flat and club and beauty
        parlour and Father's den?
    What will happen when our civilisation like a long
        pent balloon—

B. What will happen will happen; the whore and the
        buffoon
    Will come off best; no dreamers, they cannot lose
        their dream
    And are at least likely to be reinstated in the new
        régime.
    But one thing is not likely—

A.   Do not gloat over yourself
    Do not be your own vulture, high on some
        mountain shelf
    Huddle the pitiless abstractions bald about the neck

302

Who will descend when you crumple in the plains
    a wreck.
    songs
Unlike anything—

B.   The lady of the house poises the silver tongs
    And picks a lump of sugar, 'ne plus ultra' she says
    'I cannot do otherwise, even to prolong my days'—

A. I cannot do otherwise either, tonight I will book
    my seat—

B. I will walk about the farm-yard which is replete
    As with the smell of dung so with memories—

A. I will gorge myself to satiety with the oddities
    Of every artiste, official or amateur,
    Who has pleased me in my rôle of hero-worshipper
    Who has pleased me in my rôle of individual man—

B. Let us lie once more, say 'What we think, we can'
    The old idealist lie—

A.   And for me before I die
    Let me go the round of the garish glare—

B.   And on the bare and high
    Places of England, the Wiltshire Downs and the
        Long Mynd
    Let the balls of my feet bounce on the turf, my face
        burn in the wind
    My eyelashes stinging in the wind, and the sheep
        like grey stones
    Humble my human pretensions—

A.   Let the saxophones and the xylophones
    And the cult of every technical excellence, the
        miles of canvas in the galleries

And the canvas of the rich man's yacht snapping and
    tacking on the seas
And the perfection of a grilled steak—

B.   Let all these so ephemeral things
    Be somehow permanent like the swallow's tangent
        wings:
    Goodbye to you, this day remember is Christmas,
        this morn
    They say, interpret it your own way, Christ is born.

SUNDAY MORNING

Down the road someone is practising scales,
The notes like little fishes vanish with a wink of tails,
Man's heart expands to tinker with his car
For this is Sunday morning, Fate's great bazaar,
Regard these means as ends, concentrate on this Now,
And you may grow to music or drive beyond Hindhead
    anyhow,
Take corners on two wheels until you go so fast
That you can clutch a fringe or two of the windy past,
That you can abstract this day and make it to the week
    of time
A small eternity, a sonnet self-contained in rhyme.

But listen, up the road, something gulps, the church
    spire
Opens its eight bells out, skulls' mouths which will not
    tire
To tell how there is no music or movement which
    secures
Escape from the weekday time. Which deadens and
    endures.

CONVERSATION

LOUIS MAC-NEICE

Ordinary people are peculiar too:
Watch the vagrant in their eyes
Who sneaks away while they are talking with you
Into some black wood behind the skull,
Following un-, or other, realities,
Fishing for shadows in a pool.

But sometimes the vagrant comes the other way
Out of their eyes and into yours
Having mistaken you perhaps for yesterday
Or for tomorrow night, a wood in which
He may pick up among the pine-needles and burrs
The lost purse, the dropped stitch.

Vagrancy however is forbidden; ordinary men
Soon come back to normal, look you straight
In the eyes as if to say 'It will not happen again',
Put up a barrage of common sense to baulk
Intimacy but by mistake interpolate
Swear-words like roses in their talk.

BROTHER FIRE

When our brother Fire was having his dog's day
Jumping the London streets with millions of tin cans
Clanking at his tail, we heard some shadow say
'Give the dog a bone'—and so we gave him ours;
Night after night we watched him slaver and crunch
     away
The beams of human life, the tops of topless towers.

Which gluttony of his for us was Lenten fare
Who mother-naked, suckled with sparks, were chill

LOUIS Though cotted in a grill of sizzling air
MAC- Striped like a convict—black, yellow and red;
NEICE Thus were we weaned to knowledge of the Will
That wills the natural world but wills us dead.

O delicate walker, babbler, dialectician Fire,
O enemy and image of ourselves,
Did we not on those mornings after the All Clear,
When you were looting shops in elemental joy
And singing as you swarmed up city block and spire.
Echo your thought in ours? 'Destroy! Destroy!'

SLOW MOVEMENT

Waking, he found himself in a train, andante,
With wafers of early sunlight blessing the unknown
    fields
And yesterday cancelled out, except for yesterday's
    papers
    Huddling under the seat.

It is still very early, this is a slow movement;
The viola-player's hand like a fish in a glass tank
Rises, remains quivering, darts away
    To nibble invisible weeds.

Great white nebulae lurch against the window
To deploy across the valley, the children are not yet up
To wave us on—we pass without spectators,
    Braiding a voiceless creed.

And the girl opposite, name unknown, is still
Asleep and the colour of her eyes unknown

Which might be wells of sun or moons of wish
  But it is still very early.

LOUIS
MAC-
NEICE

The movement ends, the train has come to a stop
In buttercup fields, the fiddles are silent, the whole
Shoal of silver tessellates the aquarium
  Floor, not a bubble rises . . .

And what happens next on the programme we do not
      know,
If, the red line topped on the gauge, the fish will go
      mad in the tank
Accelerando con forza, the sleeper open her eyes
  And, so doing, open ours.

STEPHEN SPENDER

THE PRISONERS

Far far the least of all, in want,
Are these,
The prisoners
Turned massive with their vaults and dark with dark.

They raise no hands, which rest upon their knees,
But lean their solid eyes against the night,
Dimly they feel
Only the furniture they use in cells.

Their Time is almost Death. The silted flow
Of years on years
Is marked by dawns
As faint as cracks on mud-flats of despair.

My pity moves amongst them like a breeze
On walls of stone
Fretting for summer leaves, or like a tune
On ears of stone.

Then, when I raise my hands to strike,
It is too late,
There are no chains that fall
Nor visionary liquid door
Melted with anger.

When have their lives been free from walls and dark
And airs that choke?
And where less prisoner to let my anger
Like a sun strike?

If I could follow them from room to womb
To plant some hope
Through the black silk of the big-bellied gown
There would I win.

No, no, no,
It is too late for anger,
Nothing prevails
But pity for the grief they cannot feel.

'IN RAILWAY HALLS'

In railway halls, on pavements near the traffic,
They beg, their eyes made big by empty staring
And only measuring Time, like the blank clock.

No, I shall weave no tracery of pen-ornament
To make them birds upon my singing-tree:
Time merely drives these lives which do not live
As tides push rotten stuff along the shore.

—There is no consolation, no, none
In the curving beauty of that line
Traced on our graphs through history, where the
        oppressor
Starves and deprives the poor.

Paint here no draped despairs, no saddening clouds
Where the soul rests, proclaims eternity.
But let the wrong cry out as raw as wounds
This Time forgets and never heals, far less transcends.

STEPHEN
SPENDER

'AFTER THEY HAVE TIRED'

After they have tired of the brilliance of cities
And of striving for office where at last they may
    languish
Hung round with easy chains until
Death and Jerusalem glorify also the crossing-sweeper:
Then those streets the rich built and their easy love
Fade like old cloths, and it is death stalks through life
Grinning white through all faces
Clean and equal like the shine from snow.

In this time when grief pours freezing over us,
When the hard light of pain gleams at every street
    corner,
When those who were pillars of that day's gold roof
Shrink in their clothes; surely from hunger
We may strike fire, like fire from flint?
And our strength is now the strength of our bones
Clean and equal like the shine from snow
And the strength of famine and of our enforced idle-
    ness,
And it is the strength of our love for each other.

Readers of this strange language,
We have come at last to a country
Where light equal, like the shine from snow, strikes all
    faces,
Here you may wonder
How it was that works, money, interest, building,
    could ever hide
The palpable and obvious love of man for man.

Oh comrades, let not those who follow after
—The beautiful generation that shall spring from our
    sides—

Let not them wonder how after the failure of banks STEPHEN
The failure of cathedrals and the declared insanity of SPENDER
    our rulers,
We lacked the Spring-like resources of the tiger
Or of plants who strike out new roots to gushing
    waters.
But through torn-down portions of old fabric let their
    eyes
Watch the admiring dawn explode like a shell
Around us, dazing us with light like snow.

THE NORTH

Our single purpose was to walk through snow
With faces swung to their prodigious North
Like compass iron. As clerks in whited Banks
With bird-claw pens column virgin paper
To snow we added footprints.
Extensive whiteness drowned
All sense of space. We tramped through
Static, glaring days, Time's suspended blank.
That was in Spring and Autumn. Then Summer struck
Water over rocks, and half the world
Became a ship with a deep keel, the booming floes
And icebergs with their little birds.
Twittering Snow Bunting, Greenland Wheatear
Red throated Divers; imagine butterflies
Sulphurous cloudy yellow; glory of bees
That suck from saxifrage; crowberry,
Bilberry, cranberry, *Pyrola uniflora*.
There followed winter in a frozen hut
Warm enough at the kernel, but dare to sleep

STEPHEN With head against the wall—ice gummed my hair.
SPENDER Hate Culver's loud breathing, despise Freeman's
Fidget for washing; love only the dogs
That whine for scraps and scratch. Notice
How they run better (on short journeys) with a bitch.
In that, different from us.

Return, return, you warn. We do. There is
A network of railways, money, words, words, words.
Meals, papers, exchanges, debates,
Cinema, wireless; the worst is Marriage.
We cannot sleep. At night we watch
A speaking clearness through cloudy paranoia.
These questions are white rifts. Was
Ice our anger transformed? The raw, the motionless
Skies, were these the spirit's hunger?
The continual and hypnotized march through snow
The dropping nights of precious extinction, were these
Only the wide invention of the will,
The frozen will's evasion? If this exists
In us as madness here, as coldness
In these summer, civilized sheets: is the North
Over there, a tangible real madness
A glittering simpleton, one without towns
Only with bears and fish, a staring eye,
A new and singular sex?

AN ELEMENTARY SCHOOL CLASSROOM

Far far from gusty waves, these children's faces
Like rootless weeds the torn hair round their paleness;
The tall girl with her weighed-down head; the paper-
seeming boy with rat's eyes; the stunted unlucky heir
Of twisted bones, reciting a father's gnarled disease,

His lesson from his desk. At back of the dim class
One unnoted, mild and young: his eyes live in a dream
Of squirrel's game, in tree room, other than this.

On sour cream walls, donations; Shakespeare's head
Cloudless at dawn, civilized dome riding all cities;
Belled, flowery, Tyrolese valley; open-handed map
Awarding the explicit world, of every name but here.
To few, too few, these are real windows: world and
     words and waving
Leaves, to heal. For these young lives, guilty and
     dangerous
Is fantasy of travel. Surely, Shakespeare is wicked

To lives that wryly turn, under the structural Lie,
Toward smiles or hate? Amongst their heap, these
     children
Wear skins peeped through by bones, and spectacles of
     steel
With mended glass, like bottle bits in slag.
Tyrol is wicked; map's promising a fable:
All of their time and space are foggy slum,
So blot their maps with slums as big as doom.

Unless, dowager, governor, these pictures, in a room
Columned above childishness, like our day's future
     drift
Of smoke concealing war, are voices shouting
O that beauty has words and works which break
Through coloured walls and towers. The children
     stand
As in a climbing mountain train. This lesson illustrates
The world green in their many valleys beneath:
The total summer heavy with their flowers.

STEPHEN
SPENDER

POOR GIRL

Poor girl, inhabitant of a strange land
Where death stares through your gaze,
As though a distant moon
Shone through midsummer days
With the skull-like glitter of night:

Poor child, you wear your summer dress
And your shoes striped with gold
As the earth wears a variegated cover
Of grass and flowers
Covering caverns of destruction over
Where hollow deaths are told.

I look into your sunk eyes,
Shafts of wells to both our hearts,
Which cannot take part in the lies
Of acting these gay parts.
Under our lips, our minds
Become one with the weeping
Of the mortality
Which through sleep is unsleeping.

Of what use is my weeping?
It does not carry a surgeon's knife
To cut the wrongly multiplying cells
At the root of your life.
It can only prove
That extremes of love
Stretch beyond the flesh to hideous bone
Howling in hyena dark alone.

Oh, but my grief is thought, a dream,
Tomorrow's gale will sweep away.

314

It does not wake every day
To the facts which are and do not only seem:
The granite facts around your bed,
Poverty-stricken hopeless ugliness
Of the fact that you will soon be dead.

ALREADY

(i)

Already you are beginning to become
Fallen tree-trunk with sun-burnished limbs
In an infinite landscape among tribal bones
Encircled by encroaching ritualistic stones.

(ii)

Those that begin to cease to be your eyes
Are flowers parched of their honey where memories
Crowd over and fly out like avid butterflies.
The striped and glittering colours of lost days,
Swallow-tail, Red Admiral, fritillaries,
Feed on your eyes and then fly from our gaze.

(iii)

In the corner of the bed you are already partly ghost
A whispering scratching existence almost lost
To our blatant life which spreads through all the rooms
Our contrast transient as heaped consoling blooms.

(iv)

You are so quiet; your hand on the sheet seems a
    mouse.
Yet when we look away, the flails

STEPHEN Which pound and beat you down with ceaseless pulse
SPENDER Shake like a steam hammer through the house.

(v)

Evening brings the opening of the windows.
Now your last sunset throws
Shadows from the roots of all the trees,
Atrean hounds it unleashes
In front of a sky in which there burns a rose.
The Furies point and strain forwards
The pack of night is crowding towards us.

ICE

(To M.M.B.)

She came in from the snowing air
Where icicle-hung architecture
Strung white fleece round the baroque square.
I saw her face freeze in her fur
And my lips seemed to fetch quick fire
From the firelit corner of the room
Where I had waited in my chair.
I kissed this fire against her skin
And watched the warmth make her cheeks bloom
While at my care her smiling eyes
Shone with the health of the ice
Outside, whose brilliance they brought in.
That day, until this, I forgot.
How is it now I so remember,
Who, when she came indoors, saw not
The passion of her white December?

ANNO SANTO

STEPHEN
SPENDER

I

They bear him through the channels of the crowd
On the high chair where he sits, a radiant, bowing
    figure,
Lips alight with cherishing smile, and sensitive fingers
Threading through air towards the curving multitude
Of sun-grooved peasant faces, streaming with joy.
'*Papa! Il Papa!*' My heart weeps also. Now, when I
    shut my eyes,
I see the old pope, his grace more than a dancer's,
With a following smile, and hand like a twig touching
    waters
Which lie under hearts. The immense arches uplift
Their electric burden of candles. His robe seems
    aflame.
At one with divine compassion, I forget the enormous
    wrongs
Straddling Rome with the weight of Peter's dome.
Volcanic joys and griefs merge together in love.

II

Wood-carven peasant faces
With skin daubed by crude sun,
Rivuleted with lines
Down which storms have run.

Coarse hair like a doll's,
Eye-sockets through which shine
Tense eyes in the skull
Like quartz raw from the mine.

317

STEPHEN
SPENDER

Mumbling lips, trembling hands
Fumbling at a string of beads,
Shawls over heads, neckerchiefs
Over shoulders of black weeds.

I stand near an old peasant woman
Under the high dome:
Her body seems the fallen clay
To which her mind has come.

His finger raised before her eyes
Extends the ray her shuttered breath
Drinks into her darkness, where
Her death is life, her life is death.

CHARLES MADGE

SOLAR CREATION

The sun, of whose terrain we creatures are,
Is the director of all human love,
Unit of time, and circle round the earth,

And we are the commotion born of love
And slanted rays of that illustrious star,
Peregrine of the crowded fields of birth,

The crowded lane, the market and the tower.
Like sight in pictures, real at remove,
Such is our motion on dimensional earth.

Down by the river, where the ragged are,
Continuous the cries and noise of birth,
While to the muddy edge dark fishes move,

And over all, like death, or sloping hill,
Is nature, which is larger and more still.

AT WAR

Fire rides calmly in the air
That blows across the fields of water
That laps the papped curve of the outspread earth.

Earth is bone and builds the house
Water the blood that softly runs inside
Air is the breath by which the fire is fed.

Earth's mouth is open and will suck you down
Water climbs over earth to reach you
The assassin air is at your throat
And fire will presently split the air.

THE HOURS OF THE PLANETS

☉

The summoning sun, the sun that looks on London
See twice, sees London and unLondon sees
And leaves the sound unsounded of the leafless sky.

The rise of the   Rising along the sun's long escalier
bourgeoisie.   All equal all in inequality
Looking not one to one but each from each
Different in self-indifference.

At top of steps, some half-mile from the sea
Sat—in the morning and out of the sea up to him
Came—seeking favour and on left and right
Stood——quick as trees, then said—
These are ours and therein all that is
And the living creatures of the field and fen
Made echo sound upon the day's platface.

The little fronds, the waving sleeve and skirt
Who quickly turn aside, the animals
Of sleek two-globed marble without heart,
Stones within the middle of their eyes,
They know not what they feel.

Save passion for them.

The sun from his hauteur inclines
Upon the various crops and
The tiger hinterland. The forests of daylight.

The sun stat. And looking back
Down back upon in ewig retrograde.

The little sun fled backward through the sky
The airy cloudy cumulus split every way
The remote sea was with the remote fish.

Merciless into morsels   *The memories*
She cut her young brother and cast them   *of the past*
On the sea where each a battleship became   *become the*
In whitest blossom decked.   *images of the*
                                                     present.

The whole of London was a sea of lilies.
The captain said who stood upon the bridge
That is Absyrt.

There came a storm. The tallest cruiser
Heaven's finger touched unfolded in ros flame.

'there is no way to restore life'   *Inward*
                                                     monitions:
'glaze the dark eye that holds eternity'

The towers came nearer over the mist.   *Glimpses of*
I heard my kind pattering all about   *reality.*
The shafts, the upward and the downward shafts,
And rolling silent out in silent daylight
Innumerous pellicules.
                    Passed the X
And cliff of many windows, slept along
Crossed by the Pass of two Towers
And so ad infinitum to the stars.

                        ☿

The sun will press his hands over my eyes   *The future*
Coming unawares.   *comes.*

The silent groups are scattered in the fields   *Youth on the*
No talk goes up from them, they wave like trees.   *approach of*
                                                     age

CHARLES There will murmur as the spirits move
MADGE Two from this quarter yonder unperceived.

The ancient clocks look down
Thereupon the wise drawn into corners
Unhollow their rigid countenances.

Telegraphy Flowing quickly, quietly wisdom will be
and Killing by distance the great idiot sky.
human
generation. They wave, they falter, sisters and daughters
On the wave their motion pauses, falls, is free.

Water leaps from naked rock unafraid
Swift in twisting a garland and a smile.

Nature as the Two wanderers that were in a month
unity of Heard a cry, Oh mother I shall die
contraries. Then secretly was born
The father of death and healing
The day grew cold and still
As the embrace of enemies at war
Upon a mountain rich with copper ore.

☾

MAN MANIFORM

Real houses, real inhabitants—
One hears them coming up the daylight street
And turning into men, extraordinary,
Familiar as two hands or constant care.
The throng whose noise is always heard outside
Whose tongues are in their heels upon the stones.
In images they seem to cross a bridge
The via media of living and dead,
Thames representing their unconsciousness.

Life, more persistent than thought, continues to flow   CHARLES
Out of Europe grown gaunt and old   MADGE
Multiple genera untabulated
Carrying pouches, tufted behind ears,
Splay-footed, hammer-fingered, hooked, humped
The smooth, the rough, the freckled and the white,
The denizens of holes, the desert prowlers,
Moon-sprung, sun-hatched, dense aground, lone up
        high,
Ragged swamp dwellers, perchers in tiptops,
Insignia, plumes, bandages, clothes, flowers,
Beautifully wrapped simple forms of life;
The growing leaves are wet with primal tears
In middlesex the semi-animal kingdom.

O reich of riches, urbs of all superb
When will you break your banks? The vague of water
Is everywhere afar and every weir
Life likening to its opponent, and susurrus
Of the grey-haired waterfall.

Deep in the water eye have gazing seen
A drowned second sun, like a dissected heart.

                            ♄
Now English eyes the cancerous sun behold!   *The future of*
Bright over blackened Africa, Sahara   *mankind.*
Futurity and all paluster lakes of sewage,
Utter blackness, uttering thundercloud
On native waste and villages of hut
Far as I can see
Earth's declivity is infinite
Falling away, fading in infinite forms
Horizon added to horizon.

                          323

CHARLES Man stands black within the pause of thought
MADGE Shadowless perpendicular under beam
In deafmute equatorial solitude
When Fulmen falls, resounds among remaining
mountains.

Then might you hear like birds between
The knocking together of love sighs
Such meditation of self-gazing self
And smooth as day-divided time
A careless phantom rapture

FAR FROM THE SUN
FARTHER FROM THE SUN
FARTHEST FROM THE SUN

DEEP IN THE EARTH
DEEPER IN THE EARTH
DEEPEST IN THE EARTH

THE DREAM WILL BEGIN
THE DREAM IS BEGINNING
THE DREAM HAS BEGUN

THREE EARS OF CORN IN A SATURNIAN
FIELD
THREE STEAMERS ANCHORED IN A
NEPTUNIAN SEA
THREE SOARING SPIRES IN A URANIAN SKY

Ever they change, spires steamers ears of corn,
Ages of gloomy iron, ages of stone
And golden ages that return anew
In shadows of the darksome working man
Transmuted by the secret stone of life
No stone, the lost identity of change.

The trees expand, the chestnut floribund
Spreads ever huger, and the passers by
Melt one by one into the distant air.

24

SCENE

A coloured page, a coloured piece of glass
A reverie, a picture of a man
An element, a wand, a wandering mind

CHARACTERS

Those who plough the hollow cave
And reap the breeze

Those who rule the sky
Dividing as they will in wives and children
Plying the compasses of golden art

The brothers of earth, sea and air
And the immortal sisters who inspire
The wakeful

THE KEY

Read backwards.
Leaf by leaf
Let them fall profuse and glorious
The spectrum of the interlinear eye,
In the celestial field, the cloth of gold.
Turn backwards into white prehistory
Towards the invisible cisalpine skull.
Here pause, and look upon the title page.

It is today, when silence falls,
And all the people standing on the quay
To watch the big ship sail away
Stop waving to their friends
                                    and say
The answer to the sun is death.

IN CONJUNCTION

Now in the circulating torrent of the stars
Certain events are drawn correct and clear
That wear expressions of anguish and delight

Signs unmistakeable of the heavenly progress
The flying planet leaves the night-house
The twined figures fill the highest hemisphere

From which we conclude peace, and grateful offerings
While the bird of war, thunderless on leaden roof
No shadow shows on the galactic brilliance of the
        streaming breast

And beyond the fated, tragic, foursquare, immovable
        house
Evenings under the trees of calm, descending evenings
        of rest
Relenting over battlefields, evenings upholding us
Among alarms, rust and the dead, waiting to be blest.

LUSTY JUVENTUS

CHARLES
MADGE

The sea is an acre of dull glass, the land is a table
My eyes jump down from the table and go running
    down as far as they are able
While one is still young and still able to employ
Nerves muscles sinews eyes mouth teeth head
A giant that threw a stone at Cærodunum
Transforming England into a salty pancake
Lichen-alive governed in gametosporous colonies
Crescented with calciform corollæ, a great stone
    marsh
With the dragons of dead Hercules debating
There is no end there is no end to the labours of
    Hercules
While one is still young and still able to employ
Feet fist eyes in the head a spade a spanner
Down down we go down the emblematic abyss
Adorned with the kisses of the gentry, come out on
    primrose day
To greet the Young Bolshevik Bolus rolling up with
    banners
Across the passes of snake and ladder country
Idly I flung down pieces, but the fit is ended
When one was wery young and able to employ
The empty salads of English advent and the formulæ of
    seajoy.

A MONUMENT

All moves within the visual frame
All walks upon the ground or stands
Casting a shadow,

All grass, day's eye, the folded man
Suffer or wither up in stone
And stare there.

They call upon the end of the world
And the last waters overwhelming
To wash the unborn things

Bedded on time's distracted coast
Bald stones and smiling silences,
Severed, they shrink.

The hovering certainty of death
Unites the water and the sky,
Their small choice

Of evils on the watching shore.

DELUSIONS IV

Sometimes at evening travellers have heard
The speaking dunes of ever shifting sand
Utter a note as shrill as any bird,
While the wind creeps across the cooling land.

Sometimes the sight of gently waving green
Invites the weary traveller's footsteps on
Refracted far across the waste between,
But, one step more, the glancing palms are gone.

The secret of the desert is a stone
Because the stone contains once living things.
The fossil breccia has to marble grown,
Which to new life the chiselling sculptor brings.

Thousands who live in ignorance and pain
Build up the giant pyramid of life.
Their dust, the desert, covers all the plain
Except the uncanny sphinx, their hieroglyph.

CHARLES
MADGE

Spring, 1936

BALLAD OF HOPE AND FEAR

Have you ever seen the dawn
       Purified
By the rivers of regret?
Have you taken in your teeth
The wafer of thin bread
On a morning cold and wet
When the lines of rosy red
Were appearing overhead?

Have you ever heard the roar
Of a morning far away
In the conscience of an ear?
Have you waited for the day
While the soles of their boots
On the pavement of a city
Made a pattern of your pity
Among the limpid structures
Of mist, brick and smoke,
Sooty architectures,
Reminding you to be reminded
As you woke?

329

CHARLES
MADGE

Have you drawn the curtains back
             Scarified
By the acid and the needle
Of your hope and fear
Where those massive numbers loom
Beyond you and beyond
The little look-out room?

Did you smell the misty breath
Of their presence under heaven?
Did you go to be forgiven,
Gently close the door,
Mount the many-headed river,
Curling down the street,
(The rumour of their wail
Being loudest in the morning,
A signal and a warning,
The time of tidal feet.)
             Did you ride
On the flood?

GEORGE BARKER

SUMMER IDYLL

Sometimes in summer months, the gestate earth
Loaded to gold, the boughs arching downward
Burdened, the shallow and glucose streams
Teeming, flowers out, all gold camouflage
Of the collusive summer; but under the streams
Winter lies coldly, and coldly embedded in
The corn hunger lies germinally, want under
The abundance, poverty pulling down
The tautened boughs, and need is the seed.

Robe them in superb summer, at angles
Their bones penetrate, or with a principality
Of Spring possess them, under the breast
Space of a vacancy spreads like a foul
Ghost flower, want; and the pressure upon
The eyeballs of their spirits, upon the organs
Of their spare bodies, the pressure upon
Their movement and their merriment, loving and
Living, the pressure upon their lives like deep
Seas, becomes insufferable, to be suffered.

Sometimes the summer lessens a moment the pressure.
Large as the summer rose some rise
Bathing in rivers or at evening harrying rabbits,
Indulging in games in meadows—and some are idle,
     strewn
Over the parks like soiled paper like summer
Insects, bathed in sweat or at evening harried
By watchmen, park-keepers, policemen—indulge in
     games
Dreaming as I dream of rest and cleanliness and cash.

GEORGE And the gardens exhibit the regalia of the season
BARKER Like debutante queans, between which they wander
Blown with vague odours, seduced by the pure
Beauty, like drowned men floating in bright coral.
Summer, denuding young women, also denudes
Them, removes jackets, exposing backs—
Summer moves many up the river in boats

Trailing their fingers in the shadowed water; they
Too move by the river, and in the water shadows
Trail a hand, which need not find a bank,
Face downward like bad fruit. Cathedrals and Building
Societies, as they appear, disappear; and Beethoven
Is played more loudly to deafen the Welsh echoes,
And Summer, blowing over the Mediterranean
Like swans, like perfect swans.

TO MY MOTHER

Most near, most dear, most loved and most far,
Under the window where I often found her
Sitting as huge as Asia, seismic with laughter,
Gin and chicken helpless in her Irish hand,
Irresistible as Rabelais, but most tender for
The lame dogs and hurt birds that surround her,—
She is a procession no one can follow after
But be like a little dog following a brass band.

She will not glance up at the bomber, or condescend
To drop her gin and scuttle to the cellar,
But lean on the mahogany table like a mountain
Whom only faith can move, and so I send
O all my faith and all my love to tell her
That she will move from mourning into morning.

332

LOVE POEM

GEORGE
BARKER

Then like the ship at rest in the bay
   I drop my sails and come home
To harbour in his arms and stay
   For ever harboured from harm.

On his foot's beach my combers ride
   The vaulted corals where he stands,
And spray against his rock of side
   Showers that fill his hands.

O whirlwinds catching up the sea
   And folding islands in its shawls,
Give him to me, give him to me,
   And I will wrap him in my shallows.

O the Red Sea parted long ago
   When the angel went whistling through,
My seas rise up in pride also
   To let his chariots through.

The masculine cliff-face gazes out
   At the smile of the horizon,
And disregards the sea that flaunts
   Her beauties by the dozen.

So he looks out over my subjugation
   Where the combers coil at his feet,
And sees, the far side of adulation,
My Hesperides rise singing, one moment, from
     the ocean,
   And the next, sinking, weep.

But from the altitude of his domination
   O sometimes like waterfalls,

GEORGE His hand comes down through a gravity of
BARKER   anticipation
          And a constellation of nuptials.

Nightly to his archipelagoes where
    Apples adorn the pillar,
My kiss of fishes moves in schools and bears
    The body to him on a silver platter.

The syzygies, over our Balkan bed,
    Shed silver on the peninsula,
Against whose shores my waters beat their head
    Like rain on a red star.

The narwhal with a spike on its brow
    Spins thrashing through the wave:
His love is mine, who lashes now
    In the sweat of seas I gave.

Then morning, like a monument
    Glittering in a tree,
Reminds me of a former moment
When the first star was immanent
And the mountain, dominant,
    Leaned down and kissed me.

NEWS OF THE WORLD

Cold shuttered loveless star, skulker in clouds,
    Streetwalker of the sky,
Where can you hide? No one will take you in.
Happy the morning lights up other worlds
As from sleep they turn a family of faces
To the houseproud sun. Outraged, you, outcast,
Leading your one-eyed sister through the night,
From door to door down the locked zodiac,
    Never come home.

GALWAY BAY

GEORGE
BARKER

With the gulls' hysteria above me
I walked near these breakneck seas
This morning of mists, and saw them,
Tall the mysterious queens
Waltzing in on the broad
Ballroom of the Atlantic.

All veils and waterfalls and
Wailings of the distraught,
These effigies of grief moved
Like refugees over the water;
The icy empresses of the Atlantic
Rising to bring me omen.

These women woven of ocean
And sorrows, these far sea figures,
With the fish and skull in their
Vapour of faces, the icicles
Salting down from their eyelashes,
As I walked by the foreshore

Moved towards me, ululating:
O dragnet of the sweet heart
Bind us no longer! The cage
Bursts with passions and bones,
And every highspirited fish
Lives off our scuttled love!

I stood on a stone, the gulls
Crossed my vision with wings
And my hearing with caterwauling;
The hurdling wave, backbroken,
Died at my feet. Taller
Than the towering hour above me

The homing empresses of the sea
Came among me. And, shivering,
I felt death nuzzling in the nest
Of the diurnally shipwrecked
Drowned nocturnally breast.

SONNET OF FISHES

Bright drips the morning from its trophied nets
Looped along a sky flickering fish and wings,
Cobbles like salmon crowd up waterfalling
Streets where life dies thrashing as the sea forgets,
True widow, what she has lost; and, ravished, lets
The knuckledustered sun shake bullying
A fist of glory over her. Every thing,
Even the sly night, gives up its lunar secrets.

And I with pilchards cold in my pocket make
Red-eyed a way to bed. But in my blood
Crying I hear, still, the leap of the silver diver
Caught in four cords after his fatal strake:
And then, the immense imminence not understood,
Death, in a dark, in a deep, in a dream, for ever.

336

DYLAN THOMAS

'LIGHT BREAKS WHERE NO SUN SHINES'

Light breaks where no sun shines;
Where no sea runs, the waters of the heart
Push in their tides;
And, broken ghosts with glowworms in their heads,
The things of light
File through the flesh where no flesh decks the bones.

A candle in the thighs
Warms youth and seed and burns the seeds of age;
Where no seed stirs,
The fruit of man unwrinkles in the stars,
Bright as a fig;
Where no wax is, the candle shows its hairs.

Dawn breaks behind the eyes;
From poles of skull and toe the windy blood
Slides like a sea;
Nor fenced, nor staked, the gushers of the sky
Spout to the rod
Divining in a smile the oil of tears.

Night in the sockets rounds,
Like some pitch moon, the limit of the globes;
Day lights the bone;
Where no cold is, the skinning gales unpin
The winter's robes;
The film of spring is hanging from the lids.

Light breaks on secret lots,
On tips of thought where thoughts smell in the rain;

DYLAN When logics die,
THOMAS The secret of the soil grows through the eye,
And blood jumps in the sun;
Above the waste allotments the dawn halts.

SHOULD LANTERNS SHINE

Should lanterns shine, the holy face,
Caught in an octagon of unaccustomed light,
Would wither up, and any boy of love
Look twice before he fell from grace.
The features in their private dark
Are formed of flesh, but let the false day come
And from her lips the faded pigments fall,
The mummy cloths expose an ancient breast.

I have been told to reason by the heart,
But heart, like head, leads helplessly;
I have been told to reason by the pulse,
And, when it quickens, alter the actions' pace
Till field and roof lie level and the same
So fast I move defying time, the quiet gentleman
Whose beard wags in Egyptian wind.

I have heard many years of telling,
And many years should see some change.

The ball I threw while playing in the park
Has not yet reached the ground.

338

AFTER THE FUNERAL

DYLAN
THOMAS

In memory of Ann Jones

After the funeral, mule praises, brays,
Windshake of sailshaped ears, muffle-toed tap
Tap happily of one peg in the thick
Grave's foot, blinds down the lids, the teeth in black,
The spittled eyes, the salt ponds in the sleeves,
Morning smack of the spade that wakes up sleep,
Shakes a desolate boy who slits his throat
In the dark of the coffin and sheds dry leaves,
That breaks one bone to light with a judgment clout,
After the feast of tear-stuffed time and thistles
In a room with a stuffed fox and a stale fern,
I stand, for this memorial's sake, alone
In the snivelling hours with dead, humped Ann
Whose hooded, fountain heart once fell in puddles
Round the parched worlds of Wales and drowned each
     sun
(Though this for her is a monstrous image blindly
Magnified out of praise; her death was a still drop;
She would not have me sinking in the holy
Flood of her heart's fame; she would lie dumb and
     deep
And need no druid of her broken body).
But I, Ann's bard on a raised hearth, call all
The seas to service that her wood-tongued virtue
Babble like a bellbuoy over the hymning heads,
Bow down the walls of the ferned and foxy woods
That her love sing and swing through a brown chapel,
Bless her bent spirit with four, crossing birds.
Her flesh was meek as milk, but this skyward statue
With the wild breast and blessed and giant skull
Is carved from her in a room with a wet window

DYLAN In a fiercely mourning house in a crooked year.
THOMAS I know her scrubbed and sour humble hands
Lie with religion in their cramp, her threadbare
Whisper in a damp word, her wits drilled hollow,
Her fist of a face died clenched on a round pain;
And sculptured Ann is seventy years of stone.
These cloud-sopped, marble hands, this monumental
Argument of the hewn voice, gesture and psalm
Storm me forever over her grave until
The stuffed lung of the fox twitch and cry Love
And the strutting fern lay seeds on the black sill.

A WINTER'S TALE

It is a winter's tale
That the snow blind twilight ferries over the lakes
And floating fields from the farm in the cup of the
vales,
Gliding windless through the hand folded flakes,
The pale breath of cattle at the stealthy sail,

And the stars falling cold,
And the smell of hay in the snow, and the far owl
Warning among the folds, and the frozen hold
Flocked with the sheep white smoke of the farm house
cowl
In the river wended vales where the tale was told.

Once when the world turned old
On a star of faith pure as the drifting bread,
As the food and flames of the snow, a man unrolled
The scrolls of fire that burned in his heart and head,
Torn and alone in a farm house in a fold

Of fields. And burning then
In his firelit island ringed by the winged snow
And the dung hills white as wool and the hen
Roosts sleeping chill till the flame of the cock crow
Combs through the mantled yards and the morning men

Stumble out with their spades,
The cattle stirring, the mousing cat stepping shy,
The puffed birds hopping and hunting, the milk maids
Gentle in their clogs over the fallen sky,
And all the woken farm at its white trades,

He knelt, he wept, he prayed,
By the spit and the black pot in the log bright light
And the cup and the cut bread in the dancing shade,
In the muffled house, in the quick of night,
At the point of love, forsaken and afraid.

He knelt on the cold stones,
He wept from the crest of grief, he prayed to the
      veiled sky
May his hunger go howling on bare white bones
Past the statues of the stables and the sky roofed sties
And the duck pond glass and the blinding byres alone

Into the home of prayers
And fires where he should prowl down the cloud
Of his snow blind love and rush in the white lairs.
His naked need struck him howling and bowed
Though no sound flowed down the hand folded air

But only the wind strung
Hunger of birds in the fields of the bread of water,
      tossed

DYLAN In high corn and the harvest melting on their tongues
THOMAS And his nameless need bound him burning and lost
When cold as snow he should run the wended vales
among

The rivers mouthed in night,
And drown in the drifts of his need, and lie curled
caught
In the always desiring centre of the white
Inhuman cradle and the bride bed forever sought
By the believer lost and the hurled outcast of light.

Deliver him, he cried,
By losing him all in love, and cast his need
Alone and naked in the engulfing bride,
Never to flourish in the fields of the white seed
Or flower under the time dying flesh astride.

Listen. The minstrels sing
In the departed villages. The nightingale,
Dust in the buried wood, flies on the grains of her
wings
And spells on the winds of the dead his winter's tale.
The voice of the dust of water from the withered spring

Is telling. The wizened
Stream with bells and baying water hounds. The dew
rings
On the gristed leaves and the long gone glistening
Parish of snow. The carved mouths in the rock are
wind swept strings.
Time sings through the intricately dead snow drop.
Listen.

342

It was a hand or sound

In the long ago land that glided the dark door wide
And there outside on the bread of the ground
A she bird rose and rayed like a burning bride.
A she bird dawned, and her breast with snow and
     scarlet downed.

Look. And the dancers move
On the departed, snow bushed green, wanton in
     moon light
As a dust of pigeons. Exulting, the grave hooved
Horses, centaur dead, turn and tread the drenched
     white
Paddocks in the farms of birds.   The dead oak walks
     for love.

The carved limbs in the rock
Leap, as to trumpets. Calligraphy of the old
Leaves is dancing. Lines of age on the stones weave
     in a flock.
And the harp shaped voice of the water's dust
     plucks in a fold
Of fields. For love, the long ago she bird rises. Look.

And the wild wings were raised
Above her folded head, and the soft feathered voice
Was flying through the house as though the she bird
     praised
And all the elements of the slow fall rejoiced
That a man knelt alone in the cup of the vales,

In the mantle and calm,
By the spit and the black pot in the log bright light.
And the sky of birds in the plumed voice charmed
Him up and he ran like a wind after the kindling flight
Past the blind barns and byres of the windless farm.

343

DYLAN
THOMAS
In the poles of the year
When black birds died like priests in the cloaked
　　　hedge row
And over the cloth of counties the far hills rode near,
Under the one leaved trees ran a scarecrow of snow
And fast through the drifts of the thickets antlered
　　　like deer,

　　　　　Rags and prayers down the knee-
Deep hillocks and loud on the numbed lakes,
All night lost and long wading in the wake of the she-
Bird through the times and lands and tribes of the
　　　slow flakes.
Listen and look where she sails the goose plucked sea,

　　　　　The sky, the bird, the bride,
The cloud, the need, the planted stars, the joy beyond
The fields of seed and the time dying flesh astride,
The heavens, the heaven, the grave, the burning font.
In the far ago land the door of his death glided wide,

　　　　　And the bird descended.
On a bread white hill over the cupped farm
And the lakes and floating fields and the river wended
Vales where he prayed to come to the last harm
And the home of prayers and fires, the tale ended.

　　　　　The dancing perishes
On the white, no longer growing green, and,
　　　minstrel dead,
The singing breaks in the snow shoed villages of
　　　wishes
That once cut the figures of birds on the deep bread
And over the glazed lakes skated the shapes of fishes

Flying. The rite is shorn
Of nightingale and centaur dead horse. The springs
    wither
Back. Lines of age sleep on the stones till trumpeting
    dawn.
Exultation lies down. Time buries the spring weather
That belled and bounded with the fossil and the dew
    reborn.

    For the bird lay bedded
In a choir of wings, as though she slept or died,
And the wings glided wide and he was hymned and
    wedded,
And through the thighs of the engulfing bride,
The woman breasted and the heaven headed

    Bird, he was brought low,
Burning in the bride bed of love, in the whirl-
Pool at the wanting centre, in the folds
Of paradise, in the spun bud of the world.
And she rose with him flowering in her melting snow.

DAVID GASCOYNE

MISERERE

'*It is finished*.' The last nail
Has consummated the inhuman pattern, and the veil
Is torn. God's wounds are numbered.
All is now withdrawn: void yawns
The rock-hewn tomb. There is no more
Regeneration in the stricken sun,
The hope of faith no more,
No height no depth no sign
And no more history.

Thus may it be: and worse.
And may we know Thy perfect darkness.
And may we into Hell descend with Thee.

PIETA

Stark in the pasture on the skull-shaped hill,
In swollen aura of disaster shrunken and
Unsheltered by the ruin of the sky,
Intensely concentrated in themselves the banded
Saints abandoned kneel.

And under the unburdened tree
Great in their midst, the rigid folds
Of a blue cloak upholding as a text
Her grief-scrawled face for the ensuing world to read,
The Mother, whose dead Son's dear head

Weighs like a precious blood-incrusted stone
On her unfathomable breast:
Holds Him God has forsaken, Word made flesh
Made ransom, to the slow smoulder of her heart
Till the catharsis of the race shall be complete.

DE PROFUNDIS

Out of these depths:

Where footsteps wander in the marsh of death and an
Intense infernal glare is on our faces facing down:
Out of these depths, what shamefaced cry

Half choked in the dry throat, as though a stone
Were our confounded tongue, can ever rise:
Because the mind has been struck blind
And may no more conceive
Thy Throne . . . .

Because the depths
Are clear with only death's
Marsh-light, because the rock of grief
Is clearly too extreme for us to breach:
Deepen our depths,

And aid our unbelief.

KYRIE

Is man's destructive lust insatiable? There is
Grief in the blow that shatters the innocent face.
Pain blots out clearer sense. And pleasure suffers
The trial thrust of death in even the bride's embrace.

The black catastrophe that can lay waste our worlds
May be unconsciously desired. Fear masks our face;
And tears as warm and cruelly wrung as blood
Are tumbling even in the mouth of our grimace.

How can our hope ring true ? Fatality of guilt
And complicated anguish confounds time and place ;
While from the tottering ancestral house an angry
     voice
Resounds in prophecy. Grant us extraordinary grace,

O spirit hidden in the dark in us and deep,
And bring to light the dream out of our sleep.

LACHRYMAE

Slow are the years of light:
                 and more immense
Than the imagination. And the years return
Until the Unity is filled. And heavy are
The lengths of Time with the slow weight of tears.
Since Thou didst weep, on a remote hill-side
Beneath the olive-trees, fires of unnumbered stars
Have burnt the years away, until we see them now:
Since Thou didst weep, as many tears
Have flowed like hourglass sand.
Thy tears were all.
And when our secret face
Is blind because of the mysterious
Surging of tears wrung by our most profound
Presentiment of evil in man's fate, our cruellest
     wounds
Become Thy stigmata. They are Thy tears which fall.

EX NIHILO

Here am I now cast down
Beneath the black glare of a netherworld's
Dead suns, dust in my mouth, among
Dun tiers no tears refresh: am cast
Down by a lofty hand,

Hand that I love! Lord Light,   DAVID
How dark is Thy arm's will and ironlike   GAS-
Thy ruler's finger that has sent me here!   COYNE
Far from Thy Face I nothing understand,
But kiss the Hand that has consigned

Me to these latter years where I must learn
The revelation of despair, and find
Among the debris of all certainties
The hardest stone on which to found
Altar and shelter for Eternity.

SANCTUS

Incomprehensible—
O Master—fate and mystery
And message and long-promised
Revelation! Murmur of the leaves
Of life's prolific tree in the dark haze
Of midsummer: and inspiration of the blood
In the ecstatic secret bed: and bare
Inscription on a prison wall, 'For thou shalt persevere
In thine identity. . .': a momentary glimpsed
Escape into the golden dance of dust
Beyond the window. These are all.

Uncomprehending. But to understand
Is to endure, withstand the withering blight
Of winter night's long desperation, war,
Confusion, till at the dense core
Of this existence all the spirit's force
Becomes acceptance of blind eyes
To see no more. Then they may see at last;
And all they see their vision sanctifies.

349

Whose is this horrifying face,
This putrid flesh, discoloured, flayed,
Fed on by flies, scorched by the sun?
Whose are these hollow red-filmed eyes
And thorn-spiked head and spear-stuck side?
Behold the Man: He is Man's Son.

Forget the legend, tear the decent veil
That cowardice or interest devised
To make their mortal enemy a friend,
To hide the bitter truth all His wounds tell,
Lest the great scandal be no more disguised:
He is in agony till the world's end,

And we must never sleep during that time!
He is suspended on the cross-tree now
And we are onlookers at the crime,
Callous contemporaries of the slow
Torture of God. Here is the hill
Made ghastly by His spattered blood

Whereon He hangs and suffers still:
See, the centurions wear riding-boots,
Black shirts and badges and peaked caps,
Greet one another with raised-arm salutes;
They have cold eyes, unsmiling lips;
Yet these His brothers know not what they do.

And on his either side hang dead
A labourer and a factory-hand,
Or one is maybe a lynched Jew
And one a Negro or a Red,

Coolie or Ethiopian, Irishman,
Spaniard or German democrat.

DAVID
GAS-
COYNE

Behind his lolling head the sky
Glares like a fiery cataract
Red with the murders of two thousand years
Committed in His name and by
Crusaders, Christian warriors
Defending faith and property.

Amid the plain beneath His transfixed hands,
Exuding darkness as indelible
As guilty stains, fanned by funereal
And lurid airs, besieged by drifting sands
And clefted landslides our about-to-be
Bombed and abandoned cities stand.

He who wept for Jerusalem
Now sees his prophecy extend
Across the greatest cities of the world,
A guilty panic reason cannot stem
Rising to raze them all as He foretold;
And He must watch the drama to the end.

Though often named, He is unknown
To the dark kingdoms at His feet
Where everything disparages His words,
And each man bears the common guilt alone
And goes blindfolded to his fate,
And fear and greed are sovereign lords.

The turning point of history
Must come. Yet the complacent and the proud
And who exploit and kill, may be denied—
Christ of Revolution and of Poetry—

DAVID
GAS-
COYNE The resurrection and the life
Wrought by your spirit's blood.

Involved in their own sophistry
The black priest and the upright man
Faced by subversive truth shall be struck dumb,
Christ of Revolution and of Poetry,
And the rejected and condemned become
Agents of the divine.

Not from a monstrance silver-wrought
But from the tree of human pain
Redeem our sterile misery,
Christ of Revolution and of Poetry,
That man's long journey through the night
May not have been in vain.

SEPTEMBER SUN : 1947

Magnificent strong sun! in these last days
So prodigally generous of pristine light
That's wasted only by men's sight who will not see
And by self-darkened spirits from whose night
Can rise no longer orison or praise:

Let us consume in fire unfed like yours
And may the quickened gold within me come
To mintage in due season, and not be
Transmuted to no better end than dumb
And self-sufficient usury. These days and years

May bring the sudden call to harvesting,
When if the fields Man labours only yield
Glitter and husks, then with an angrier sun may He
Who first with His gold seed the sightless field
Of Chaos planted, all our trash to cinders bring.

Additional Poets
CHARLES WILLIAMS

THE CROWNING OF ARTHUR

The king stood crowned; around in the gate,
midnight striking, torches and fires
massing the colour, casting the metal,
furnace of jubilee, through time and town,
Logres heraldically flaunted the king's state.

The lords sheathed their swords; they camped
by Camelot's wall; thick-tossed torches,
tall candles flared, opened, deployed;
between them rose the beasts of the banners;
flaring over all the king's dragon ramped.

Wars were at end; the king's friend stood
at the king's side; Lancelot's lion
had roared in the pattern the king's mind cherished,
in charges completing the strategy of Arthur;
the king's brain working in Lancelot's blood.

Presaging intelligence of time climbed,
Merlin climbed, through the dome of Stephen,
over chimneys and churches; from the point of
    Camelot
he looked through the depth to the dome of Sophia;
the kingdom and the power and the glory chimed.

He turned where the fires, amid burning mail,
poured, tributaried by torches and candles,
to a point in a massive of colour, one
aureole flame; the first shield's deep azure,
sidereally pointed, the lord Percivale.

CHARLES Driving back that azure a sea rose black;
WILLIAMS on a fess of argent rode a red moon.
The Queen Morgause leaned from a casement;
her forehead's moon swallowed the fires,
it was crimson on the bright-banded sable of Lamorack.

The tincture changed; ranged the craft
of the king's new champion in a crimson field;
mockery in mockery, a dolphin naiant;
a silver fish under bloody waters,
conquered or conquering, Dinadan laughed.

A pelican in golden piety struck well
The triple bloody drops from its wound;
in strong nurture of instinct, it smote
for its young its breast; the shield of Bors
bore its rich fervours, to itself most fell.

Shouldering shapes through the skies rise and run,
through town and time; Merlin beheld
the beasts of Broceliande, the fish of Nimue,
hierarchic, republican, the glory of Logres,
patterns of the Logos in the depth of the sun.

Taliessin in the crowd beheld the compelled brutes,
wildness formalized, images of mathematics,
star and moon, dolphin and pelican,
lion and leopard, changing their measure.
Over the mob's noise rose gushing the sound of the
      flutes.

Gawaine's thistle, Bedivere's rose, drew near:
flutes infiltrating the light of candles.
Through the magical sound of the fire-strewn air,

354

spirit, burning to sweetness of body,
exposed in the midst of its bloom the young queen
    Guinevere.

Lancelot moved to descend; the king's friend kneeled,
the king's organic motion, the king's mind's blood,
the lion in the blood roaring through the mouth of
    creation
as the lions roar that stand in the Byzantine glory.
Guinevere's chalice flew red on an argent field.

So, in Lancelot's hand, she came through the glow,
into the king's mind, who stood to look on his city:
the king made for the kingdom, or the kingdom made
    for the king?
Thwart drove his current against the current of Merlin:
In beleaguered Sophia they sang of the dolorous blow.

Doom in shocks sprinkled the burning gloom,
molten metals and kindling colours pouring
into the pyre; at the zenith lion and dragon
rose, clawed, twisted, screamed;
Taliessin beheld a god lie in his tomb.

At the door of the gloom sparks die and revive;
the spark of Logres fades, glows, fades.
It is the first watch; the Pope says Matins in Lateran;
the hollow call is beaten on the board in Sophia;
the ledge of souls shudders, whether they die or live.

EDWIN MUIR

THE ROAD

There is a road that turning always
    Cuts off the country of Again.
Archers stand there on every side
    And as it runs Time's deer is slain,
    And lies where it has lain.

That busy clock shows never an hour.
    All flies and all in flight must tarry.
The hunter shoots the empty air
    Far on before the quarry,
    Which falls though nothing's there to parry.

The lion couching in the centre
    With mountain head and sunset brow
Rolls down the everlasting slope
    Bones picked an age ago,
    And the bones rise up and go.

There the beginning finds the end
    Before the beginning ever can be,
And the great runner never leaves
    The starting and the finishing tree,
    The budding and the fading tree.

There the ship sailing safe in harbour
    Long since in many a sea was drowned.
The treasure burning in her hold
    So near will never be found,
    Sunk past all sound.

There a man on a summer evening
Reclines at ease upon his tomb
And is his mortal effigy.
And there within the womb,
The cell of doom,

The ancestral deed is thought and done,
And in a million Edens fall
A million Adams drowned in darkness,
For small is great and great is small,
And a blind seed all.

THE FACE

See me with all the terrors on my roads,
The crusted shipwrecks rotting in my seas,
And the untroubled oval of my face
That alters idly with the moonlike modes
And is unfathomably framed to please
And deck the angular bone with passing grace.

I should have worn a terror-mask, should be
A sight to frighten hope and faith away,
Half charnel field, half battle and rutting ground.
Instead I am a smiling summer sea
That sleeps while underneath from bound to bound
The sun- and star-shaped killers gorge and play.

THE OLD GODS

Old gods and goddesses who have lived so long
Through time and never found eternity,
Fettered by wasting wood and hollowing hill,

357

EDWIN You should have fled our ever-dying song,
 MUIR The mound, the well, and the green trysting tree
       They are forgotten, yet you linger still.

       Goddess of caverned breast and channelled brow
       And cheeks slow hollowed by millenial tears,
       Forests of autumns fading in your eyes,

       Eternity marvels at your counted years
       And kingdoms lost in time, and wonders how
       There could be thoughts so bountiful and wise

       As yours beneath the ever-breaking bough,
       And vast compassion curving like the skies.

THE TRANSFIGURATION

So from the ground we felt that virtue branch
Through all our veins till we were whole, our wrists
As fresh and pure as water from a well,
Our hands made new to handle holy things,
The source of all our seeing rinsed and cleansed
Till earth and light and water entering there
Gave back to us the clear unfallen world.
We would have thrown our clothes away for lightness,
But that even they, though sour and travel stained,
Seemed, like our flesh, made of immortal substance,
And the soiled flax and wool lay light upon us
Like friendly wonders, flower and flock entwined
As in a morning field. Was it a vision?
Or did we see that day the unseeable
One glory of the everlasting world
Perpetually at work, though never seen

Since Eden locked the gate that's everywhere
And nowhere? Was the change in us alone,
And the enormous earth still left forlorn,
An exile or a prisoner? Yet the world
We saw that day made this unreal, for all
Was in its place. The painted animals
Assembled there in gentle congregations,
Or sought apart their leafy oratories,
Or walked in peace, the wild and tame together,
As if, also for them, the day had come.
The shepherds' hovels shone, for underneath
The soot we saw the stone clean at the heart
As on the starting-day. The refuse heaps
Were grained with that fine dust that made the world;
For he had said, 'To the pure all things are pure.'
And when we went into the town, he with us,
The lurkers under doorways, murderers,
With rags tied round their feet for silence, came
Out of themselves to us and were with us,
And those who hide within the labyrinth
Of their own loneliness and greatness came,
And those entangled in their own devices,
The silent and the garrulous liars, all
Stepped out of their own dungeons and were free.
Reality or vision, this we have seen.
If it had lasted but another moment
It might have held for ever! But the world
Rolled back into its place, and we are here,
And all that radiant kingdom lies forlorn,
As if it had never stirred; no human voice
Is heard among its meadows, but it speaks
To itself alone, alone it flowers and shines
And blossoms for itself while time runs on.

EDWIN
MUIR

EDWIN   But he will come again, it's said, though not
MUIR   Unwanted and unsummoned; for all things,
        Beasts of the field, and woods, and rocks, and seas,
        And all mankind from end to end of the earth
        Will call him with one voice. In our own time,
        Some say, or at a time when time is ripe.
        Then he will come, Christ the uncrucified,
        Christ the discrucified, his death undone,
        His agony unmade, his cross dismantled—
        Glad to be so—and the tormented wood
        Will cure its hurt and grow into a tree
        In a green springing corner of young Eden,
        And Judas damned take his long journey backward
        From darkness into light and be a child
        Beside his mother's knee, and the betrayal
        Be quite undone and never more be done.

THE TOY HORSE

See him, the gentle Bible beast,
With lacquered hoofs and curling mane,
His wondering journey from the East
Half done, between the rock and plain,

His little kingdom at his feet
Through which the silver rivulets flow,
For while his hoofs in silence beat
Beside him Eden and Canaan go.

The great leaves turn and then are still.
Page after page through deepening day
He steps, and from each morning hill
Beholds his stationary way.

360

His lifted foot commands the West,
And, lingering, halts the turning sun;
Endless departure, endless rest,
End and beginning here are one.

Dumb wooden idol, you have led
Millions on your calm pilgrimage
Between the living and the dead,
And shine yet in your golden age.

MICHAEL ROBERTS

SHINING DARK

Scatter grey ash to the darkness, break
The jar, the brittle urn, to the bleak
Inhuman north, and the dark wind—

Crumble the trivial husk, the shell
And claim, O firm substantial Earth,
The living pulse and the quick sap
From the green shoot and the cunning skull,

Take it; and take the unsullied lake,
The song, the unconquered hill, the alert
Touch, and the glance, and a man's strength—

Take it; you can but take it once—
The gentian hour and the sun's light;
Pride of young earth and living limb,

Take: Calcine the amorphous dust,
Destroy the inert substratum, break
Too late, the pattern: dust attains,
Quicker than tardy death, the shining dark—

Beethoven deaf and Milton blind,
Melville, forsaken of the valiant mind,
Beyond the inhuman pattern, men,
Broken, ephemeral, undismayed.

IN THE STRANGE ISLE

MICHAEL
ROBERTS

In the strange isle,
In the green freckled wood and grassy glade,
Strangely the man, the panther and the shadow
Move by the well and the white stones.

Voices cry out in trees, and fingers beckon,
The wings of a million butterflies are sunlit eyes,
There is no sword
In the enchanted wood.

Branches bend over like a terror,
The sun is darkened,
The white wind and the sun and the curling wave
Cradle the coral shore and the tall forest.

Ceaseless the struggle in the twining circles,
The gulls, the doves, and the dark crows;
The fangs of the lily bleed, and the lips
Of the rose are torn.

Trees crash at midnight unpredicted,
Voices cry out,
Naked he walks, and with no fear,
In the strange isle, the wise and gentle.

THE WORLD'S END

Those who have visited the North Pole
Or other pubs beyond a two-mile limit
Will know, at least by hearsay, this one, too.
Here is no glory of the Star and Garter,
Nor the obscure theology of the Goat and Compasses,
But a somewhat plain home truth,
That the world lives by labour and barter,
And all things, in the long run, end up shabby.

Here is the ash of history. But we recall
When fire came down from heaven and the house
    rocked
(A sensation mildly exhilarating to those in love with
    life)
And we remember tracer-bullets and the white flares,
And a general atmosphere of form and colour,
With possible extinction giving flavour to the stewed
    pears.

Well, here is the World's End, or so it seems;
But Oh, my love, tenacity is all:
'Her years of pain and glory' are not ended.
Silent, invisible, the bombs explode,
The dead and wounded walk the cancelled streets,
Colour and form run through the brittle pages,
And Time can crumble all, but cannot touch
The book that burns, faster than we can read.

VERNON WATKINS

THE TURNING OF THE LEAVES

Not yet! Do not yet touch,
Break not this branch of silver-birch,
Nor ask the stealthy river why it laves
Black roots that feed the leaves.

Ask first the flickering wren.
He will move further. Ask the rain.
No drop, though round, through that white miracle
Will sink, to be your oracle.

Not yet! Do not yet bend
Close to that root so tightly bound
Loosened by creeping waters as they run
Along the fork's rough groin.

Ask not the water yet
Why the root's tapering tendrils eat
Parched earth away that they may be
Nearer the source those fibres must obey.

Behind the bark your hands will find
No Sycorax or flying Daphne faned
And the brown ignorant water bindweed breeds
Not caring there what brows it braids.

Light in the branches weaves.
Hard is the waiting moment while it waves,
This tree whose trunk curves upward from the stream
Where faltering ripples strum.

VERNON See how it hangs in air.
WATKINS The leaves are turning now. We cannot hear
The death and birth of life. But that disguise,
Look up now, softly: break it with your eyes.

MUSIC OF COLOURS—WHITE BLOSSOM ...

White blossom, white, white shell; the Nazarene
Walking in the ear; white touched by souls
Who know the music by which white is seen,
Blinding white, from strings and aureoles,
Until that is not white, seen at the two poles,
Nor white the Scythian hills, nor Marlowe's queen.

The spray looked white until this snowfall.
Now the foam is grey, the wave is dull.
Call nothing white again, we were deceived.
The flood of Noah dies, the rainbow is lived.
Yet from the deluge of illusions an unknown colour is
        saved.

White must die black, to be born white again
From the womb of sounds, the inscrutable grain,
From the crushed, dark fibre, breaking in pain.

The bud of the apple is already forming there.
The cherry-bud, too, is firm, and behind it the pear
Conspires with the racing cloud. I shall not look.
The rainbow is diving through the wide-open book
Past the rustling paper of birch, the sorceries of bark.

Buds in April, on the waiting branch,
Starrily opening, light raindrops drench,
Swinging from world to world when starlings sweep,

Where they alight in air, are white asleep.
They will not break, not break, until you say
White is not white again, nor may may.

White flowers die soonest, die into that chaste
Bride-bed of the moon, their lives laid waste.
Lilies of Solomon, taken by the gust,
Sigh, make way. And the dark forest
Haunts the lowly crib near Solomon's dust
Rocked to the end of majesty, warmed by the low
    beast,
Locked in the liberty of his tremendous rest.

If there is white, or has been white, it must have been
When His eyes looked down and made the leper clean.
White will not be, apart, though the trees try
Spirals of blossom, their green conspiracy.
She who touched His garment saw no white tree.

Lovers speak of Venus, and the white doves,
Jubilant, the white girl, myth's whiteness, Jove's,
Of Leda, the swan, whitest of his loves.
Lust imagines him, web-footed Jupiter, great down
Of thundering light; love's yearning pulls him down
On the white swan-breast, the magical lawn,
Involved in plumage, mastered by the veins of dawn.

In the churchyard the yew is neither green nor black
I know nothing of Earth or colour until I know I lack
Original white, by which the ravishing bird looks wan.
The mound of dust is nearer, white of mute dust that
    dies
In the soundfall's greatest light, the music in the eyes,
Transfiguring whiteness into shadows gone,
Utterly secret. I know you, black swan.

FOAL

Darkness is not dark, nor sunlight the light of the sun
But a double journey of insistent silver hooves.
Light wakes in the foal's blind eyes as lightning
    illuminates corn
With a rustle of fine-eared grass, where a starling
    shivers.

And whoever watches a foal sees two images,
Delicate, circling, born, the spirit with blind eyes
    leaping
And the left spirit, vanished yet here, the vessel of ages
Clay-cold, blue, laid low by her great wide belly the
    hill.

See him break that circle, stooping to drink, to suck
His mother, vaulted with a beautiful hero's back
Arched under the singing mane,
Shaped to her shining, pricked into awareness
By the swinging dug, amazed by the movement of suns;
His blue fellow has run again down into grass,
And he slips from that mother to the boundless
    horizons of air,
Looking for that other, the foal no longer there.

But perhaps
In the darkness under the tufted thyme and down-
    trodden winds,
In the darkness under the violet's roots, in the darkness
    of the pitcher's music,
In the uttermost darkness of a vase
There is still the print of fingers, the shadow of waters.
And under the dry, curled parchment of the soil
    there is always a little foal
Asleep.

So the whole morning he runs here, fulfilling the track VERNON
Of so many suns; vanishing the mole's way, moving WATKINS
Into mole's mysteries under the zodiac,
Racing, stopping in the circle. Startled he stands
Dazzled, where darkness is green, where the sunlight
    is black,
While his mother, grazing, is moving away
From the lagging star of those stars, the unrisen
    wonder
In the path of the dead, fallen from the sun in her hooves
And eluding the dead hands, begging him to play.

A CHRISTENING REMEMBERED

(for Rhiannon)

Water of life no prophet could divine,
Whose eyes now know a month more light than shade:
The font in your awakening is waylaid,
Where fell that christening moment from the vine.
If I look deeply there, I see time fade
And light grow perfect, dark; and darkness shine.
Again I see the curve her body made,
Bearing you like a pitcher doomed to wine.

That ancient miracle makes moist your lip
With Cana's feast; and babblings none could spell
Recall great buckets that a chain let slip
Down the dark, echoing walls of some deep well
Where a stone, plunging, woke you from your sleep:
Your angel spoke the moment that it fell.

E. J. SCOVELL

THE FIRST YEAR

II

Before she first had smiled or looked with calm
Light-answering eyes and claimed to be of man
I put my finger in her shadowy palm,
And her own whispering ones from their chestnut fan
Closed again (as they must) on mine, to a bud.
Then I was where strong currents piled and slackened.
Like a pulse telling all the power of blood
This palm seemed the cavern where alone her darkened
And secret rock-roofed river showed to man
(Except when one inside half-raised the blind
Of her inky eyes, and fierce a dark beam ran
Searchlighting day). So I strayed on her mind;
And thought I trespassed in that covered land.
Her hand seemed private, still an unborn hand.

XI

When the old sleep, a sadness moves beholders;
And when the strong mature, whose shoulders
Support the world in their generation's hour—
Strangely sleep's weakness lies with power;
But when you sleep, sleep only seems your other
Self, your flower's leaf, your brother.

Sleep's unknowing, where so little's known,
Is a lamb with a lamb lying down,
And sleep's imprudence and unguarded nature
You wear like any thornless creature,

Open, upturned to dangerous nights and days
Like scabious where the cattle graze.

E. J.
SCOVELL

Not fast like ours your categories seem;
Your dreams play with your waking dream.
And bold all visions come into your net—
The rage of thought not on you yet,
That frightens the many to a standing stone
So it may seize and have the one.

Not at the pillow end of your big bed
You sleep, but where your wandering head
Happens to tire and rest. So sometimes, thrown
Far out on your blue eiderdown,
You seem a sleeping sea-bird, guarded best
By yielding to the sea, wild sea its friend and nest.

THE SWAN'S FEET

Who is this whose feet
Close on the water,
Like muscled leaves darker than ivy
Blown back and curved by unwearying wind?
They, that thrust back the water,
Softly crumple now and close, stream in his wake.

These dank weeds are also
Part and plumage of the magnolia-flowering swan.
He puts forth these too—
Leaves of ridged and bitter ivy
Sooted in towns, coal-bright with rain.

He is not moved by winds in air
Like the vain boats on the lake.

371

E. J. Lest you think him too a flower of parchment,
SCOVELL Scentless magnolia,
See his living feet under the water fanning.
In the leaves' self blows the efficient wind
That opens and bends closed those leaves.

EVENING SCENE

The waves lay down their trail,
On the brown water feathers of foam.
Over the dark bituminous sands
The stragglers loiter home.

Where the stream seeps to sea
And the sands are tarnished glass to the sky
They walk as if on evening light,
They run and seem to fly.

The shallow acre-wide
Waves of low tide swathe their feet like a meadow.
Surely they feel themselves unmade,
Spirits that cast no shadow.

I see them small, distinct,
Dark, and see on the sheen of what wings they fly,
The two lit wings of land and sea,
The one vane of the sky;

And see, not near nor far,
The black-brown cliffs stand with their slopes of green
Stippled with darkness. All of space
Is the sand's width between.

KATHLEEN RAINE

THE CRYSTAL SKULL

At the focus of thought there is no face,
the focus of the sun is in crystal with no shadow.
Death of the victim is the power of the god.

Out of the eyes is the focus of love,
the face of love is the sun, that all see,
the skull of the victim is the temple of sight.

The eyes of the victim are the crystal of divination.
Sun clears the colours of life.
The crystal of the skull is the work of the sun.

The stone of my destruction casts no shadow.
The sun kills perfectly with the stroke of noon.
The clarity of the crystal is the atonement of the god.

The perfection of man is the pride of death,
the crystal skull is the perpetuity of life.
The power of the god is the taking of love.

The perfection of light is the destruction of the world,
death and love turn the faces of day and night.
The illumination of the skull is the joy of the god.

THE SILVER STAG

My silver stag is fallen—on the grass
Under the birch-trees he lies, my king of the woods,
That I followed on the mountain, over the swift
        streams,
He is gone under the leaves, under the past.

KATH- On the horizon of the dawn he stood,
LEEN The target of my eager sight; that shone
RAINE Oh from the sun, or from my kindled heart—
       Outlined in sky, shaped on the infinite.

       What, so desiring, was my will with him,
       What wished-for union of blood or thought
       In single passion held us, hunter and victim?
       Already gone, when into the branched woods I
              pursued him.

       Mine he is now, my desired, my awaited, my beloved,
       Quiet he lies, as I touch the contours of his proud
              head,
       Mine, this horror, this carrion of the wood,
       Already melting underground, into the air, out of the
              world.

       Oh, the stillness, the peace about me
       As the garden lives on, the flowers bloom,
       The fine grass shimmers, the flies burn,
       And the stream, the silver stream, runs by.

       Lying for the last time down on the green ground
       In farewell gesture of self-love, softly he curved
       To rest the delicate foot that is in my hand,
       Empty as a moth's discarded chrysalis.

       My bright yet blind desire, your end was this
       Death, and my winged heart murderous
       Is the world's broken heart, buried in his,
       Between whose antlers starts the crucifix.

ISIS WANDERER

KATH-
LEEN
RAINE

This too is an experience of the soul
The dismembered world that once was the whole god
Whose broken fragments now lie dead.
This passing of reality itself is real.

Gathering under my black cloak the remnants of life
That lie dishonoured among people and places
I search the twofold desert of my solitude,
The outward perished world, and the barren mind.

Once he was present, numinous, in the house of the
        world,
Wearing day like a garment, his beauty manifest
In corn and man as he journeyed down the fertile
        river
With love he filled my distances of night.

I trace the contour of his hand fading upon a cloud,
And this his blood flows from a dying soldier's wound.
In broken fields his body is scattered and his limbs lie
Spreadeagled like wrecked fuselage in the sand.

His skull is a dead cathedral, and his crown's rays
Glitter from worthless tins and broken glass.
His blue eyes are reflected from pools in the gutter,
And his strength is the desolate stone of fallen cities.

Oh in the kitchen-midden of my dreams
Turning over the potsherds of past days
Shall I uncover his loved desecrated face?
Are the unfathomed depths of sleep his grave?

KATH- Beyond the looming dangerous end of night
LEEN Beneath the vaults of fear do his bones lie,
RAINE And does the maze of nightmare lead to the power
        within?
        Do menacing nether waters cover the fish king?

        I piece the divine fragments into the mandala
        Whose centre is the lost creative power,
        The sun, the heart of God, the lotus, the electron
        That pulses world upon world, ray upon ray
        That he who lived on the first may rise on the last day.

THE PYTHONESS

(For John Hayward)

I am that serpent-haunted cave
Whose navel breeds the fates of men.
All wisdom issues from a hole in the earth:
The gods form in my darkness, and dissolve again.

From my blind womb all kingdoms come,
And from my grave seven sleepers prophesy.
No babe unborn but wakens to my dream,
No lover but at last entombed in me shall lie.

I am that feared and longed-for burning place
Where man and phoenix are consumed away,
And from my low polluted bed arise
New sons, new suns, new skies.

376

BERNARD SPENCER

DELOS

Wealth came by water to this farmless island;
Dolphins with backs like bows swim in mosaic
Floors where the Greek sea-captains piled up money;
And the jagged circular patterns spin with the rush of
The impetus and fling of waves.

Steps go down to the port. And in this area
You could buy corn and oil or men and women.
Above on the windy hill Leto the human
Bore her birth pains, gave two gods to a legend
Glittering and loveless like the sea.

Slavery, we know, was not of the market only.
Here specially were rich and poor, priests and their
        pennies.
Imperial slavery we know. But the salt Aegean
Rolled waves of flame and killing, quarrels of aliens,
Till life here burst and was quiet.

In the boulevards of these dead you will think of
        violence,
Holiness and violence, violence of sea that is bluer
Than blue eyes are; violence of sun and its worship;
Of money and its worship. And it was here by the
        breakers
 That strangers asked for the truth.

OLIVE TREES

The dour thing in olive trees
   is that their trunks are stooped like never dying
      crones,
   and they camp where roads climb, and drink with
      dust and stones.

The pleasant thing is how in the heat
   their plumage brushes the sight with a bird's-wing
      feeling:
   and perhaps the gold of their oil is mild with dreams
      of healing.

The cold thing is how they were
   there at the start of us; and one grey look surveyed
   the builder imagining the city, the historian with his
      spade.

The warm thing is that they are
   first promise of the South to waking travellers:
   of the peacock sea, and the islands and their boulder-
      lumbered spurs.

SARCOPHAGI

Excellent ritual of oils, of anointing,
office of priests;
everything was paid before these dead put on
the armless dress of their sarcophagi,
lying down in Phoenicia,

pillowing their heavy sculptured heads, their broad
foreheads like rides of sand, the rock of the chin,

the mouth, the simple map of the face, the carved
hair in full sail.

Surrender of sunlight and market and the white
loops of the coast,
was simply a journey, a bargain rigid as stone:
though youth took passage.

Stretched by the salt and echoing roads to the West
twenty-six bargain-makers of Phoenicia;
twenty-six dead with wide eyes,
confident of harbour.

W. R. RODGERS

LIFE'S CIRCUMNAVIGATORS

Here, where the taut wave hangs
Its tented tons, we steer
Through rocking arch of eye
And creaking reach of ear,
Anchored to flying sky,
And chained to changing fear.

O when shall we, all spent,
Row in to some far strand,
And find, to our content,
The original land
From which our boat once went,
Though not the one we planned.

Us on that happy day
This fierce sea will release,
On our rough face of clay,
The final glaze of peace.
Our oars we all will lay
Down, and desire will cease.

NEITHER HERE NOR THERE

In that land all Is, and nothing's Ought;
No owners or notices, only birds;
No walls anywhere, only lean wire of words
Worming brokenly out from eaten thought;
No oats growing, only ankle-lace grass
Easing and not resenting the feet that pass;

No enormous beasts, only names of them;
No bones made, bans laid, or boons expected,
No contracts, entails, hereditaments,
Anything at all that might tie or hem.

W. R.
RODGERS

In that land all's lackadaisical;
No lakes of coddled spawn, and no locked ponds
Of settled purpose, no netted fishes;
But only inkling streams and running fronds
Fritillaried with dreams, weedy with wishes;
Nor arrogant talk is heard, haggling phrase,
But undertones, and hesitance, and haze;
On clear days mountains of meaning are seen
Humped high on the horizon; no one goes
To con their meaning, no one cares or knows.

In that land all's flat, indifferent; there
Is neither springing house nor hanging tent,
No aims are entertained, and nothing is meant,
For there are no ends or trends, no roads,
Only follow your nose to anywhere.
No one is born there, no one stays or dies,
For it is a timeless land, it lies
Between the act and the attrition, it
Marks off bound from rebound, make from break, tit
From tat, also to-day from to-morrow.
No Cause there comes to term, but each departs
Elsewhere to whelp its deeds, expel its darts;
There are no homecomings, of course, no good-byes
In that land, neither yearning nor scorning,
Though at night there is the smell of morning.

LAWRENCE DURRELL

IN ARCADIA

By divination came the Dorians,
Under a punishment composed an arch.
They invented this valley, they taught
The rock to flow with odourless water.

Fire and a brute art came among them.

Rain fell, tasting of the sky.
Trees grew, composing a grammar.
The river, the river you see was brought down
By force of prayer upon this fertile floor.

Now small skills: the fingers laid upon
The nostrils of flutes, the speech of women
Whose tutors were the birds; who singing
Now civilised their children with the kiss.

Lastly, the tripod sentenced them.

Ash closed on the surviving sons.
The brown bee memorised here, rehearsed
Migration from an inherited habit.
All travellers recorded an empty zone.

Between rocks 'O death', the survivors.
O world of bushes eaten like a moon,
Kissed by the awkward patience of the ant.
Within a concave blue and void of space.

Something died out by this river: but it seems
Less than a nightingale ago.

COPTIC POEM

LAW-
RENCE
DURRELL

A Coptic deputation, going to Ethiopia,
Disappeared up one morning like the ghost in Aubrey

'With a Sweet Odour and a Melodious Twang'.
Who saw them go with their Melodious Odour?

I, said the arrow, the aboriginal arrow,
I saw them go, Coptic and Mellifluous,

Fuzzy-wig, kink-haired, with cocoa-butter shining,
With stoles on poles, sackbuts and silver salvers

Walking the desert ways howling and shining:
A Coptic congregation, red blue and yellow,

With Saints on parchment and stove-pipe hats,
All disappeared up like the ghost in Aubrey

Leaving only a smell of cooking and singing,
Rancid goat-butter and the piss of cats.

SWANS

Fraudulent perhaps in that they gave
No sense of muscle but a swollen languor
Though moved by webs: yet idly, idly
As soap-bubbles drift from a clay-pipe
They mowed the lake in tapestry,

Passing in regal exhaustion by us,
King, queen and cygnets, one by one,
Did one dare to remember other swans
In anecdotes of Gauguin or of Rabelais?
Some became bolsters for the Greeks,
Some rubber Lohengrins provided comedy.

The flapping of the wings excited Leda.
The procession is over and what is now
Alarming is more the mirror split
From end to end by the harsh clap
Of the wooden beaks, than the empty space
Which follows them about,
Stained by their whiteness when they pass.

We sit like drunkards and inhale the swans.

GREEN COCONUTS

At insular café tables under awnings
Bemused benighted half-castes pause
To stretch upon a table yawning
Ten yellow claws and
Order green coconuts to drink with straws.

Milk of the green loaf-coconuts
Which soon before them amputated stand,
Broken, you think, from some great tree of breasts,
Or the green skulls of savages trepanned.

Lips that are curved to taste this albumen,
To dredge with some blue spoon among the curds
Which drying on tongue or on moustache are tasteless
As droppings of bats or birds.

Re-enacting here a theory out of Darwin
They cup their yellow mandibles to shape
Their nuts, tilt them in drinking poses,
To drain them slowly from the very nape:
Green coconuts, green
Coconuts, patrimony of the ape.

A WATER-COLOUR OF VENICE

LAW-
RENCE
DURRELL

Zarian was saying: Florence is youth,
And after it Ravenna, age,
Then Venice, second-childhood.

The pools of burning stone where time
And water, the old siege-masters,
Have run their saps beneath
A thousand saddle-bridges,
Puffed up by marble griffins drinking,

And all set free to float on loops
Of her canals like great intestines
Now snapped off like a berg to float,
Where now, like others, you have come alone,
To trap your sunset in a yellow glass,
And watch the silversmith at work
Chasing the famous salver of the bay . . .

Here sense dissolves, coheres to print only
These bitten choirs of stone on water,
To the rumble of old cloth bells,
The cadging of confetti pigeons,
A boatman singing from his long black coffin . . .

To all that has been said before
You can add nothing, only that here,
Thick as a brushstroke sleep has laid
Its fleecy unconcern on every visage,

At the bottom of every soul a spoonful of sleep.

ROY FULLER

MEDITATION

Now the ambassadors have gone, refusing
Our gifts, treaties, anger, compliance;
And in their place the winter has arrived,
Icing the culture-bearing water.
We brood in our respective empires on
The words we might have said which would have
    breached
The Chinese wall round our superfluous love
And manufactures. We do not brood too deeply.
There are our friends' perpetual, subtle demands
For understanding: visits to those who claim
To show us what is meant by death,
And therefore life, our short and puzzling lives,
And to explain our feelings when we look
Through the dark sky to other lighted worlds—
The well-shaved owners of sanatoria,
And raving, grubby oracles: the books
On diet, posture, prayer and aspirin art:
The claims of frightful weapons to be investigated:
Mad generals to be promoted: and
Our private gulfs to slither down in bed.

Perhaps in spring the ambassadors will return.
Before then we shall find perhaps that bombs,
Books, people, planets, worry, even our wives,
Are not at all important. Perhaps
The preposterous fishing-line tangle of undesired
Human existence will suddenly unravel
Before some staggering equation

386

Or mystic experience, and God be released
From the moral particle or blue-lit room.
Or, better still, perhaps we shall, before
Anything really happens, be safely dead.

ROY
FULLER

THE HERO

When the hero's task was done
And the beast lay underground,
In the time that he had won
From the fates that pushed him round

He had space to contemplate
How the peasants still were bled
And that in the salvaged state
Worms continued at the head.

Little space: already, where
Sweetly he enjoyed his fish,
Seeing through the shouldered hair
Loosening sails and dirty dish,

Gasped a pale new plea for aid.
Cleaning his gun later, he
Felt with awe the old beast's shade
Fall across the wine-dark sea.

387

F. T. PRINCE

THE TEARS OF A MUSE IN AMERICA

I

Call out, celebrate the beam
Imprisoning and expressing him.
Fix the mature flash for the end but in advance
Fix in the glow of that sense what shall pass.

II

Give him a pale skin, a long hand
A grey eye with deep eyelids, with deep lids.
Complete with a dark mouth the head
Of Veronese's equerry; though of too confident a grace
His gestures, less fine than his limbs. Allow him also
    to sleep much
As with an effect of wantonness. Then he should
    swim and run
Jump horses and touch music, laugh willingly and
    grow
Among plain manners and legalities, and yet
Say where Monongahela and Alleghany
Have woven preparatives, glistening fall or where
New York assembles brittle towers. And let him,
Pleased to accomplish purposes
Alight in loose dress from a car.

III

He arrives thus with the ray of his intelligence
With what may cluster about it, dispositions

Recollections and curiosity, the state
Of reason and vision, the deceits of passion
Play of reserves, reflections, admirations
I am luminously possessed of. And all of which am
    anxious
To acknowledge makes him another of the many-
    minded, another
Exposed and assaulted, active and passive mind
Engaged in an adventure and interesting and interested
In itself by so being. But here solutions bristle
For the case seems to shine out at me from the moment
I grant him all the mind I can; when I in short
Impute to him an intemperate spirit, a proud wit
And in a springing innocence that still cannot undo
    itself
The pallid fire I cannot if I wish, with-hold. He shall
As he does, overpraise and underprize
And outvalue and contemn all those purities and
    powers
Of sight and speech, the so true so rich fleece
Covertly and attentively and often too
Fastidiously and rashly to neglect.
Here the position, action on his part, his going
In a still preserved uncertainty of light
Waits only for my touch: and there I have him
Amid the impunities of the polluted city
I see him in the stale glare of those follies,
Illiterate illuminations run to seed
Irreconcilables and abominables
Of all kinds swallowed, neither good nor bad
Either remembered or forgotten. In the dusk
There appears the full pallor of his looks
Desiring and desiring to desire.
And in fine he proceeds, fanned by this dubious flush

389

F. T. In the way I know. It comes to me afresh
PRINCE There glimmers out of it upon me that I want
Nothing to come of it at once. It glimmers,
It glimmers from the question of how, how shall it fall
The moment of the simple sight? and where
In what green land the simple sorrow? and
Under what boughs beneath whose hand wherever,
As in a fog upon the perfumed Cape,
A falling together of many gleams
Neither remembered nor forgotten and neither
Undesiring nor desiring the moment of despair?
Only say it should all as it will fall, as it fell
Or will have fallen, hanging back but to take place
All at once in the tacit air and on the ground
Of this period: the process
Of confrontation, reflection, resolution
That follows, it is this that will ascend
To the last point of fitted and related clarity.

IV

Caught in that leisurely and transparent train
Of the soft ostensibility of story
His motions and his thoughts are their own net
And while the beam folds on itself I'll not
Deny it is indefensibly too fine.
For as in smooth seas under dawn, whatever
He does he cannot do amiss
Being in these eyes seen aright
As he questionlessly is
In the white air under dawn
If he lives if he dies
He but plays at all escapes
As a dolphin or salmon leaps
And exquisite heresies

390

But leave the musing surface with a gleam.
So if all else be but conceivable yet
Of a lucidity that lives, himself
Mirrored may be the same,
Antecedents and foils will palliate. For
How idly miraculous
Or of what tortuous glory
In fact this creature was
How should my mere ingenuity relate?
In the great sweetness of which light
I ask if may be I have made
Though in an ecstasy of loss
At the last too little of it? But at least
Since I have seen him clear,
Whether he fondle a golden mare
Which he has ridden through wet woods
Or in the sunlight by the water
Stand silent as a tree, this verse no longer weeps.

ANNE RIDLER

PIERO DELLA FRANCESCA

The body is not fallen like the soul:
For these are godlike, being
Creatures of flesh, and in that being whole.
Founded on earth, they seem to be built not painted—
These huge girls, the mountain marble and
The valley clays were mixed for them,
The cleanness of lavender and the coolness of sand,
Also the tints of the deep sea;
And from the sea were made
The shell-like apse, and the pillars that echo each other
As waves do, in the Virgin's grey colonnade.

This gentle Jerome, with his Christ nailed
To the brown hill behind his head,
In speech with a stolid Donor, could not be—
Surely—by Manichaean doubts assailed;
In bodily peace this Solomon is wise:
Nothing is tortured, nothing ethereal here,
Nor would transcend the limits of material
Being, for in the flesh is nothing to fear
And nothing to despise.
The singing choir is winged, but who would wish
To fly, whose feet may rest on earth?
Christ with his banner, Christ in Jordan's water,
Not humbled by his human birth.

DEUS ABSCONDITUS

ANNE
RIDLER

I selfish and forsaken do still long for you
God for whom I was born and should have died:
Like lovers over miles and miles of sea
I lean my heart toward my comfort uselessly;
Did man or God weep out this sundering tide?

Cut off each sense, withdraw to the inmost secret
     place:
This God absconds from every promised land.
To shrink like a mollusc and to find no grace
This is the lot his lovers face.

And yet the worst is, not to seek you; yet the worst
Is not to know our lack of you. O, Love,
By what cords will you draw us? As at first
The cords of a man? Not splendour but the penal flesh
Taken for love, that moves us most.

Who breaks his tryst in a passionate ritual
May burn in a dry tree, a cold poem,
In the weak limbs of a child, so instant and perpetual,
In the stranger's face of a father dying,
Tender still but all the while departing.

Here he is endured, here he is adored.
And anywhere. Yet it is a long pursuit,
Carrying the junk and treasure of an ancient
     creed,
To a love who keeps his faith by seeming mute
And deaf, and dead indeed.

LAURIE LEE

THE THREE WINDS

The hard blue winds of March
shake the young sheep
and flake the long stone walls;
now from the gusty grass
comes the horned music of rams,
and plovers fall out of the sky
filling their wings with snow.

Tired of this northern tune
the winds turn soft
blowing white butterflies
out of the dog-rose hedges,
and schoolroom songs are full
of boys' green cuckoos
piping the summer round

Till August sends at last
its brick-red breath
over the baking wheat and blistered poppy,
brushing with feathered hands
the skies of brass,
with dreams of river moss
my thirst's delirium.

DAY OF THESE DAYS

Such a morning it is when love
leans through geranium windows
and calls with a cockerel's tongue.

When red-haired girls scamper like roses
over the rain-green grass,
and the sun drips honey.

When hedgerows grow venerable,
berries dry black as blood,
and holes suck in their bees.

Such a morning it is when mice
run whispering from the church,
dragging dropped ears of harvest.

When the partridge draws back his spring
and shoots like a buzzing arrow
over grained and mahogany fields.

When no table is bare,
and no breast dry,
and the tramp feeds off ribs of rabbit.

Such a day it is when time
piles up the hills like pumpkins,
and the streams run golden.

When all men smell good,
and the cheeks of girls
are as baked bread to the mouth.

As bread and beanflowers
the touch of their lips,
and their white teeth sweeter than cucumbers.

NORMAN NICHOLSON

TO THE RIVER DUDDON

I wonder, Duddon, if you still remember
An oldish man with a nose like a pony's nose,
Broad bones, legs long and lean but strong enough
To carry him over Hardknott at seventy years of age.
He came to you first as a boy with a fishing-rod
And a hunk of Ann Tyson's bread and cheese in his
    pocket,
Walking from Hawkshead across Walna Scar;
Then as a midde-aged Rydal landlord,
With a doting sister and a pension on the civil list,
Who left his verses gummed to your rocks like lichen,
The dry and yellow edges of a once-green spring.
He made a guide-book for you, from your source
There where you bubble through the moss on Wrynose
(Among the ribs of bald and bony fells
With screes scratched in the turf like grey scabs),
And twist and slither under humpbacked bridges—
Built like a child's house from odds and ends
Of stones that lie about the mountain side—
Past Cockley Beck Farm and on to Birk's Bridge,
Where the rocks stride about like legs in armour,
And the steel birches buckle and bounce in the wind
With a crinkle of silver foil in the crisp of the leaves;
On then to Seathwaite, where like a steam-navvy
You shovel and slash your way through the gorge
By Wallabarrow Crag, broader now
From becks that flow out of black upland tarns
Or ooze through golden saxifrage and the roots of
    rowans;

Next Ulpha, where a stone dropped from the bridge
Swims like a tadpole down thirty feet of water
Between steep skirting-boards of rock; and thence
You dribble into lower Dunnerdale
Through wet woods and wood-soil and woodland
    flowers,
Tutson, the St. John's-wort with a single yellow bead,
Marsh marigold, creeping jenny and daffodils;
Here from hazel islands in the late spring
The catkins fall and ride along the stream
Like little yellow weasels, and the soil is loosed
From bulbs of the white lily that smells of garlic,
And dippers rock up and down on rubber legs,
And long-tailed tits are flung through the air like darts;
By Foxfield now you taste the salt in your mouth,
And thrift mingles with the turf, and the heron stands
Watching the wagtails. Wordsworth wrote:
'Remote from every taint of sordid industry'.
But you and I know better, Duddon lass.
For I, who've lived for nearly thirty years
Upon your shore, have seen the slagbanks slant
Like screes sheer into the sand, and seen the tide
Purple with ore back up the muddy gullies
And wiped the sinter dust from the farmyard
    damsons.
A hundred years of floods and rain and wind
Have washed your rocks clear of his words again,
Many of them half-forgotten, brimming the Irish sea.
But that which Wordsworth knew, even the old man
When poetry had failed like desire, was something
I have yet to learn, and you, Duddon,
Have learned and re-learned to forget and forget
    again.
Not the radical, the poet and heretic,

NORMAN
NICHOL-
SON To whom the water-forces shouted and the fells
Were like a blackboard for the scrawls of God,
But the old man, inarticulate and humble,
Knew that eternity flows in a mountain beck—
The long cord of the water, the shepherd's numerals
That run upstream, through the singing decades of
  dialect.
He knew beneath mutation of year and season
Flood and drought, frost and fire and thunder,
The frothy blossom on the rowan and the reddening
  of the berries,
The silt, the sand, the slagbanks and the shingle,
And the wild catastrophes of the breaking mountains,
There stands the base and root of the living rock,
Thirty thousand feet of solid Cumberland.

THE TAME HARE

She came to him in dreams—her ears
Diddering like antennae, and her eyes
Wide as dark flowers where the dew
Holds and dissolves a purple hoard of shadow.
The thunder clouds crouched back, and the world
  opened
Tiny and bright as a celandine after rain.
A gentle light was on her, so that he
Who saw the talons in the vetch
Remembered now how buttercup and daisy
Would bounce like springs when a child's foot stepped
  off them.
Oh, but never dared he touch—
Her fur was still electric to the fingers.

Yet of all the beasts blazoned in gilt and blood

In the black-bound missal of his mind,
Pentecostal dove and paschal lamb,
Eagle, lion, serpent, she alone
Lived also in the noon of ducks and sparrows;
And the cleft-mouthed kiss which plugged the night
    with fever
Was sweetened by a lunch of docks and lettuce.

THE UNDISCOVERED PLANET

Out on the furthest tether let it run
Its hundred-year-long orbit, cold
As solid mercury, old and dead
Before *this* world's fermenting bread
Had got a crust to cover it; landscape of lead
Whose purple voes and valleys are
Lit faintly by a sun
No nearer than a measurable star.

No man has seen it; nor the lensed eye
That pin-points week by week the same patch of sky
Records even a blur across its pupil; only
The errantry of Saturn, the wry
Retarding of Uranus, speak
Of the pull beyond the pattern:—
The unknown is shown
Only by a bend in the known.

399

HENRY REED

LESSONS OF THE WAR
To Alan Michell

JUDGING DISTANCES

Not only how far away, but the way that you say it
Is very important. Perhaps you may never get
The knack of judging a distance, but at least you know
How to report on a landscape: the central sector,
The right of arc and that, which we had last Tuesday,
      And at least you know

That maps are of time, not place, so far as the Army
Happens to be concerned—the reason being,
Is one which need not delay us. Again you know
There are three kinds of tree, three only, the fir and
      the poplar,
And those which have bushy tops to; and lastly
      That things only seem to be things.

A barn is not called a barn, to put it more plainly,
Or a field in the distance, where sheep may be safely
      grazing.
You must never be over-sure. You must say, when
      reporting:
At five o'clock in the central sector is a dozen
Of what appear to be animals; whatever you do,
      Don't call the bleeders *sheep*.

I am sure that's quite clear; and suppose, for the sake
      of example,
The one at the end, asleep, endeavours to tell us

What he sees over there to the west, and how far away, HENRY
After first having come to attention. There to the west, REED
On the fields of summer the sun and the shadows bestow
          Vestments of purple and gold.

The still white dwellings are like a mirage in the heat,
And under the swaying elms a man and a woman
Lie gently together. Which is, perhaps, only to say
That there is a row of houses to the left of arc,
And that under some poplars a pair of what appear to
      be humans
          Appear to be loving.

Well that, for an answer, is what we might rightly call
Moderately satisfactory only, the reason being,
Is that two things have been omitted, and those are
          important.
The human beings, now: in what direction are they,
And how far away, would you say? And do not forget
          There may be dead ground in between.

There may be dead ground in between; and I may not
          have got
The knack of judging a distance; I will only venture
A guess that perhaps between me and the apparent
          lovers,
(Who, incidentally, appear by now to have finished,)
At seven o'clock from the houses, is roughly a distance
          Of about one year and a half.

G. S. FRASER

SUMMER AND WINTER

I

Summer can ripen common flesh on sea-shores
And makes its whorlings whisper like sea-shells:
Summer grows roses from the mouths of whores
And rings the changes on the seaside belles.
Summer, the dank, exhausted and too pliant,
Can wash her sins away within the sea:
Summer the stones and grasses find compliant,
The waters flatter her ductility.
Summer, at evening, on her basket chair,
A blowsy frump, her glass of beer before her,
Can change her frock, put scent upon her hair,
And in the cool night we again adore her.
Be to her frailties a little blind:
Summer's a harlot but her heart is kind.

II

Winter has a diminishing sky:
And a perspective other than retrospect
That hurts and holds the eye.
Winter does not offer escape
Forward or backward from its final landscape
And on all sides its skies fall
As if the whole world were a theatre
Where the round year had taken its curtain call.
Winter offers us, for instance,
The nerves of a leaf on a puddle of ice
And the terrible nearness of distance.

As if, being aware, one stood
At the wrong, the small end of a corridor.
And Winter has no analogy to war
Except the view of it the dying may have,
But is not unlike an unhappy love:
I love, but I do not like winter at all.

G. S.
FRASER

ON A MEMORY OF BEAUTY

How can the heart for sea and stone
    Be cumbered, and forget a face
That moved it once to fret and moan—
    Forget the woman, see the place?

But was it one or was it two,
    Was it a statue or a girl?
Might every spring her form renew,
    And the white sea-froth be her curl?

Beauty but for a moment shone,
    The likeness of a cloud or wave
Whose momentary aspect, gone,
    The sieve of memory cannot save.

Right at the back of my head I know
    Incredible wild things
Struggle like swans half-blind with snow—
    And the dying swan sings.

ALUN LEWIS

DAWN ON THE EAST COAST

From Orford Ness to Shingle Street
The grey disturbance spreads
Washing the icy seas on Deben Head.

Cock pheasants scratch the frozen fields,
Gulls lift thin horny legs and step
Fastidiously among the rusted mines.

The soldier leaning on the sandbagged wall
Hears in the combers' curling rush and crash
His single self-centred monotonous wish;

And time is a froth of such transparency
His drowning eyes see what they wish to see;
A girl laying his table with a white cloth.

.   .   .   .

The light assails him from a flank,
Two carbons touching in his brain
Crumple the cellophane lanterns of his dream.

And then the day, grown feminine and kind,
Stoops with the gulfing motion of the tide
And pours his ashes in a tiny urn.

From Orford Ness to Shingle Street
The grey disturbance lifts its head
And one by one, reluctantly,
The living come back slowly from the dead.

THE PEASANTS

ALUN
LEWIS

The dwarf barefooted, chanting
Behind the oxen by the lake,
Stepping lightly and lazily among the thorntrees
Dusky and dazed with sunlight, half awake;

The women breaking stones upon the highway,
Walking erect with burdens on their heads,
One body growing in another body,
Creation touching verminous straw beds.

Across scorched hills and trampled crops
The soldiers straggle by.
History staggers in their wake.
The peasants watch them die.

TERENCE TILLER

BATHERS

They flutter out of white, and run
through the electric wind to bathe,
giggling like rivers for the fun
of smacking mud in the toes, of lithe
and sliding bodies like their own
—sharp rushes, good to battle with.

The child knows all delight to be
naked and queer as his own name,
foreign as being loved; but he
feels as a kind of coming home
the flags that slap his plunging knee,
and the cold stocking of the stream.

Coiling in wombs of water, bent
backwards upon the sheets of air,
his wand of sexless body lent
to all that was or casts before,
he strips to either element
a fœtus or a ravisher.

So gladly virgin rivers rush
down to their amniotic seas,
children of cold and glittering flesh
that promise harvest as they pass
panics of tiny fertile fish
in the fast pale of boisterous thighs.

PERFUMES

TERENCE
TILLER

Not every ghost has died before it haunts:
perfumes it seems have shadows, and will throw
days before them those thin beckoning scents:
unnamed, as the first sounds of poems grow
—formless and soft, like far-off instruments.

Mistily three days round me, blind men's trees,
changing as eyes, bodiless odours have lain:
the lemon-garden or the heat of bees;
November beaches' salt and iodine;
plushy church-air; lips' faint fragrances.

Now as the poem read, creating more
than word or reader were, grows firm and thrills
like a cello between thighs, the form is here:
your perfume round me like the death of bells,
and you moving the sweetness of the air.

Because our hands trail in each other as though
a child's through water, and refuse goodnight,
I carry perfume back with me, and you,
your body the bell's singing heart: the sweet
perpetual ghost again; but this time true.

W. S. GRAHAM

LOVE POEM

Where you (in this saying) lag in the waving woods
Under climber moon tonight under branching
    industry
Of all my homing opposites, this paidout saying
Serves us again the upward legging oaks
Heaving in air. This fastened fire awakes,
Filament between us full of the sleeping rooks.
This wood's around us under the curlew's loveweep.
Glowormed in the myrtle beds, under the stoop
Of the starry harrier boughs, we kindle this memory
    up.

To still lie low together, heart and hand fast,
We hear the windkindling trees around us move.
These words bribe words away. Man and woman
Lie at their best, lifeline crossed on lifeline
And all signs sail in their holygranted garden.
Kept in one element, devoured in an ore of Heaven,
They're lifebled back to this now double night.
So are we bedded burning in our infinite
Immortal filament where continually our dead cry out.

So you (in this flame-fastened saying) beneath
Bullhorned goatbearded oak, look up at the night
Falling away across the staining sky.
Our branching veins remember us and flower
The morning's first bright resins burning over
Our two kissed lives. Our present morning ever
Handing us back to forgiveness lands us back

408

To under a stiller sky. The daybreak cock W. S.
GRAHAM
Fixed in the calyx east crows seven bright heavens
    awake.

GIGHA

That firewood pale with salt and burning green
Outfloats its men who waved with a sound of
    drowning
Their saltcut hands over mazes of this rough bay.

Quietly this morning beside the subsided herds
Of water I walk. The children wade the shallows.
The sun with long legs wades into the sea.

NIGHT'S FALL UNLOCKS THE DIRGE
OF THE SEA

Night's fall unlocks the dirge of the sea
To pour up from the shore and befriending
Gestures of water waving, to find me
Dressed warm in a coat of land in a house
Held off the drowned by my blood's race
Over the crops of my step to meet some praise.

The surge by day by night turns lament
And by this night falls round the surrounding
Seaside and countryside and I can't
Sleep one word away on my own for that
Grief sea with a purse of pearls and debt
Wading the land away with salt in his throat.

By this loud night traded into evidence
Of a dark church of voices at hand

I lie, work of the gruff sea's innocence
And lie, work of the deaths I find
On the robbed land breathing air and
The friendly thief sea wealthy with the drowned.

AT WHOSE SHELTERING SHALL
THE DAY SEA

At whose sheltering shall the day sea
Captain his ships of foam to save
Them weary of air, their hair gently
Afloat above them on prongs of water?
Now, prince in the seacircling tower,
Emigrant to grief, furious seafarer swept over

The seven wounds and multiple five
Senses of drowning; he fills his voice
With land-dry prayers and the sea above.
His 'help' or 'save me' like a bird
Bore back only the stretched whitefingered
Hand of the swelling sea and found him sheltered,

Sheltered in soon all of us to be
That memory against the scuppering rocks,
The spilling aprons of the sea.
Grief fills the voice with water, building
Ruin on the ruining land. Sheltering
In sea he breathes dry land, dry grave and dwelling.

JOHN HEATH-STUBBS

MARIA AEGYPTIACA

Thrust back by hands of air from the sanctuary door,
Mary of Egypt, that hot whore,
Fell on the threshold-stone. Priest, candles, acolyte
Shivered in flame upon her failing sight—
She swooned, and lay there like one dead. And then
    she fled
In the black Thebaïd. For forty years
She hid among the rocks splintered with heat;
The greedy desert to its own pitiless drought
Sucked all her body's beauty—which had spread
A wildfire death in kisses through brown limbs
Of sailormen at Alexandria,
Or Syrian fig-merchants with small dull eyes.
          All night she would display
Her naked skin and bones to the harsh red moon
To be her only lover; through the day,
(While she was kneeling on the white hot sand)
Hairy and ithyphallic,
The dancing satyrs would distract her prayer;
The memory of her lust
Split open the rock-tombs, and buried kings
Whose brown dead flesh was like dried dates, with eyes
Of emerald glittering in a gilded mask,
Tripped forth, their grave-bands looped fantastically,
And made their court to her with antic bows.

   .   .   .   .

And when at last she died,
With burning tender eyes, hair like dark flame,

JOHN The golden lion came;
HEATH- And with his terrible claws scooped out a tomb,
STUBBS Gently, in the loose soil,
And gave that dry burnt corpse to the earth's womb.

THE MERMAID AT ZENNOR

Half fish, half fallen angel, none of you
Human at all—cease your lust's
Cold and insatiate crying from the tangled bay;
Nor, sea-hag, here
Stretch webbed and skinny fingers for your prey.

This is a hideous and a wicked country,
Sloping to hateful sunsets and the end of time,
Hollow with mine-shafts, naked with granite, fanatic
With sorrow. Abortions of the past
Hop through these bogs; black-faced, the villagers
Remember burnings by the hewn stones.

Only the saints,
Drifting on oak-leaves over the Irish sea,
To sing like pipits from their crannied cells
With a thin stream of praise; who hear the Jennifer
Sob for her sins in a purgatory of foam—
Only these holy men
Can send you slithering from the chancel steps,
And wriggling back to your sunken paradise
Among the hollow-eyed and the capsized.

ALEX COMFORT

THE ATOLL IN THE MIND

Out of what calms and pools the cool shell grows
dumb teeth under clear waters, where no currents
fracture the coral's porous horn
grows up the mind's stone tree, the honeycomb,
the plump brain-coral breaking the pool's mirror,
the ebony antler, the cold sugared fan.

All these strange trees stand downward through the
     water,
the mind's grey candied points tend to the surface—
the greater part is out of sight below:

but when on the island's whaleback spring green blades,
new land on water wavers, birds bring seeds
and tides plant slender trunks by the lagoon

I see the image of the mind's two trees cast
     downward,
one tilting leaves to catch the sun's bright pennies,
one dark as water, its root among the bones.

FIFTH ELEGY

In the round park the old men sitting on benches
move their feet in leaves. From their pink open lips
curls the white breath, when seeds are dropping, and
     bright
ranks of shields hang from the poplar's rods—
reckoning chances. Leaves are underfoot.

ALEX Their hands are closed. Their palms are furrowed
COMFORT   as children's.
            Their heads are polished in the streams of wind.
            Under the dripping tree and the colours of creepers
            the benches stand, and drops hang down from straws:
            gold shields are struggling in the birches' net.

            Their minds are quiet, reckoning the chance of spring.
            One cannot ask them what is in their minds.
            The leaves with voiceless rivers in their hands
            come round their feet, and the children's balls leap up
            spinning above the bushes, into a clear sky.

            These are the watchers that no summer touches,
            sitting beside the restless tides of air—
            whose feet like rocks the leaves have drifted up:
            beaches of cloud that go above the trees
            whiten and hiss with the invisible foam:

            whether the clouds will graze again, and the limes
                  flower—
            the swallows' faces brush at the window-panes—
            whether the gardens will open to their slow steps;
            or the dull horn blow, later, in colder days,
            the pillows' landscape darken into stone.

            The furrows of these faces map in autumn
            unknown countries, the hills and paths of the dead.
            It is the hunters' land, whose mossy heads
            lie round the springs, and drink in deepest valleys
            the perpetual green water, the spinning grains of the
                  brook.

Their knowledge reads the leaves: the dead and the
            children
speak to them voice and voice beside the lawns.
Under their waiting feet old lovers lie
in a bridal sleep below the pools of leaves
while on their eyes fall spinning the winged seeds.

THE POSTURES OF LOVE

II

There is a white mare that my love keeps
unridden in a hillside meadow—white
as a white pebble, veined like a stone
a white horse, whiter than a girl.

And now for three nights sleeping I have seen
her body naked as a tree for marriage
pale as a stone that the net of water covers

and her veined breasts like hills—the swallow islands
still on the corn's green water: and I know
her dark hairs gathered round an open rose

her pebbles lying under the dappled sea.
And I will ride her thighs' white horses.

KEITH DOUGLAS

MERSA

This blue half circle of sea
moving transparently
on the sand as pale as salt
was Cleopatra's hotel:

here is a guesthouse built
and broken utterly since
an amorous modern prince
lived in this scoured shell.

Now from the ruined hive of a town
the cherry-skinned soldiers stroll down
to undress to idle on the white beach.
Up there, the immensely long road goes by

to Tripoli: the wind and dust reach
the secrets of the whole
poor town whose masks would still
deceive a passer by,

faces with sightless doors
for eyes, with cracks like tears
oozing at corners. A dead tank alone
leans where the gossips stood.

I see my feet like stones
underwater. The logical little fish
converge and nip the flesh
imagining I am one of the dead.

TIME EATING

KEITH DOUGLAS

Ravenous Time has flowers for his food
in Autumn, yet can cleverly make good
each petal: devours animals and men,
but for ten dead he can create ten.

If you enquire how secretly you've come
to mansize from the smallness of a stone
it will appear his effort made you rise
so gradually to your proper size.

But as he makes he eats; the very part
where he began, even the elusive heart
Time's ruminative tongue will wash
and slow juice masticate all flesh.

That volatile huge intestine holds
material and abstract in its folds:
thought and ambition melt and even the world
will alter, in that catholic belly curled.

But Time, who ate my love, you cannot make
such another; you who can remake
the lizard's tail and the bright snakeskin
cannot, cannot. That you gobbled in
too quick, and though you brought me from a boy
you can make no more of me, only destroy.

IAIN FLETCHER

ADOLESCENTS IN THE DUSK

About this time when dusk falls like a shutter
Upon the decomposition of the time,
Eliding eye and day and surfaces and shapes,
Whitening of faces like stoles in the twilight . . .
When the gardens between the houses are rose-
Encumbered with sidereal roses
And the roads like gorges grey in the tired light of
     falling . . .
They come then as birds in an irresponsible plumage
Moulting their childhood for always,
Half-predatory, half
Laughing . . .
Ripeness that dares not open, that fears its own
Promise, skin mercilessly
Alive with star-points of sensation, angel-
Senses aroused like petals outcurving
After the first prolongation of the look in impossible
     mirrors
With disquiet and admiration . . .
                   The daily evening descends then
And the air about them seems now
Crumpled with the great winged lover,
That absent lover whom their drifting gaze
Can never quite encounter . . .
                      They are aware
Of absence, as I am aware
Of the creeping essence of unsleeping presence,
And would refuse the engagement
Leaving their laughing to glide still farther and farther
              (Like a flying away of doves . . .)
Ironic as shadows that mimic the conceptual pleasures
     of man.   418

SIDNEY KEYES

ELEGY

(*In Memoriam* S. K. K.)

April again and it is a year again
Since you walked out and slammed the door
Leaving us tangled in your words. Your brain
Lives in the bank-book, and your eyes look up
Laughing from the carpet on the floor:
And we still drink from your silver cup.

It is a year again since they poured
The dumb ground into your mouth:
And yet we know, by some recurring word
Or look caught unawares, that you still drive
Our thoughts like the smart cobs of your youth—
When you and the world were alive.

A year again, and we have fallen on bad times
Since they gave you to the worms.
I am ashamed to take delight in these rhymes
Without grief; but you need no tears.
We shall never forget nor escape you, nor make
     terms
With your enemies, the swift-devouring years.

EARLY SPRING

Now that the young buds are tipped with a falling sun—
Each twig a candle, a martyr, St. Julian's branched
     stag—
And the shadows are walking the cobbled square like
     soldiers
With their long legs creaking and their pointed hands
Reaching the railings and fingering the stones
Of what expended, unprojected graves:
The soil's a flirt, the lion Time is tamed,
And pain like a cat will come home to share your
     room.

GLAUCUS

The various voices are his poem now.

Under the currents, under the shifting lights
Of midway water, rolls his fleshy wreck:
Its gurnard eye reflects those airy heights
Where once it noted white Arcturus set.

Gull-swift and swerving, the wet spirit freed
Skims the huge breakers. Watching at the prow
Of any southbound vessel, sailor, heed
Never that petrel spirit, cruel as pride.

Let no cliff-haunting woman, no girl claim
Kinship with Glaucus, neither sow
The tide with daffodils, nor call his name
Into the wind, for he is glorified—
And cold Aegean voices speak his fame.

THE KESTRELS

SIDNEY
KEYES

When I would think of you, my mind holds only
The small defiant kestrels—how they cut
The raincloud with sharp wings, continually circling
About a storm-rocked elm, with passionate cries.
It was an early month. The plow cut hard.
The may was knobbed with chilly buds. My folly
Was great enough to lull away my pride.

There is no virtue now in blind reliance
On place or person or the forms of love.
The storm bears down the pivotal tree, the cloud
Turns to the net of an inhuman fowler
And drags us from the air. Our wings are clipped.
Yet still our love and luck lies in our parting:
Those cries and wings surprise our surest act.

ACKNOWLEDGEMENTS

For permission to reprint copyright material, the following acknowledgements are made:

For poems by Conrad Aiken, to the author, Messrs. Charles Scribner's Sons and Messrs. A. M. Heath & Co.
> *Preludes for Memnon* (Scribners) 1931.
> *Time in the Rock* (Scribners) 1936.

For poems by W. H. Auden, to the author and Messrs. Faber & Faber.
> *For the Time Being* (Faber) 1945.
> *Collected Shorter Poems* (Faber) 1950.

For poems by George Barker, to the author and Messrs. Faber & Faber.
> *Eros in Dogma* (Faber) 1944.
> *News of the World* (Faber) 1950.
> *Summer Idyll* is reprinted from the first edition: it does not appear in any of Mr. Barker's books.

For poems by Alex Comfort, to the author and Messrs. Routledge & Kegan Paul.
> *A Wreath for the Living* (Routledge) 1942.
> *Elegies* (Routledge) 1944.
> *The Signal to Engage* (Routledge) 1946.

For poems by Hart Crane, to the poet's family and Mr. Horace Liveright.
> *Collected Poems* (Liveright) 1933.

For poems by E. E. Cummings, to the author, Mr. Horace Liveright, the Oxford University Press and Messrs. A. M. Heath & Co.
> *is 5* (Boni & Liveright) 1933.
> *50 Poems* (O.U.P.) 1940.

For poems by H.D., to Mrs. H. D. Aldington, Mr. Horace Liveright and Messrs. Chatto & Windus.

    Collected Poems (Boni & Liveright) 1925.

    Red Roses for Bronze (Chatto & Windus) 1931.

For poems by Keith Douglas, to the author and Editions Poetry London.

    Collected Poems (Editions Poetry London) 1951.

For poems by Lawrence Durrell, to the author and Messrs. Faber & Faber.

    A Private Country (Faber) 1943.

    Cities, Plains and People (Faber) 1946.

    On Seeming to Presume (Faber) 1948.

    Another version of 'Water Colour of Venice' appeared in *The New Statesman & Nation*.

For the poem by Richard Eberhart, to the author and Messrs. Chatto & Windus.

    Reading the Spirit (Chatto & Windus) 1936.

For poems by T. S. Eliot, to the author and Messrs. Faber & Faber.

    Collected Poems 1909-1935 (Faber) 1936.

    Four Quartets (Faber) 1944.

For poems by William Empson, to the author, Messrs. Chatto & Windus and Messrs. Faber & Faber.

    Poems (Chatto & Windus) 1935.

    The Gathering Storm (Faber) 1940.

For the poem by Iain Fletcher, to the author.

    'Adolescents in the Dusk' appeared in *Poetry London*.

For poems by G. S. Fraser, to the author and Editions Poetry London.

    The Traveller has Regrets (Editions Poetry London) 1948.

For poems by Roy Fuller, to the author and Messrs. John Lehmann.
> *Epitaphs and Occasions* (Lehmann) 1949.

For poems by David Gascoyne, to the author, Editions Poetry London and Messrs. John Lehmann.
> *Poems 1937–1942* (Editions Poetry London) 1943.
> *A Vagrant* (John Lehmann) 1950.

For poems by W. S. Graham, to the author and Messrs. Faber & Faber.
> *The White Threshold* (Faber) 1949.

For poems by Robert Graves, to the author, the Seizin Press, Messrs. Cassell & Co. and Messrs. A. P. Watt & Son.
> *Collected Poems* (Cassell) 1938.
> *Poems 1938–1945* (Cassell) 1946.

For poems by John Heath-Stubbs, to the author, Messrs. Eyre & Spottiswoode and Messrs. Pearn, Pollinger & Higham.
> *The Swarming of the Bees* (Eyre & Spottiswoode) 1950.
> 'The Mermaid' appeared in *Time & Tide*.

For poems by Gerard Manley Hopkins, to the poet's family and the Oxford University Press.
> *Poems: Edited by Robert Bridges.* Second Edition (O.U.P.) 1930.

For poems by T. E. Hulme, to Mr. Herbert Read and Messrs. Routledge & Kegan Paul.
> *Speculations* (Kegan Paul) 1924. Hulme's five poems had previously been printed as an addendum to Ezra Pound's *Ripostes* (Elkin Mathews).

For poems by Sidney Keyes, to the poet's family and Messrs. Routledge & Kegan Paul.

Collected Poems of Sidney Keyes (Routledge) 1945.

For poems by D. H. Lawrence, to Mrs. Frieda Lawrence, Messrs. Heinemann and Mr. Martin Secker.

Collected Poems (Secker) 1932.
Last Poems (Secker) 1933.

For poems by Laurie Lee, to the author, the Hogarth Press and Messrs. John Lehmann.

The Sun My Monument (Hogarth Press) 1944.
Bloom of Candles (Lehmann) 1947.

For poems by Alun Lewis, to the poet's family and Messrs. Allen & Unwin.

Ha! Ha! Among the Trumpets (Allen & Unwin) 1945.

For poems by C. Day Lewis, to the author, the Hogarth Press and Messrs. Jonathan Cape.

Collected Poems (Hogarth Press) 1935.
A Time to Dance (Hogarth Press) 1935.
Overtures to Death (Cape) 1938.
Poems 1943–1947 (Cape) 1948.

For the poem by Vachel Lindsay, to Mrs. Lindsay and The Macmillan Company.

Collected Poems (Macmillan) 1922.

For poems by Louis MacNeice, to the author and Messrs. Faber & Faber.

Collected Poems (Faber) 1949.

For poems by Charles Madge, to the author and Messrs. Faber & Faber.

The Disappearing Castle (Faber) 1937.
'Ballad of Hope and Fear' appeared in the *Irish Times*.

425

'At War' and 'Lusty Juventus' are reprinted from the first edition but do not appear in either of Mr. Madge's books.

For poems by Harold Monro, to Mrs. Alida Monro and Mr. Cobden-Sanderson.
Collected Poems (Cobden-Sanderson) 1933.

For poems by Marianne Moore, to the author and Messrs. Faber & Faber.
Collected Poems (Faber) 1951.

For poems by Edwin Muir, to the author, Messrs. J. M. Dent & Sons and Messrs. Faber & Faber.
Journeys and Places (Dent) 1937.
The Narrow Place (Faber) 1943.
The Labyrinth (Faber) 1949.

For poems by Norman Nicholson, to the author and Messrs. Faber & Faber.
Five Rivers (Faber) 1943.
Rock Face (Faber) 1948.
'The Undiscovered Planet' has not previously been printed in book form.

For poems by Wilfred Owen, to Mrs. Susan Owen and Messrs. Chatto & Windus.
Poems (Chatto & Windus) 1931.

For poems by Ezra Pound, to the author and Messrs. Faber & Faber.
Selected Poems (Faber) 1948.
Homage to Sextus Propertius (Faber) 1934.
Seventy Cantos (Faber) 1950.

For the poem by F. T. Prince, to the author and Messrs. Faber & Faber.
Poems (Faber) 1938.

426

For poems by Peter Quennell, to the author and Messrs. Chatto & Windus.

 Poems (Chatto & Windus) 1926.

For poems by Kathleen Raine, to the author, Editions Poetry London and Messrs. Hamish Hamilton.

 Stone and Flower (Editions Poetry London) 1943.

 The Pythoness (Hamish Hamilton) 1949.

For poems by John Crowe Ransom, to the author, Messrs. Alfred A. Knopf, Inc., Messrs. Eyre & Spottiswoode and Messrs. Pearn, Pollinger & Higham.

 Selected Poems (Eyre & Spottiswoode) 1947.

For poems by Herbert Read, to the author and Messrs. Faber & Faber.

 Collected Poems (Faber) 1946.

For the poem by Henry Reed, to the author and Messrs. Jonathan Cape.

 A Map of Verona (Cape) 1946.

For poems by Laura Riding, to the author, the Seizin Press and Messrs. Cassell & Co.

 Collected Poems (Cassell) 1938.

For poems by Anne Ridler, to the author and Messrs. Faber & Faber.

 The Golden Bird (Faber) 1951.

For poems by Michael Roberts, to Mrs. Michael Roberts, Messrs. Jonathan Cape and Messrs. Faber & Faber.

 Poems (Cape) 1936.

 Orion Marches (Faber) 1939.

 'The World's End' has not previously been printed in book form in this country.

For poems by W. R. Rodgers, to the author and Messrs. Secker & Warburg.

Awake and Other Poems (Secker & Warburg) 1941.

'Neither Here nor There' has not previously been printed in book form.

For poems by Isaac Rosenberg, to Mrs. I. Wynick and Messrs. Chatto & Windus.

Collected Poems (Chatto & Windus) 1950.

For poems by E. J. Scovell, to the author and Messrs. Routledge & Kegan Paul.

Shadows of Chrysanthemums (Routledge) 1944.

'Evening Scene' has not previously been printed in book form.

For poems by Edith Sitwell, to the author, Messrs. Macmillan & Co. and Messrs. Pearn, Pollinger & Higham.

The Canticle of the Rose (Macmillan) 1949.

For poems by Sacheverell Sitwell, to the author and Messrs. Faber & Faber.

Canons of Giant Art (Faber) 1933.

For poems by Bernard Spencer, to the author and Editions Poetry London.

Aegean Islands (Editions Poetry London) 1946.

For poems by Stephen Spender, to the author and Messrs. Faber & Faber.

Poems: Revised Edition (Faber) 1933.

The Still Centre (Faber) 1939.

Poems of Dedication (Faber) 1947.

The Edge of Being (Faber) 1949.

'Anno Santo' has not previously been printed in book form.

For poems by Wallace Stevens, to the author and Mr. Alfred Knopf.

    Harmonium (Knopf) 1931.

    The lines from 'Esthétique du Mal' are reprinted from *Transport to Summer* by Wallace Stevens, by permission of Alfred A. Knopf Inc. Copyright 1942, 1947 by Wallace Stevens.

For the poems by Allen Tate, to the author and Messrs. Eyre and Spottiswoode.

    Selected Poems (Eyre & Spottiswoode) 1947.

For poems by Dylan Thomas, to the author, to the *Sunday Referee*, the Parton Press and Messrs. J. M. Dent & Sons.

    18 Poems (*Sunday Referee* and Parton Press) 1934.

    25 Poems (Dent) 1936.

    The Map of Love (Dent) 1939.

    Deaths and Entrances (Dent) 1946.

For poems by Terence Tiller, to the author and the Hogarth Press.

    The Inward Animal (Hogarth Press) 1943.

    Unarm Eros (Hogarth Press) 1948.

For poems by Vernon Watkins, to the author and Messrs. Faber & Faber.

    Ballad of the Mari Llwyd (Faber) 1941.

    The Lady with the Unicorn (Faber) 1948.

For the poem by Charles Williams, to the author's family and the Oxford University Press.

    Taliessin Through Logres (O.U.P.) 1938.

For poems by W. B. Yeats, to the author's family and Messrs. Macmillan & Co.

    Collected Poems (Macmillan) 1933.

INDEX OF AUTHORS

431